Mostly on Martha's Vineyard

BOOKS BY HENRY BEETLE HOUGH

Tuesday Will Be Different 1971
Martha's Vineyard (with Alfred Eisenstaedt) 1970
The Road 1970
Vineyard Gazette Reader (editor) 1967
The Port 1963
Lament for a City 1960
Melville in the South Pacific 1960
Great Days of Whaling 1958
The New England Story 1958
Thoreau of Walden 1956
An Alcoholic to His Sons (as told to) 1954
Whaling Wives (with Emma Mayhew Whiting) 1953
Singing in the Morning 1951
Once More the Thunderer 1950
Long Anchorage 1947
Roosters Crow in Town 1945
All Things Are Yours 1942
That Lofty Sky 1941
Country Editor 1940
Martha's Vineyard, Summer Resort 1936

Mostly on Martha's Vineyard

A Personal Record

Henry Beetle Hough

HARCOURT BRACE JOVANOVICH

New York and London

Library of Congress Cataloging in Publication Data

Hough, Henry Beetle, 1896–
Mostly on Martha's Vineyard.

1. Hough, Henry Beetle, 1896–   I. Title.
PN4874.H67A33   070.4′092′4   74-22494
ISBN 0-15-106800-3

First edition

B C D E

To the Past

Mostly on Martha's Vineyard

1

Gladys Reid, who is of a fairly advanced age, though not so much further advanced than I, has been looking through her father's papers and throwing some of them away—most of them, I suppose, because that's what happens when afternoons grow long. In his daybook she found the entry, "Married today," then "Loafed today," and the next day he worked ten hours.

So when we talk together we share a long view that will soon be everybody's or nobody's dim record—misunderstood, of course. Perhaps that's best, for then our prejudices and experiences will be laid away intact.

Gladys has been rigorously punctual all her life, and so have I. Now she's pushing eighty-one, she says, and I'm pushing seventy-eight but no harder than I can help. I like too much the golden sunlight of September and October, and I count on early morning walks to the Harbor Light with Graham, who is a collie two and a half years old.

Gladys Reid's father was Benjamin W. Pease of Tom's Neck Farm on Chappaquiddick, as handsome a man as I ever saw, who spoke with good sense at town meeting and was as able at carpentering as at farming. The Indian name "Chappaquiddick" means "Separated Island," and Chappaquiddick is separated from the rest of Martha's Vineyard by Edgartown Harbor, Katama Bay, and usually by an opening through the barrier of South Beach to the uninterrupted Atlantic, which has Spain and its castles on the other side. One can stand on the beach and see far, but not that far.

The beach opens and closes erratically with the forces of wind, tide, surf, and season, helping or hindering the shell-fishing in Katama Bay, and I have seen several openings made by human ingenuity, usually under the leadership of Captain Antone King Silva. The beach is now closed while the Army Engineers have its future under advisement.

I remember Ben Pease's stories about Chappaquiddick. Back when pilots kept a lookout from Sampson's Hill for vessels to guide around Cape Cod and into Boston there used to be a store in the Handy house. The pilots would walk back from Boston as far as the packet landing at Woods Hole, and they considered it little trouble to bring salable items with them. That was how the Handy house was kept stocked.

One night a customer was directed to go upstairs to look for something he had come after. He came down without the candle that had lighted his way up.

"Oh, I stuck it in that barrel of turnip seed," he said.

"Turnip seed!" yelled Mr. Handy. "That isn't turnip seed. That's gunpowder. Run for your life!"

They all got out as the roof blew off. This is one of the links we have with old times, and we can still date things by reference to the time the roof blew off the Handy house.

In a class Dr. Talcott Williams taught in the Columbia School of Journalism when I was a student there, he spoke of ancient civilizations. "Professor James Harvey Robinson says the Greeks were our contemporaries," a member of the class volunteered. Dr. Williams looked at him benignly and said, "Never quote professorial rivals."

I wonder with whom Gladys Reid and I are really contemporaries. Not with the Greeks, of course, but not with many other human beings alive today, either.

This morning the sun rose just south of Main Street, which serves as a fixed point where street joins wharf and wharf reaches into harbor. Graham and I stood beside the Harbor Light observing the bright-orange flush in the sky, then the fading and paling, then the sun itself, a little at a time. The quality of the light was as informative as the calendar. When we reached home a soft white reek hid Sheriff's Meadow Pond, and a great blue heron flew up from John Butler's Mud Hole.

"Life is real, life is earnest," my mother said as she sat with her sewing on many an afternoon during my childhood in our house at 85 Campbell Street in New Bedford. Her sewing box was made of a wide band of whalebone turned upon itself and studded to keep the ends joined. The dark whalebone, almost black, was scratched with drawings I never deciphered, the lid was stuffed plumply to receive pins and needles, and some of the stuffing escaped through the red cloth top. The words my mother spoke were from Longfellow but she had long lost track of that—they were her own reminder of life's truth, and sometimes but not always an expression of the mood I found her in when I came home from school.

My father was different. He might say, "God damn it!" or "God damn it, Louise!" if the matter happened to concern the household. From his teens he had been a newspaperman in the making; he soon became the city editor, and then for many years was managing editor of the New Bedford *Evening Standard*.

A teacher at the Parker Street Grammar School read to us one day the words of Abraham Lincoln: "All that I am, all that I hope to be, I owe to my angel mother." I decided that this was the case with me, my judgment swayed by my father's temper the previous evening when a can of shoe polish

had resisted his efforts to open it. As a younger son, often left
at home with my mother, I was partial to her tenderness.

My childhood remains in a mythology of its own. The
dahlia bulbs were always kept in the front cellar. This was one
of the facts of life. A fat man named Potter worked in Ryan's
grocery store, and I thought he was quite logically named
Potter Ryan. When an ice-cream cart, horse-drawn, of course,
came through the streets in spring, a bell guaranteed the excellence of the product, but a whistle warned us off. The most
delicious waffle I ever ate was uncooked in the inside, but I
got it by running all the way across the Common, uphill, to
ask my mother for a nickel when the circus parade would be
coming by.

In February, 1908, soon after the *Standard* had established
a Sunday edition, the telephone rang in our house at a late
hour on Saturday evening. My father answered, and so we
learned ahead of the rest of the city that King Carlos and the
Crown Prince of Portugal had been assassinated in the streets
of Lisbon. This was typical of the advantages my brother and
I enjoyed as members of a newspaperman's family.

The night staff would have telephoned my father in any
case, considering the importance of the event to the large
Portuguese population of New Bedford, but he would always
get calls because of his hoard of clippings and all manner of
reference material. From the age of fourteen he had kept
scrapbooks, and late in life he was able to turn to Scrapbook
No. 1 for relevant information about John L. Sullivan, the
Strong Boy of Boston.

It was he who had begun the morgue in the *Standard* office.
At home I looked in on him in a third-floor room, working in
odd hours with big shears, files of newspapers, and *Harper's
Weekly,* a mammoth wastebasket beside him, surrounded by
cigar smoke and the air thin-dried by an old-fashioned gas
heater.

At the time of the assassination of King Carlos, I was eleven years old and therefore at a noticing age, but there had been countless instances that added piquancy to our lives without my having the remotest idea of the reason. My brother, George, and I were growing up in an unfolding, eccentric, often marvelous day-by-day account of the world at large. A time came when I thought, without consulting anyone, that the biggest of all news would be the discovery of the North Pole, but it didn't turn out so.

I awoke in the mornings of my childhood to hear the Angelus ring out from the granite clock tower of St. Lawrence Church, a few blocks distant on County Street, which had been the old County Road. The Angelus, its bright clear chime of three-and-three-and-three, put us on notice that it was six o'clock, a year-round fixed point of earliness. I did not know until much later that it also affirmed the incarnation.

The gaslight—we had Welsbach burners—would be on in the dining room; my mother's footsteps moved back and forth to the kitchen, and I smelled the fragrance of coffee and toast. I knew while I lay in bed that my father was sitting at the table with the *Morning Mercury* beside him, marking it boldly here and there with an editorial black pencil.

The *Mercury*, under the same ownership as the *Standard*, was a quite different paper, though the editor, Zephaniah W. Pease, had worked as a reporter with my father and had been best man at his wedding. Mr. Pease, in a fifty-year reminiscence, described the *Mercury* as a "newspaper of demeanour." The noun implied a degree of cultivation, which he exemplified, for he wore spats, dressed punctiliously, and admired literary stylists. My father's taste ran to the macabre side; his bookplate symbolized the weird in literature, and *Crime and Punishment* was a good example of his chosen reading.

Many years passed before I knew why he marked up the *Mercury* at the breakfast table. I accepted a lot of things without asking questions. What he was doing, of course, was beginning his day's work as city editor, picking out stories or leads for stories that would need following up in the busy hours ahead.

Although breakfast was at six, lunch—which, since we were in New England, was called "dinner"—did not come until one-thirty. Just so were we regulated by edition times. My father had a newspaperman's occupational nervous indigestion, but he could relish Tabasco, horse-radish, strong mustard, and the hottest of peppers, which made him perspire on the top of his head.

In the evening we sat around the table in the sitting room sharing the light of a kerosene lamp my mother thought important as a supplement to the gaslight overhead, my mother sewing, my father reading. At intervals he would tap with one foot or walk from room to room, until my mother said, "George, I wish you'd stop walking quarter-deck." These things "nerved" her even disposition.

Our arrangements were generally tranquil, but my mother occasionally let it be known that she would have liked one room in the house free from impinging bookcases. One room was free—the kitchen. Most of the others, including the corridor, had as many books as they could hold. Early in life my father had become interested in Daniel Defoe as journalist, and had gone on to collect editions of Defoe's works, from *Robinson Crusoe* to *Moll Flanders* and *A Journal of the Plague Year*. His zeal for George Borrow and Dostoevski came later.

George and I read Mayne Reade, Captain Marryat, and R. M. Ballantine, but not Oliver Optic or Alfred George Henty, except that I exposed myself to *Frank on a Gunboat* once when I was at Aunt Emma's. I suppose that we passed into adult literature by way of Robert Louis Stevenson and Mark Twain. Our set of Dickens was in discouragingly small type, but we were enthralled by *David Copperfield* and, in a different way, by *Oliver Twist*.

We were privileged with free tickets to baseball games, concerts, the theater, and even for a time rode free on my father's pass for travel on the side-wheelers between New Bedford and Martha's Vineyard.

There was then a golden age of the theater, though I may have been the only one who knew it. Lester Lonergan came to the New Bedford Theatre in a road company of *If I Were King*, some of the lines of which are with me still: "The king is great in the eyes of the people but the people are great in the eyes of God" and of course "Where are the snows of yester-year . . ." Lonergan was quickly aware that New Bedford was a good theater town, and he soon launched a stock company, which celebrated its thousandth performance in March, 1914.

The plays I saw and loved were rife with the qualities of the traditional stage: *Trilby, David Garrick, Raffles, Sherlock Holmes, The Old Homestead, The Mummy and the Hummingbird*. But Lonergan put on Shakespeare, too, and we saw *Hamlet, The Merchant of Venice, Romeo and Juliet,* and *Othello*.

All one spring when my brother was convalescent from an illness I was allowed to occupy a box seat at Hathaway's Theatre on Saturday nights, and I'm not sure how much my mind was expanded and illuminated—a good deal, I should hope—but mostly I had a wonderful time. Whether one effect can be counted a serious loss I do not know, but I sacrificed at the outset any high-hushed critical sense I might have had. Everything on the stage was wonderful, and a missed line or so made no particle of difference.

For many years I did not realize that I was tone deaf, and that the best chamber music of the day, the Kneisel Quartet and the Flonzaley Quartet, brought to New Bedford at least once a year, was necessarily wasted on me. I saw the rapt expression on the faces of listeners around me and expected to be educated to the same degree of raptness. I never was.

Musical shows were fine—*The Merry Widow*, on its first tour of one-night stands, *The Bohemian Girl*, and so on—and I retained some memory of the "Merry Widow Waltz" and

"I Dreamt that I Dwelt in Marble Halls." But my most distinct musical memory always has been of my father singing "The Minstrel Boy" while he was shaving in the bathroom in the morning. This seems odd, for he wasn't musical, either, though he spoke fondly of "Gypsy John" and "Father O'Flynn" as sung by his friend Win Goff, a New Bedford-born baritone.

I was excused from the Parker Street School, not by the teacher, but by my father, to hear Sousa's Band. An *Uncle Tom's Cabin* company came to New Bedford, with street parade, two Topsys, and two of Marks, the lawyer, but only one Little Eva to ascend to heaven in puffed-up stage clouds. Lew Dockstader's Minstrels came also, a style of folk entertainment that meant no harm but deserves its present banishment.

My father had been a circus fan from boyhood, and he passed along his enthusiasm to George and me. We turned out early on Circus Day, took the trolley to the North End, and saw the stakes driven with perfect timing by crews with sledge hammers, and the canvas raised for the big top and the side shows. The early morning feeling was mixed with smells of crushed grass, hay, animals, and brewing coffee. We watched the elephants at work pushing gaily painted wagons, boys carrying water, all the magnificent disorder which daily proved a triumph of organization.

In the afternoon my father took George and me into the side show before the public was admitted, and so tender was my age that I bawled loudly on being introduced to the almost naked man who was blue all over. Some years later, when George and I went alone to Ringling Brothers Circus, we were astonished but not terrified when we came face to face with Lionel the Dog-faced Boy in a canvas-bordered passage we had thought suitable for our purpose. "What are you peeing here for?" Lionel demanded. I don't think we replied.

When Buffalo Bill's Wild West Show came to New Bedford, I sat uneasily, always ready to be terrified by the shoot-

ing in the Battle of the Little Big Horn, but I admired Colonel
Cody, all in white with white mane and goatee astride his
beautiful white horse. I didn't much mind the exhibition of
sharpshooting.

Ours was always a baseball family. New Bedford had a club
in what was called the International League, and my paternal
grandfather, Dr. George T. Hough, used to drive out in a two-
wheeled chaise to see the games. The *Morning Mercury* had
no one to score, so my grandfather did it until the chore became a nuisance and he recommended his son. My father
showed so much aptitude as baseball reporter that the *National
Baseball Gazette* in New York offered him a job at $15 a week
as a starter "and pay you as much more as your ability shows
you are worth." This was on the recommendation of Frank
Bancroft, manager of the Athletics, the same Bancroft who
managed the Cincinnati Reds in the year of the Black Sox
scandal in Chicago. Since my father was only nineteen, his
family kept him in New Bedford; but baseball got him into
the newspaper profession, as this record shows:

Mercury Publishing Co. to George A. Hough, Dr., For scoring
44 baseball games at 50¢ from May 10 to Oct. 11, $22. Rec'd
payment, George A. Hough, Jan. 8, 1885.

I was a lot younger than nineteen when my father thought
it would be a good idea for me to follow the pattern of his
career. George, two and a half years my senior, was already
a capable horseman and was reporting sulky races held at outlying tracks. So I was introduced to scoring baseball by an
older boy at Buttonwood Park, where neighborhood games
were played. I was not an apt pupil. When my first box score
appeared in the *Standard*, my father noticed a discrepancy.
Before it had begun, my career was suspended. I have known
ever since that every nine-inning game played to completion
must have the symmetry of twenty-seven put-outs.

The other day a rector on Martha's Vineyard asked an
adroitly casual question about my relationship with my father,

and I could sense the inquiring spirit of Freud. Every minister nowadays has Freudian insights, and I guessed that in this instance the rector was construing my combativeness, or whatever cross-grained behavior I exhibit, as possibly the result of early parental fixation. I almost denied the suggestion, but remembered that in Freudian reference denial is tantamount to confession, so I said that maybe there had been something between me and my father, as between father and son there quite commonly is.

Beside my typewriter now, in the year 1974, is a scrapbook my father made and presented to me on my fifth birthday in 1901. It is a big scrapbook of the sort used for pasting up invoices in a day of simpler business procedures. I turn the pages and once more come upon the assassination of President McKinley. Here are newspaper portraits of the martyred President, of Mother McKinley, of the assassin Czolgosz (my father told us how to pronounce his name), and pictures of the death chamber in which he was electrocuted. Here is McKinley's favorite hymn, "Lead, Kindly Light."

Theodore Roosevelt smiles from an old page, ready to say, "Bully!" Here are Li Hung Chang, General Grant, the East Room of the White House, the grand dome of the Capitol, the old and new Minot's Ledge Lighthouse, Bolivar in the Venezuelan countryside, parade inspection at West Point—all in the scrapbook a newspaperman made for his five-year-old son.

From this scrapbook I learned several stanzas of Theodore O'Hara's poem "The Bivouac of the Dead," and having learned them have been unable to get free of them in all the years since, though "Yon marble minstrel's voiceless stone" is an obsolete kind of poesy and "the vengeful blood of Spain" is painfully unhistoric.

My father clipped some advertising of the time: the man in the moon shouting down for some Pear's Soap to be sent up to him, the Uneeda Biscuit kid in yellow oilskins, Cream of

Wheat, Edison's Gramophone. Who and what else? Queen Victoria in youth and age, Christ on the Cross as painted by Rubens, an opium den, ships at sea, a romantic cadet singing "Good-By, Dolly, I Must Leave You."

Theodore Roosevelt, first brought to my attention through the scrapbook, became a life-size figure. A time came when I heard my father say to my mother at breakfast, "He says his hat is in the ring." The year was 1912, and the metaphor of the hat and the ring had to be explained to everyone.

My brother and I learned much important news at the breakfast table, and also on odd or casual occasions. We were watching the play *The Witching Hour* when someone leaned in and said that the *Titanic* had been sunk.

It was a different sort of thing when I came home from the Mary B. White School on an afternoon in 1906 and found my brother, recently ill with diphtheria, sitting on the piazza in the warm April sunlight. He told me there had been an awful earthquake in San Francisco and nobody knew whether Aunt Addie and Aunt Ettie were alive or dead. They were my mother's older sisters, and they had been visiting in San Francisco, where Aunt Ettie had lived for many years before her widowhood.

It turned out that they had survived the catastrophe.

There is a choice now of going backward or forward in time, and I skip for a moment to 1920, when Betty and I, hardly remembering our few days of honeymoon at Lake Mohonk, went to live in Edgartown, a small place of 1,200 inhabitants on a small island, Martha's Vineyard, not yet populated year round by as many as 6,000, situated thirty miles by sea from the nearest city, and sojourned there for forty-five years, supporting ourselves mainly and as best we could from the labors of a country newspaper. At present, Betty having died in 1965, I am living alone with Graham in a sort of semi-retirement, though still performing many of the duties of editor of the *Vineyard Gazette*.

But this Thoreauvian paraphrase does not explain just how it really was. We did not look upon the Island as our Concord, though we appreciated its character and insular self-sufficiency. I did not know Thoreau in 1920, though Betty did, and neither of us had any notion of forsaking the world. We were both young, and youth is often exalted by love and fantasy. But youth is also a time of enterprise, and I considered myself as enterprising as anybody. When it was settled that we were to own, edit, and publish the *Vineyard Gazette*, I was still holding my first job with the meat packers in Chicago, and I walked in Jackson Park, evening after evening, scheming how the paper could be made to pay. For instance, we would print complete fishing news and get advertising from businesses that had things to sell to commercial fishermen.

Thoreau couldn't have lived at Walden if he had had children, and it was evident at the start that Betty and I couldn't take on a weekly newspaper and also raise a family. This calculation grew on us, hardening into decision and relief; and neither of us—so far as I can remember—ever had reason to be sorry. We could see that the world even then was overabundant with children, and there were choices in the paths to fulfillment in life.

Before I left Chicago I often walked with my first employer, and lifetime counselor and friend, Pendleton Dudley. He had not wanted me to leave the meat packers and had offered to have my name lettered on the office door if I chose to stay. I resisted this worldly temptation, and finally he accepted my decision. As we walked along, perhaps under those tall, straight trees on Stony Island Avenue, he said, "Yes, Henry, go ahead and raise your little family. . . ."

Inwardly I resisted the prescription he took for granted. Why should I do what everybody else did? A long time afterward I noticed that Shakespeare, running through the seven ages of man, omitted any mention of parenthood or even of marriage.

So, leaving Chicago behind, I was detaching myself from

the world but not forsaking it, and Betty and I were clear about going ahead on our own, to the extent that circumstances allowed. Betty, with a childhood experience and love of the Pennsylvania mountains, had only a recent acquaintance with the Island, though already an attachment to it. My own Vineyard background could hardly have had greater depth, though it did not relieve me of doubts about the *Gazette.*

One other choice for me would have been a job on the *Standard*. The business manager had written me in Chicago to suggest that I join the advertising department. I knew I didn't want that, though for a while a scheme hung in the air for the Houghs somehow to acquire a newspaper, or control of one, with my father and George on the editorial side and me on the business end. It wouldn't have worked.

But would the *Gazette* open a large enough opportunity? Everyone said it wouldn't—except my father, and to him the business prospect figured only as a detail. I said firmly that the *Gazette* was too small. In the beginning Betty agreed, but she listened to my father and the lure of the Island.

Certainly she knew, when we were rowing on the lake at Mohonk and the fact happened into our conversation, that if every inch of space in every issue of the paper were to be sold for advertising at the rate of 35 cents an inch, a year's entire revenue would come to only $22,400. But the rate of 35 cents an inch was only the one recommended to us, and it might not be possible to maintain. The old editor's rate was 10 cents an inch except for a few contracts such as that for Fletcher's Castoria, which netted $25 a year.

I pulled gently on the oars and said that the *Gazette* would have to be enlarged. Betty wasn't really convinced, but soon she became cheerful again.

And so the decision about our future seemed to be my father's, because he gave the *Vineyard Gazette* to us as a wedding present, along with a contract for Charles H. Marchant, the Old Editor, to stay on for a term that turned out to be eleven years. We accepted with gratitude so remarkable a gift, and I think Betty credited my father with much greater realism in this matter than he possessed. But he did have the gleam of a high heart.

I am writing still in 1974, and yesterday I was invited by Pare and Elizabeth Lorentz to see a showing in the Edgartown town hall of Pare's famous pioneering documentary, *The Plough That Broke the Plains,* filmed in the dust bowl and depression year of 1936, now as then the life and action of history and more, too, because of its gripping sense of continuity.

Tom and Rita Benton were Pare's principal guests, those old and good friends of my father's, and mine also, I realized warmly. Pare and Elizabeth had us to lunch, and Tom and Pare talked of *The Plough* and of how Tom had painted the very things Pare had filmed—the sad, skinny horses and mules, the canting shacks, the defeated men and women retreating through unending swirls of dust.

Tom Benton at eighty-four—what gusto, what vitality and independence; he and Rita were on a great height of achievement, keenly aware of possessing that rarest thing of all, the moment, the very moment, on their own terms. They spoke of old and good times with my father at Fish Hook in the later days, when he lived alone. That was when Tom painted my father's portrait for the Boston Museum of Fine Arts. "New England Editor," he called it. After the portrait was done, Tom and Rita invited my father and Betty and me to their place in Chilmark to see it, and Tom said, "What do you think of it? Not that I give a God damn." But he was pleased that we did like it and said so enthusiastically. Rita had cooked a wonderful dinner, which we ate in a spirit of shared triumph and comradeship.

The morning after seeing *The Plough,* I sat down at the typewriter and said to myself that what I am writing will be a documentary of a sort, whether I make it so deliberately or not. And I reflected that if I am alive in 1976, as I now expect to be, I shall have lived and experienced only twenty years less than half the life span of the republic. This is not a weighty reflection, but it justifies some looking back over my shoulder.

2

My mother was born in the village of Holmes Hole, now Vineyard Haven, in the year 1858, so she would have been seven years old when Lincoln was assassinated. It never occurred to me to ask what, if anything, she remembered about that far-off time, for in all my years of growing up she not only seemed young, she was young.

Holmes Hole rose on a hillside facing east, above a deeply indented, well-formed blue harbor which served as an important port of call and refuge for vessels in the carrying trade. Though the village remained small, the dimensions of its concern were extended through long voyages made by my grandfather and others of his time to the Pacific and Indian Oceans, and through the peripheral journeying of mariners such as Uncle Press, Aunt Addie's husband, who commanded vessels in the China and Australian trade and owned a Newfoundland dog that licked the nap of his beaver hat all the wrong way.

My grandfather's family came from Maine but he was born in New Bedford in 1815, son of an older Henry Beetle and his wife, Martha Hillman, sister of the Hillman shipwrights who built the famous whaleship *Charles W. Morgan*. Both parents died when he was six, and he went to live with an uncle, James H. Beetle, on the East Side (as it was called) of Holmes Hole harbor, also known, for reason enough, as the Barbary Coast.

James Beetle held appointment as a notary and had much to do with ship surveys, wreck reports, and the like. His house was a considerable distance from the one-room school at Farm Neck to which my grandfather went on foot. I have my grandfather's powder horn, his initials carved on the wooden plug, and a few of his books. *The Sunday Service of the Methodists,* dated London, 1792, is inscribed "William Daggett, Gibraltar, 1827, Given to Capt. Henry Beetle."

At the age of seventeen my grandfather went to sea, and I know of him next eight years later, when he called with a letter of introduction to a young woman at Topham, Maine, not far from Farmington and the Smoky River Valley. This was the letter, dated at Farmington, August 25, 1840:

Miss Eliza Ann Eaton,—
Dear Girl,

I write this to inform you that I am now at this place. I arrived on the Sabbath, was too late on Saturday to take the stage, otherwise could have been in time at your house to have seen you at home. We went out to your house yesterday and dined there but how great my disappointment not finding you at home. There seems to be some ill fate about the matter.

I wrote to you about a month since and have this day found the letter in the office at this place. The bearer of this, my Nephew, will hand you that as well as this. You will now find me as good as my word. I have now to a letter fulfilled my promise and by this introduced to you my Nephew, Henry W. Beetle, this is him, how do you like him?

I regret in the deepest sense that I am not situated to come down with him and see you, but business precludes the propriety. I have said to him and now say to you that should there be a mutual exchange of sentiment by you and him that I am extremely desirous that you should come up with him on Friday next. I shall probably be here until Sunday. I am not willing to go home without seeing you.

I will say to you without hesitancy that you may place implicit

confidence in him, for I believe that he will not deceive you. I
hope that you both may and will be of one mind. If you are
otherwise inclined, you will have the goodness to hand him
back this epistle. Whatever the result, I ever remain your friend
and well wisher. It now only remains, I think, for you to be
as punctual as myself.

Jas. H. Beetle

N.B. I have mentioned my views to your grandmother which
she cordially agrees with. I mean all that I said I mean.

Eliza was as punctual as Uncle James. She did not hand the
letter back, and she at twenty-four and my grandfather at
twenty-five were married in December, 1840.

From December to April is only three months, and it was
in April, so soon after the wedding, that my grandfather received an important letter from Jireh Perry, a New Bedford
agent and owner of whaleships:

Mr. Henry Beetle: Sir, Being in want of a mate for the ship
John Adams and from the knowledge I have of you, should very
much like to have you go mate of her. She will be ready for
sea the first of July. The John Adams is a small ship, will carry
1850 barrels, in perfect order, and our intention is for her to go
sperm whaling for two years and if you do not succeed in filling
her with sperm oil to fill up with whale oil. . . . Please answer
immediately.

There could be only one answer, and my grandfather left
home in the first summer of his marriage for an address beyond
the sunset and the baths of all the western stars: "Mr. Henry
Beetle, Indian Ocean, Ship John Adams, Bradford, Master."

My grandfather's letters home are still evocative. In one of
them after he became captain, he wrote to Eliza Ann from the
Canary Islands: "I sent you a letter by the brig Wheaton of
Nantucket. I want to know if you receive it. I trusted to a
Nantucket man. I never trusted one yet but deceived me." In
another: "Have got a good mate if he would let gin alone. I
like the bark very well but she leaks a little (don't tell anyone). . . ." And in still another: "My chief mate I have put
on shore today. Had a fall but I think he will get over it. He

has been no use to me at all. I have wished him on Nantucket many a time and I could have stuck up a cord wood stick and put a hat on it. Then I should have known what I had to help me. . . ."

Back on the Vineyard at about this time, a young man named Edgar Marchant was establishing the *Vineyard Gazette*, which seventy-four years later his great-nephew would sell to my father as a wedding gift to Betty and me. In 1920 I called upon one of the original subscribers, Aunt Rebecca Manter, who, with her husband, had run the gristmill on Roaring Brook in Chilmark. She was very old but she laughed as she remembered how Chilmark people had ridiculed that young fellow down in Oldtown who thought he could start a paper.

My grandfather was stopping at the Society Islands in March of 1847. He didn't say whether he went ashore at Tahiti or Papeete, but by this time Herman Melville and Dr. Long Ghost had left for good.

"Been 6 miles in a boat after potatoes and yams," my grandfather wrote. "Came on to rain and got a regular soakin. . . ."

From Fayal, lying offshore: "My bread and flour goes from bad to worse. Have hove overboard 4 casks of Bread all rotten (don't tell anybody, Mr. Hitch won't like it). Worms can't live in the flour, it is too sour and musty. . . ." Worms were one thing, foremast hands another; Mr. Hitch and other New Bedford ship owners expected flour to be eaten.

Now I turn to the lonesomeness of that first voyage as mate in the *John Adams*, not two years as proposed, but almost three. From Capetown in January, 1844, my grandfather addressed his "Affectionate Wife":

Every day I feel more anxious to be with you and in hopes to be by April. . . . It is past 9 o'clock in the evening with us, and I sit writing to you and the second mate to his father. We came in last evening, today employed cleaning ship. . . . I have not been on shore yet, and whether I go is quite uncertain. If I was sure I would not have the scurvy I am sure I would not. What more to write I do not know, for news I have none.

I hear the wind a-whistling on deck and the Capt. ashore which gives me double duty tonight, but if I could while away one moment of your time from pain or sorrow I would write until midnight.

My grandfather was not a tourist. He would never have read the *National Geographic*. But he did go ashore.

The Captain on shore, the second mate turned in, and I am lonesome and homesick. . . . It is my liberty tomorrow and I have some thought of going to church for I have not seen the inside of one since I went with you. I hope we shall be able to go more than we have yet, for I am tired of going to sea and I think if I could find some other way of getting a livelihood and be with my Eliza, we should see more comfort and happiness than we do now, none.

I don't expect to make my fortune this voyage. It is too far gone. What little oil we have got, I know who has got it, which gives me some satisfaction. . . . The nine o'clock gun has fired and when the daylight gun fires I shall have to turn out.

The *John Adams* ended her voyage at New Bedford in May, and my grandfather hurried home to his wife of three and a half years who, factually, was still a bride of a few months. Their first child, Martha Adeline, my Aunt Addie—she did not care for the "Martha"—was born on May 5, 1845, an important date for me because I knew her long and well and could look back through her eyes upon the manners of the past. Now, in 1974, I have been reading the memoir of a man who spent years looking around for his identity. I was not born at the end of a line as slack as that.

In May, 1846, my Aunt Addie a year old, the first edition of the *Vineyard Gazette* just published at Edgartown, the ship *Hercules*, Henry W. Beetle, master—at the age of thirty —lay in the roadstead at Lahaina, where he found letters that troubled him. He wrote to his wife:

Dear Eliza, you gave me a small description of a day's work you done. I fear you will shorten your days if you do so. . . . No, I do not want my wife to work so hard. Is there no one you could get to cut your wood? . . . If you want money, Eliza, Mr. Perry will let you have $150, I think, without hesitation. . . .

You wish to know how I get along. Very well. I have had very little difficulty as yet. I discharged two the worst men I had today, and in hopes of getting along well with the rest. If I can get oil I have nothing to fear. . . .

The *Hercules* made a summer cruise on the North West grounds in the bight formed by Alaska as it juts far out and trails off in the Aleutians. She came south in the fall, cruised on the line or off New Zealand, and recruited at the Society Islands the following March. There was no letter from my grandfather until he reached Más Afuera, in the Juan Fernández group, in February, 1848. He finally made port at New Bedford again in May of 1849.

The *Vineyard Gazette* that year, "A Family Newspaper, Neutral in Politics, Devoted to General News, Marine Intelligence, Literature, Morality, Agriculture and Amusement," filled many of its columns with the excitement of gold and California. At first, the tales of fortune, "golden rocks," wealth accumulated overnight, plenty of gold to enrich 100,000 miners for years to come; then, more sobering letters home, reports of hard labor and small return, illness, high prices for all necessities.

My grandfather bought a share in the schooner *Helen M.* and sailed around the Horn for El Dorado. The *Helen M.* was a trading schooner, but my grandfather wrote from Paita, which he naturally called "Payty," to say, "If Sis will be a good girl and do as you want, you may buy her a new dress and I will send you the first California gold I get to pay for it."

Since he wasn't a tourist, he didn't mention the sandy bluff at Paita, as high as the Gay Head cliffs at home, or the dry barren look of a rainless port, or the iron customs house that had been brought in sections from England. But he supplied items of neighborhood news that should have got into the *Vineyard Gazette:*

The calculation now is to stop here to get potatoes which will be the middle of August. . . . Grafton Hillman is here fitting his vessel, taking all the comfort in the world. He has a nice brig of 150 tons. Capt. Consider Fisher is here with his wife. . . .

On October 12, 1850, at Holmes Hole, my Aunt Henrietta was born, and on October 10 her father was writing from San Francisco:

Dear W. — I write to inform you that I have sold out of the sch Helen M. and send you a Bill of Exchange for $500 which you can get cashed at any of the banks in New Bedford. I don't know hardly what to do, whether to go home or not. I have not seen the prospect of making anything yet. . . . I shall write next mail or start myself if it is healthy on the Isthmus. Last accounts it was sickly there.

So now it was back to whaling for Captain Beetle, and his ship was the *James Andrews,* which sailed from New Bedford on June 6, 1851, for the Atlantic and Indian Oceans. For a few months he had been a husband and father of two daughters separated in age by four years, the usual span of a whaling voyage, living in a white house near the top of a hill in Holmes Hole. I knew the house well, and I don't think it changed much in character through the years. Conch shells stood at either side of the front door, and a row of box bushes responded to the sunlight with a scent I identified as that of sunlight itself.

After almost a year at sea, my grandfather made port at St. Catherine's, Brazil, and wrote home.

I had 3 men to run away, one I discharged spitting blood, 2 more tried to run but I catched them in the act. I can't depend on my mate at all. I don't pretend to believe a word he says. My second got as drunk as a beast a number of times in port, the last 4 days I had my hands full, could not sleep nights for fear the crew would steal a boat and run for it. There is no comfort for me nor happiness. If I get oil enough to make a saving voyage and get home in 30 months I may feel a little better than I do now. . . .

I want to hear what you are doing, etc., whether Adeline goes to school or not, and how much, how much tax you have to pay, whether the oil got home safe, and how much it brought. . . .

He had shipped home 331 barrels of sperm, but I do not know what the oil gauger found or the going price of sperm.

Now I am confronted with a family void. My grandfather arrived home on November 4, 1853, and stayed nine months. A son was born to him and Eliza but there is no telling when.

I went to the graveyard in Vineyard Haven, the renamed Holmes Hole, this afternoon and left Graham in the car while I walked down an empty path under the bare wintry oaks. I found the Beetle lot easily enough though I had not been there since Aunt Addie's funeral in 1928.

Long after the death of Eliza Ann, my grandfather married Lottie, whose surname was also Beetle and who was hated by my mother. His weathered granite stone stands upright between those of his two wives, which are somewhat smaller, as custom dictated. I don't suppose there is any sex parity in gravestones even in this day of women's lib.

Aunt Ettie's grave is here, too, in a long and far separation from her closed-off years of marriage in San Francisco. The obituaries of her Scotsman husband called him a "capitalist," though my understanding had been that he was a ship's outfitter. Perhaps he was both.

The only other stone is deprecatingly small, bearing one word, "Infant." Here lies the boy who might have been my uncle.

The January light followed increasingly strong puffs of wind, changing the shadows as they slanted to long patterns on the slope beyond the path where I stood. Winter was here, and loneliness, and the infinite patience of time.

Eliza Ann Beetle died in July, 1872, at the age of fifty-three, having never known the best of married life and a scant ten years of uninterrupted companionship with her husband. A picture of her in her youth suggests that she may have been tall, perhaps with a large frame and long arms and legs; but her reserve was too much for the camera. A crayon enlargement of long ago made her seem quietly beautiful. In her last picture she had become a woman dwindled of feature and spirit, the more pitiful because of a flush the daguerreotypist added to her shrunken cheeks.

I chose another path, which took me to the burial lot of Uncle Press, who married Aunt Addie in 1863, when she was seventeen and he was forty-two. This was six years after the death of his first wife, Sophronia, at sea aboard the bark *Carrie Leland* of New York. He is generally identified as Capt. Presbury L. Smith, but he preferred the spelling "Pressberry" and this form was used on his gravestone and on an obelisk in the center of the lot.

One more burial place I turned aside to visit, a modest, narrow location of rest, where the graves of my father and mother are marked with boulders from their beloved North Tisbury hills.

Back at the gate, Graham's long head was thrust out through the car window as he watched for me.

An item in the Marine News in the *Vineyard Gazette* completes the record of the bark *Fortune*, so far as I have been able to reconstruct it: "Ar, at N.B., May 4, 1856, bark Fortune, Beetle, Ochotsk Sea, Lahaina, Dec. 13, via Roratonga, with 128 bbls spm, 1850 do whale, 200,000 bone. Took 50 bbls wh oil on passage."

So my grandfather had been to the Ochotsk (the modern spelling is "Okhotsk"), which almost might have been the end of the world, far up against Kamchatka, in a region of sudden gales, pack ice, and raw fog. He left his ship at New Bedford and hastened home.

My mother was born June 2, 1858, the length of a four-year voyage from the unnamed son, two four-year voyages from Aunt Ettie, and three four-year voyages from Aunt Addie. Aunt Emma, my mother's younger sister, was born after another four years, in 1862, and the family was complete. But I have no idea where my grandfather may have voyaged between my mother and Aunt Emma.

All this I claim as a valid part of my documentary as I write it now, though at the same time it seems to have little to do with me. Rootstock and genes, the changing times, birth and age—there they are, and the nation also growing older. This heritage of mine embodied a sort of Puritanism, and I have tried to pin the subject down. I have looked into dictionaries, encyclopedias, and histories—so little of close relevance. I have reread *The Last Puritan* without finding a kinship between old Boston and the old Vineyard.

This from Richard H. Tawney applies somewhat: "It would be misleading to dwell on the limitations of Puritan ethics without emphasizing the enormous contribution of Puritanism to political freedom and social progress. The foundation of democracy is the sense of spiritual independence which nerves the individual to stand against the powers of the world. The virtues of enterprise, diligence and thrift are the indispensable foundation of any complex and vigorous civilization. . . ."

The lives of Martha's Vineyard were lived not more narrowly but more frugally than most. Their quality was suntanned and lean. It will not do to assert too much, and in the end I come to a definition stated negatively and in modern idiom: You have to settle for less. That was what was really in my mother's mind as she sat with her whalebone sewing box and said aloud to herself, "Life is real, life is earnest."

Of course there were men and women active on Martha's Vineyard when Betty and I joined the *Gazette* who had been young when my mother was young.

Charles H. Brown, known to Vineyarders as Charlie Brown or Lawyer Brown, was a year younger than she. He had attended the Dukes County Academy at West Tisbury, gone on to Dartmouth College, and had taken his law degree at Boston University, after which he was admitted to the bar by Justice Oliver Wendell Holmes. By 1920 he had given up a law practice in Boston and was settled in easygoing retirement in Vineyard Haven, taking what cases might come along. He appeared in the celebrated bathing beach case in district court at Edgartown during our first summer.

The case really began with this paid notice in the *Gazette*, inserted by James E. Chadwick, owner of the beach, whose friendship we prized as soon as we knew him well:

Bare legged women will not be tolerated.
Women bathers must wear stockings.
One-piece bathing suits are forbidden both for men and women
Skirts (bathing suits) must cover the knees.

These rules helped produce the atmosphere that led two summer youths to frolic on the beach raft in such a way that Mr. Chadwick had them up before Judge Eldridge on a complaint charging malicious mischief. Retained for the prosecution was young Arthur W. Davis, who made a classical and complete preparation.

But here came Lawyer Brown, quickly casting loose from the law of the land and veering out to sea with admiralty law. Judge Eldridge happened to be the last judge in the state who had never been admitted to the bar, and the farther Lawyer Brown went to sea, the more he fidgeted. He found the defendants not guilty.

Lawyer Brown, a gifted controversialist, wrote communications to the *Gazette* opposing a hard-surfaced highway across the plains between Edgartown and West Tisbury. Beriah T. Hillman, white-bearded veteran of the Civil War and present Register of Probate, championed the other side of the argument—naturally, for he was up-Island born, in Chilmark.

Mr. Brown threw in a red herring of irrelevance by advocating a different highway route in defiance of sportsmen, clubs, and individuals who "probably would wish to keep these miles of beautiful and once productive country for their own pleasure and that of their friends. This is an economic crime, for these seemingly barren fields were once the granary of the early settlers of the Island; and their descendants, like the Crofters of Scotland, have been dispossessed and their homesteads turned into hunting lodges for the rich."

Mr. Hillman was surprised that Mr. Brown should be "so blind to the beauties that may be seen in traveling the Edgartown and West Tisbury road. I am afraid that when traveling that road he has been like my friend Capt. George Fred Tilton, too much absorbed in contemplating the sand in the roadway to look away at the distant hills and behold their beauty. One of the most charming pictures is a sunset of a hazy October evening viewed from this roadway. The sun sinking behind the western hills touching up the heavens with a glow of magnificence and splendor. . . . There is a quaint beauty in the level plain with clumps of trees fringing its margin, and here and there a lonesome tree standing forth like a sentinel."

Mr. Brown returned to the encounter: "Mr. Hillman does me honor when he couples my name with that of Capt. George Fred Tilton, but I think he has got the wrong Tilton. If I remember rightly, the one who perpetrated the bon mot on the sandy roads of the Vineyard was an uncle of the captain, John Lawrence Tilton. Peace to his ashes and may he find a worthy biographer, for he was a leaner and wittier Falstaff, a stronger and braver Cyrano all in one. When he met the inquisitive Mr. Chonfeldt on the sandy old road, he was driving an ancient stallion whose pedigree he was wont to recite as follows: 'The Morgan hoss Trustee, sired by the third Bulrush Morgan and damned by the only John L. Tilton.'

"When I drive over the road it is in ancient car sired by E. R. Thomas and damned by the entire community. The Tiltons and I do well to watch the road for our steeds are like to stumble, but Mr. Hillman may look aloft. He is traveling that way, and his road, albeit straight and narrow, is secure. . . .

"The charm of the plain is the charm of the desert places— the scant and thorny herbage, the parching winds by day, the frosts by night, the soaring hawk and even the whirring prairie chicken. . . . This is no place for a scenic highway. The roar of the Packard would drown the booming of the cock heath hen, and the stench of gasoline would offend the rabbits, chewinks, and all our timid desert friends. Leave us to our solitude."

I don't suppose anyone knew who Mr. Chonfeldt was, but this didn't matter. The outwash plain of the Vineyard, extending southward from the glacial hills up-Island, which Mr. Hillman saw in blue autumnal haze, was not a desert, though it was largely given over to scrub oak, chewinks, brown thrashers, secret wildflowers, and the still surviving heath hen or eastern prairie chicken, remnants of flocks Charlie Brown had hunted in his youth.

Hardly anyone writes such letters to the *Gazette* any more. Grace of writing, not to mention appropriate allusions, are not only dated, but damned by the Age of Communication. Not to mention, for that matter, the advance of modern education.

A momentous event for George and me was the marriage of our parents in the white-towered Methodist church in Vineyard Haven. Before me now is the letter my grandfather directed to my mother on March 3, 1893:

Dear Louise,—
I write you a few lines this morning to tell you that I have written a few lines to G giving my consent to your marriage.
I never was so bothered to know what to write him. I have no objection to your marrying him if that is the best for you both. Now what are your plans, when & so forth and all the particulars, just write.
I have not heard from Addie for a week. Emma has gone to Cambridge. . . . With much love. Excuse haste.
Father

In the margin of the letter he had written: "(Rather hard for me to give away my baby.)" Since his "baby" was then thirty-five years old, this comment is remarkable. Remarkable also was the willingness of my forthright and seldom patient father to submit to what he must have recognized as a strained observance of an obsolete convention. For that matter, my mother had shown unusual initiative and independence for her time by training as a nurse and becoming head nurse at St. Luke's, the principal New Bedford hospital.

Anyway, I can readily understand why my grandfather felt "so bothered." Once again, this time on November 22, 1896, his resources were put to a test:

My Dear Daughter Louise,—
Every day since I received George's very kind and interesting letter I thought I would write and thank him for it but I did not do it, so tonight after many days I am trying to write you a few lines to let you know that I appreciate your kindness in naming your baby for me. I only wish I was good enough to be so honored and to hear you are getting along so well which I hope you will continue to do and that you will soon be able to be up and around.

Mr. Howland and Dr. B's wife seemed very much pleased and said they thought it was named as it should be. You must excuse me to George for my negligence in not writing before. For the last three weeks I have had a Bad cold and most of the time I did not have Life and energy enough to do anything. . . .
                                        Affectionately from Father

Of course I was the "it" who was named as it should be.

I know my grandfather only from photographs which show him with white hair and beard and gentle eyes. But a young ship captain of today looks over my shoulder and says, "I'd hate to have sailed under him." So now I notice the straight line of my grandfather's lips, the furrows from his nose that form a triangle with this line as a base, and when I cover the upper part of his face I can see the grim spirit of determination below.

He died on January 24, 1898, and the minister in the white church on the hill used the old familiar image, "A cedar of Lebanon has fallen."

During my childhood, Aunt Addie and Aunt Ettie lived in my grandfather's house and had made it their own. There was a swing in the great apple tree in the back yard in which George and I by turns rode higher and higher, until, excited and satisfied, we let the old cat die. Rhubarb grew in that yard, and climbing roses against the kitchen ell.

In the hall were a multitude of baskets Aunt Addie had collected, woven by Eskimos and South Sea Islanders and I know not by what other primitive artists of basketry. On the parlor wall hung one of Aunt Ettie's paintings, the Cliff House and Seal Rock on the California coast, and I supposed always that Seal Rock must be among the great national landmarks. If a *Gazette* correspondent, especially the late Lucinda Norton St. John, had been asked to describe that room, she would have said that it was "sumptuously furnished."

An elaborately decorated lacquer cabinet had drawers in which sandalwood fans were kept, nearby stood a tall and lovely Chinese screen, and in one corner was displayed the fine china brought home by Uncle Press. I don't think anyone sat on the voluptuously silken and overstuffed sofa, but it deserved its prominence.

There were oriental rugs of worth and beauty, and fine old tables with fascinating knickknacks and ornaments. On Chinese stools stood Aunt Addie's plants, mainly a maidenhair fern and an aspidistra. Aunt Ettie's gloxinias lived in the dining room, with a sunny southern exposure. When it came time to divide family possessions, Betty and I took the maidenhair fern, a choice I now consider to have been a mistake. The aspidistra would have been just the thing in our house to repel the counterculture.

When we visited Aunt Addie and Aunt Ettie as children, George and I read *Mrs. Wiggs of the Cabbage Patch* and, much later, Florence I. Barclay's *The Rosary* and *Mistress of Shenstone*, which of course we did not have at home. The aunts were also long on Gene Stratton Porter—*Freckles, A Girl of the Limberlost,* and the colorfully decorated *Moths of the Limberlost.*

We used to hear stories about Uncle Press, in particular the one about his shipboard cook who prepared an excess number of potatoes for the cabin table in order to make use of the leftovers himself. Uncle Press had the cook stand against a bulkhead and threw the surplus at him as one bombards an artful dodger at a country fair. I inherited a journal kept by Uncle Press on the brig *Brownsville City* on a passage from Sydney to San Francisco with cargo and passengers in 1853. One entry reads: "Mrs. Gale at 3 a.m. awoke and found she had a baby, a son. Lat by obs 18:45 S. Long by Chron 155: 53:30."

My mother was not a year old, living in my grandfather's house, when a young doctor newly graduated from medical school in New York City arrived to take up practice in Holmes Hole. He put this announcement in the *Vineyard Gazette:*

DR. GEORGE T. HOUGH
Physician and Surgeon
Holmes Hole, Mass.
N.B. All the Drugs and Medicines Usually Kept in
Drug Stores Are for Sale at His Office.

This was my paternal grandfather. Martha's Vineyard was thus woven into my family twice over.

I doubt if Dr. Hough had made preliminary trips of any account to the Island, yet between April and December, 1859, he courted and married Maria Presbury Smith, daughter of Captain Nathan Smith and niece of Uncle Press. Maria's mother was Jane de Neuville, daughter of a French émigré of 1770, a detail I record out of respect to the sea-borne cosmopolitanism of what was at the same time a tightly bound insular community.

George Thomas Hough was the son of Garry Andrew and Julia Wright Hough, and was born in a house at the corner of the Bowery and Hester Street in New York City. After the early death of his mother, he lived with the Wright family upstate until he chose to be a doctor rather than a circuit-riding elder like his Wright grandfather. At medical school he met a Vineyard-born physician, Dr. Leroy Milton Yale, who told him about Martha's Vineyard and Holmes Hole.

The young Dr. Hough, twenty-four years old in 1861, was deeply concerned about the impending conflict between North and South. He wrote to an old college friend in Mississippi to ask about the *other side*, and sent the reply to the *Gazette*.

What would the South do without money and without credit? If the Negroes loved their masters so well, and would fight for them, why did they run away? What would the South do in case of an insurrection? Dr. Hough expressed his own opinion that the troubles of the day meant the end of slavery.

His friend answered pridefully, as would be expected of a Mississippian. He had voted for secession, though unwillingly. He was confident about the South's finances, said the question of a navy would be settled to A. Lincoln's satisfaction, and doubted that there would be an insurrection as far south as Mississippi. He advised any "John Brown friends" of Dr. Hough to proceed carefully, the South was united, and anyone who conquered it would conquer the best blood of the South. It was not planned to have Negroes fight, for they could be used to better advantage raising corn and so on. As to slavery, he himself had just returned from Natchez, where his errand had been to purchase six Negroes.

So the lines were drawn in my grandfather's convictions, as in the news that Fort Sumter had been fired upon in April, the same month a son was born to him and Maria. Lincoln called for volunteers, and Dr. Hough left for service in the Medical Corps of the Northern Army.

While he was away, his wife died.

My father's paternal grandfather, Garry Andrew Hough, died when I was a year old. I wish I might have known him.

He was born in Potsdam, New York, in 1814, one year earlier than Henry W. Beetle in New Bedford. At fourteen he became an apprentice in the print shop of the Saint Lawrence *Republican,* which despite its name was a Democratic newspaper. After working for this and other small papers and becoming proprietor for a time of the *Monroe Standard* at Honeydew Falls, he decided to become an actor. He found small parts in a stock company in Syracuse at $15 a week, a stipend increased to $17 when he married Julia Asbury Wright, whose middle name honored Bishop Asbury, who had christened her.

Garry Hough took another turn at newspaper work, until, according to an old Detroit newspaper, "there was an attempt to rouse Canada against the English government in what was known as the Patriot War, and Mr. Hough associated rather picturesquely in that rebellion." I wonder what he did.

Anyway, he was soon back in theatricals, playing towns in the Shenango Valley—Utica, Binghamton, Oswego, Elmira, Bath, and so on—the performances being given in halls. The company carried its own scenery, consisting of five or six drops and one set of wings. The drops showed a street, a prison interior, a forest, a parlor, and a kitchen. Jumps were made by stagecoach, except for towns on lakes or canals.

In 1843 came the emotional wave of the temperance movement led by John B. Gough, and Garry Hough was quick to ride the crest with shows such as *The Drunkard's Reform. Ten Nights in a Bar-Room* came later.

An innkeeper in Ripley, Ohio, complained of the troupe for performing without a license. The rival inn, down the street, had been chosen for its accommodation, and the manager tipped off Garry Hough as to impending trouble with the law. In fast time the actors were hiking down a lane to a landing on the Ohio River, their baggage coming after them in a wagon.

Garry peered in both directions along the river—no boat in sight. He stationed a man on the bluff above the landing, and soon the alarm was raised—a horseman approaching. Baggage and props were loaded into a skiff and shoved off from the riverbank. But the sculling oar stuck in the mud, leaving only a boat hook for any sort of propulsion.

The horseman reined up, saw that all attachable properties were adrift in navigable waters on the Ohio, looked on for a while, and remarked that he had done his duty. He wheeled his horse about and trotted off.

Soon the steamboat *Swiftsure No. 3* came around a bend, and in response to a signal picked up the baggage and crew of the skiff from the Kentucky shore, where they had managed to land, then crossed over and took on the rest of the troupe. The *Swiftsure*'s captain transported them on trust and even offered the sort of hospitality a temperance company was bound to decline.

Business proved to be bad. Three performances in Marietta were no help. Up the river, then, to Pittsburgh, where rain washed out festivities planned for the Fourth of July, with six performances in a hall known as the "Temperance Ark" as a climax. Only one performance could be given, and that produced receipts of less than $20.

But Cleveland, where three weeks had been played to crowded houses in April, now brought a return of fortune in September.

The temperance shows yielded to tours with *Uncle Tom's Cabin* through towns of the Middle West. The first *Uncle Tom* dramatization had been made by an actor named Akin, a member of the Garry Hough company. This stage version included a comedy character not found in Harriet Beecher Stowe's novel, a Yankee named Gumption Cute. Garry Hough played the role many times, and I have a sketch from a Detroit newspaper showing him so, hat on the back of his head, finger thrust forward, inquiring, "Say, you, is this the place where human chattels are sold at public auction?"

My great-grandfather's *Uncle Tom* played a year at the Chatham Theatre in New York City, drew crowds in Milwaukee and at the Buffalo Museum, and in 1865 began a tour under canvas. At Elkhart, Indiana, a sudden squall collapsed the tent.

According to the Elkhart *Review,* "The living mass struggled beneath the canvas, bent on self-preservation, the cries of fear and anguish ringing on the air, the loud calls of friends and more subdued accents of endearment may be imagined by nonparticipants." But "in a brief space of time the last person had succeeded in escaping, and we are happy to record with no other harm than fright, and in a few instances, contusions. . . . Articles of apparel left in the excitement were carefully secured by Mr. Hough's employees and taken to the Clifton House where the owners may find them."

Milton Nobles, an actor of old-time repute, caught on with the *Uncle Tom* company while it was playing under canvas, but in ten weeks he had not been paid. He mustered his courage for a complaint, he said later, and approached Garry Hough in Ypsilanti. He had a speech all prepared. But my great-grandfather grasped his hand cordially and slapped him on the back. " 'Young man,' said he, 'I have been watching you carefully. I have made up my mind that there is something in you.' I started to say I didn't know how it got there but Garry was too quick for me. 'Yes, young man, there is a future before you.' Before I could say it couldn't very well be behind me, he added, 'Keep your eyes and ears open and your mouth shut. Things are cooking.' Then he winked mysteriously, slapped me on the back and left me standing on the corner with my mouth open. Garry was a dandy. We shall not look upon his like again."

In Detroit my great-grandfather became the first manager of the Opera House, and continued until he had achieved the mellow afternoon status of a patriarch. His nearest approach to my own time came in 1894, when he wrote to my father in quavery handwriting. My brother, George, had just been born. "My Dear Boy," the letter to my father began. "I congratulate you on your first production. Nine pounds! What a whopper! And a boy, too. Most parents take pride in genders but why it is so I could never understand. Little boys and little girls are always sweet in my eyes—the un-winged angels of earth, the only true type of heavenly perfection. . . ."

When this lively ancestor died in 1897 at the age of eighty-three, one of the Detroit dailies printed a long obituary under a black headline:

CURTAIN DOWN
ON THE LIFE OF GARRY A. HOUGH, THE VETERAN
ACTOR MANAGER
He Has Made His Last Exit
Death Came to Him This Morning at His Home
and Carried Him On Its Wings to Make His
Entrance in a New Part on a New Stage

In history's odd way, roughly half a century after Garry Andrew Hough's death, his great-great-grandson, my nephew George A. Hough III, began an early stage of his newspaper career in Detroit as a reporter for the *Free Press*.

My Grandmother Hough always waited until after the cold May storm before she took the steamer from New Bedford for another summer at 7 County Park on the Camp Ground at Cottage City, the town that became Oak Bluffs in 1907. It had grown from a half-circle of tents pitched for a camp meeting in the summer of 1835, the surroundings chosen for their seclusion and idyllic loveliness—an oak grove, a pond reaching to the Sound, tall bluffs, an expanse of open pasture. Then, after the Civil War, the camp meeting had become a place of recreation, the tents yielding to gingerbread cottages, and a worldly resort rising outside and beyond the grove.

When Dr. George T. Hough returned from the war, he soon settled in New Bedford, with its larger opportunities, but he did not desert Martha's Vineyard entirely. He visited the home of Captain Nathan Skiff Smith, who had been his father-in-law, until the captain's death in 1868. The captain, I note by way of further deepening a sense of the old life of Holmes Hole, had been "an exile from home for nearly 35 years, having passed but 5 years of the time with his family, and had just returned to spend the rest of his life with loved ones at home. . . ." The quotation is from his obituary in the *Vineyard Gazette*.

It was on a visit to the Island that my grandfather met Lydia Winslow Anthony, who was to become my grandmother. Her home was in Westport, some seven miles from New Bedford, in a region of river, marshes, and green fields. The Anthonys were Quakers who kept a station on the Underground Railroad for escaping slaves during the Civil War. They were apparently well-to-do, for I once saw a marriage settlement paper protecting the right of her possessions in her own name. Her supply of sheets, table linen, and so on, all with the initials L.W.H., has worn through two more family generations and still persists in plenty.

How quiet and unchanging and how comfortable in her principles my grandmother was as she sat in a corner of her dark, neat living room on the second floor at 95 Elm Street in New Bedford. Her "nice things" were different from those of Aunt Addie and Aunt Ettie—an old grandfather clock, paintings by R. Swain Gifford, an artist esteemed at the time, who was born on Naushon Island and was a friend of my grandfather's, an etching or two by Dr. Leroy Milton Yale, two enormous blue-and-gilt Chinese vases with rippled rims, oriental rugs, fine old mahogany things.

My grandmother dressed always in black, becoming to her age and bulk. She was not at all fat, but it couldn't be denied that she was "fleshy." One of her shoes was built up an inch or so higher than the other, but I never asked why. She didn't walk a great deal, but when she did walk she didn't limp.

She was always with us at Campbell Street for Thanksgiving and Christmas, and often at other times. A friend had given my father a silver cocktail mixer inscribed with words from *Othello:* "O God! that men should put an enemy into their mouths to steal away their brains." My grandmother asked me to explain this, and I almost did, while my father waited nervously. She didn't know he "drank." When she asked me what I wanted to be when I grew up, I thought it funny to say I wanted to be a brewer. She took the witticism well, laughing in her succession of rumbles. She said once that Henry would be a good lawyer because he was so quick with a reply.

The fact was that I had no idea what I wanted to be. I did not even know what choices there were. I was waiting around to find out what I was going to be, for sooner or later someone would certainly tell me. After a while I heard my father remark to my mother, "I may want both my boys to go into the newspaper business." But although I expected to hear more on the subject, I never did.

My mother often remarked in later years, "I never could understand why Grandma Hough didn't care about seeing the boys in their bath." She had too much sense—that was why.

The veranda at her summer cottage at 7 County Park was shaded by a rampant Dutchman's-pipe vine, one of the gloomiest aberrations known to horticulture. It was much admired in my boyhood, but it isn't there any longer, so at least it did not have the curse of immortality.

My grandmother died in 1914, and our family rode by automobile followed by a motor hearse, a new thing then, not generally considered proper, over a long whaleback of a road to the burying ground at Westport, where she would lie with her Quaker ancestors. My father pointed out to us the Anthony homestead, a clean-lined, stately house, and I remembered that runaway slaves had been sheltered there. On the way home, as we passed the crest of the great hill, I looked back at Westport and then ahead at the smoking stacks of the cotton mills of New Bedford.

3

So this is how my brother and I came into the stream of history, as nearly as possible an accounting of our genes and the threads we were to pick up as we went along, as well as some account of the influences at work around us, most of them only partly exposed. When my Grandfather Beetle was born he was, according to the nearest census, one of 7,240,000 Americans; my mother appeared as one of 31,400,000, the number rounded off a little; and my brother and I as one each of about 63,000,000 Americans. Now each of us is one of some 203,000,000 Americans.

These figures inspire awe. I think their influence upon our lives will best be seen in relation to the times. The clock strikes, a year ends, a year begins, and the times make some of us, if not what we are, what we otherwise might not have been. We did have some choice, though, didn't we?

I was born not in the best of times or in the worst of times, but in a transitional era. I was destined to see the despoiling and degradation of a rural place, Martha's Vineyard, a small city, New Bedford, and a great city, New York.

I heard the rattle of wagon wheels on rocky roads, I wore a

red cap with "1903" in white letters above the visor, I walked safely through Central Park at night, I saw the mighty elms when they still stood in front of the New Bedford City Hall, I saw Lester Lonergan as Svengali, and night after night one gentle fall I watched Halley's Comet in its travels across eons and the sky. All this was a long time ago.

When I reached an age of understanding, this country and much of the Old World had reached the age of the benevolent bourgeoisie. This phrase was uttered with satiric delight by Professor Carlton J. H. Hayes when he taught history courses, mine included, at Columbia University shortly before the United States plunged into World War I. I could see its appropriateness to the city of New Bedford during my growing up.

The spirit of the times rested on possessions but not upon inordinate acquisitiveness. The middle class was benevolent because it had begun to get along so nicely. It went to church with a dollar bill in its hand and sympathized with the lot of the poor. The wonder of technical marvels lay in the future unsuspected, while the hand of the bourgeoisie reached with satisfaction for familiar things, so many within reach—the only things, really, proper to a gratifying standard of living.

The new arc light at the corner of Campbell and County Streets sputtered, and its carbons needed continually to be adjusted or replaced. Gas lights, after all, were more dependable.

I was attending the Parker Street Grammar School when the first Woolworth's 5 and 10 Cent Store opened on Purchase Street near Hathaway's Theatre. Policemen wore helmets and a goodly percentage of them had paunches, the paunches being more reassuring than not. A motorist, wanting gasoline, drew up in front of McGowan's blacksmith shop on Pleasant Street, and a man wheeled out a tank; the demand was supplied by means of a hand pump and crank.

Still a small boy, I walked with my father past the Kirby & Hicks livery stable while we discussed the impending introduction of photo-engraving to the *Standard* plant. Up to that time pictures had been reproduced by means of chalk plates etched by an able newspaper artist, Ed Ashley, a good friend of my father's. Photo-engraving would make possible many more pictures in the paper, and I was all for that. My father asked why the printed word was not enough. I couldn't think of an answer, but I still favored pictures.

I arrived at my first independent aesthetic judgment by deciding that the tulip beds on the Common, symmetrically and stiffly arranged, and so blatant in color, were ugly. I still think so. The same goes for the Public Garden in Boston.

I admired the iron drinking cup dangling at the end of its chain at the fountain on the Common and regretted that I was not permitted to drink from it. Hygiene was coming in, bringing bubble fountains, outdoor sleeping porches, and fad diets now mostly forgotten. They couldn't have worked out.

Herman Melville's panegyric of old New Bedford still had a good deal of vitality, though few people knew of it. He wrote: ". . . nowhere in all America will be found more patrician-like houses; parks and gardens more opulent. . . ."

"Whence came they?" he asked, and replied, "All these brave houses and flowery gardens came from the Atlantic, Pacific and Indian Oceans. One and all, they were harpooned and dragged up hither from the bottom of the sea—In summer time the town is sweet to see: full of maples—long avenues of green and gold, and in August, high in the air, the beautiful and bountiful horse chestnuts, candelabra-wise, proffer the passer-by their upright cones of congregated blossoms. So omnipotent is art which in many a district of New Bedford has superinduced bright terraces of flowers upon the barren refuse thrown aside at creation's natal day."

The horse chestnuts bloom in May, soon after the lilacs, but that doesn't matter.

Even in Melville's time New Bedford was no longer entirely duty-bound to the sea. The Honorable Joe Grinnell in 1840 had put through the New Bedford and Taunton Railroad

against the opposition of the stagecoach people. There hadn't
been money enough to carry the tracks all the way into town,
so they stopped short at Pearl Street, only one block north
from Campbell, and as a child I thought the depot had been
located for our convenience.

The town was reaching northward, beyond the Wamsutta
Mills, which had been launched by Joe Grinnell and Tom
Bennett in 1846, the same year in which Edgar Marchant was
establishing the *Gazette*. It reached past Weld Street and the
new car barn, almost to Brooklawn Park, which had been the
estate of Thoreau's friend Daniel Ricketson.

One day my mother said the Bennett house was to be torn
down, and why didn't George and I join in the opportunity
offered to the public to inspect it. This had been the John
Avery Parker mansion in the early maritime age of riches, later
sold to Thomas Bennett of the Wamsutta Mills, surely a symbol
of the city's change. It stood on County Street a short block
around the corner from our house, its grounds following the
descent of the hillside toward the railroad tracks and the Acushnet River.

Daniel Ricketson left a description of John Avery Parker:
"Among those who carried great weight on change in our
community . . . he rose by his own industry and ability from
a poor boy to one of our wealthiest merchants. Few men possessed more energy or enterprise than he. . . . In person he
was rather stout, and his countenance mild. His manners were
a little hasty for dignity, but there was much of the old-fashioned gentility about him when not harassed with business."

His mansion was built in 1834 on what had been the farm of
Ebenezer Willis, and therefore it was only twelve years in
being when Melville saw it in its greatness, and perhaps seventy
years when I turned in at the gateway, looking aloft at a
massive portico, a pediment supported by six Ionic columns
rising boldly. All this grandeur was flanked and completed by
pillared wings at either side.

I entered the bare and ravaged rooms, still grand in proportion and scope, from which the furnishings had been removed to make way for the arrival of the wrecker. A great hall ran through the center of the mansion with an imposing staircase at the end, and beyond that another portico and terraces descending in orderly grace.

I remember too little of that imported classic style of domestic architecture but I can attest that what the *Mercury* reported was true: "Untenanted, with the process of disintegration already at work, its two façades plastered with the bills of an agent, the once magnificent estate awaits ignoble demolition by dealers in second hand materials." So was to end "the finest adaptation of Greek temple architecture to a dwelling ever created." This I dare believe to be true. I at least saw the mansion whole, and there are not many extant who did.

Soon all was gone except one denuded south wing made into a house for the chief of police. Fronting the hillside and the Common developers put up a crowded succession of dwellings modern enough for the prospering new generation of the middle class.

As I grew older I realized that our family belonged to the middle class, though all along I had assumed we were members of the proletariat. From my reading and nonconformist existence in a crusading editor's household, I could think of no other satisfactory affiliation.

Our block on Campbell Street was unpretentious. Our house faced an empty lot encumbered with granite slabs intended for future use in foundation work; and the lot opened into a lane where the DeTerra boys lived—Joe, Frank, Vit, and round-eyed Manuel. Brick McDermott lived at the Smith Street end of the lane. The Blossom Brothers, partners in a woodworking mill, occupied a double house on the west side of the lot. Mr. and Mrs. Charles Blossom were the parents of Carleton, Jamie, and Ruth. The house on the corner of Summer Street belonged to one of the Killigrew Brothers, partners in a saloon, the family brood including John, Lily, Willie, and Harold.

Next to us toward County Street, in a shingled house painted dark, splendid red, lived Mr. Conant, a merchant tailor, patronized by my father in his bachelor days. When the side-wheeler *Martha's Vineyard* was in a collison along about 1905, my mother went next door to tell Mrs. Conant, for sensations were always to be shared. One time Mr. Conant addressed a rebuke to some of the neighborhood boys, and Louis McBay, a policeman's son, yelled out, "It's only old Coconut."

Two blocks downhill at the corner of Pleasant and Campbell stood the house of warm brown stone where Hetty Green, the world's richest woman, had been born. In my day it was a Catholic hospital. Vines grew over the sides, and a sloping lawn gave dignity to a fine portico which must once have had a view of the river.

Across the street stood another stone dwelling, occupied by the Tabers, good enough friends of my family for George and me to call Mr. Taber "Uncle Joe." Once I asked my mother if he was really our uncle, and she said, "No." On a day of chill, driving rain she sent me to the Taber house on some errand. I was admitted and stood in the high-ceilinged hall, which must have run almost the full width of the house, watching torrents of rain water seeping and streaming from the ceiling into buckets and tubs placed to receive it. The roof must have been in grave disrepair, and the gardens on the hillside behind the house were gone into neglect.

On Sundays my father and George and I went for walks along the wharves below the round slope of Johnnycake Hill, at the center of New Bedford. Most of them were earthen wharves contained within wooden bulkheads, the earth and planking saturated with oil, whale and sperm. Some whale ships still sailed, and we looked at them in various stages of outfitting. Tier upon tier of oil casks waited on the wharves for the oil gauger or for a proper market price, covered with seaweed as protection from the sun. Other ships, spars partly removed, waited to be sold and broken up.

Sometimes we walked northward along the railroad tracks past the piers where the Vineyard and New York steamers dock, toward the Wamsutta Mills, built in littoral marshland where the Indians in time immemorial had taken shellfish and game. The Wamsutta railroad yard was where the circus came in.

Miss Pasho, who taught the fourth grade at the Mary B. White School, told us that the moist air of New Bedford made it possible for the mills to spin cotton yarn of exceeding fineness. We were ahead of all the cities of the world in manufacturing the choicest of cotton textiles. Miss Pasho was right in her day. No one dreamed that inventive minds would think up artificial humidity.

The boast of the cotton mills impressed me, but I also knew scraps and fancies from the whaling past:

> Strike up the band
> Here comes a sailor
> Cash in his hand
> Just off a whaler—
> Stand in a row
> Don't let him go. . . .

While George and I were growing up, the city grew up—or at least grew. It had assumed city government in 1847, but when I was born there were only 60,000 inhabitants. By the time I left high school the Chamber of Commerce could, and did, boast of 125,000.

This was cotton-mill growth—and cotton-textile prosperity. The shift from a whaling and maritime economy had not come quickly, or painlessly. There had been off years in the price of oil. Longer voyages to remoter seas became necessary. Confederate raiders destroyed many whale ships during the Civil War, and the federal government had sunk a whole fleet of them, loaded with stone, in a vain attempt to blockade Savannah and Charleston harbors. And a new capitalism rose after the war—ships more costly to build, youth no longer willing or driven to hard exploitation before the mast. Besides all this, Drake had discovered rock oil in Pennsylvania.

So came the turn to cotton manufacture. When the semi-

centennial of New Bedford's incorporation as a city was celebrated, Thomas B. Reed, Speaker of the House, wrote from
Washington: "The earth has got to be mighty shifty to get
out of the grasp of people equally at home on land or water."
This sounded well, and it was what I grew up more or less
believing. Anyway, New Bedford was one of the original and
stirring cities of the United States, and a lively place for a
newspaperman.

I looked last night at one of my father's scrapbooks and
found this headline:

**WHERE IS
THIS CITY?**

George A. Hough Tells of Police
Corruption

In a City with Which He Is
Familiar

Interesting Paper Read Before Medico-
Legal Society

Reminiscences of New Bedford Murder
Cases

The headline appeared in the New Bedford *Morning Mercury*. There is no doubt that my father blistered the police. He
recalled the case of Peter Johnson, a Gay Head Indian, who
was brutally murdered. The district attorney had arranged to
have Johnson's body exhumed and the skull prepared as a
courtroom exhibit. Obviously the digging up and mutilation
of the victim's body would outrage public opinion, especially
since Johnson was a Civil War veteran. My father found out
what was up and published the story, for which his newspaper
was denounced in terms more familiar today than ever before
for "defeating the ends of justice."

In his talk to the Medico-Legal Society he paid his respects to the "ends of justice" cry as "a specter conjured up by drones among the police headquarters detectives" and "as unworthy the consideration of more intelligent men."

A question persisted as to how he had found out about Peter Johnson's skull. He might have found out about it when he arrived home on an October evening and noticed a huge tin pail oddly placed just inside the front door. Uncle Garry had recently been appointed Medical Examiner, and he and my father were both living in the family home on Elm Street. If my father had lifted the lid of the pail—but he didn't. The telephone distracted him at the very instant. My brother and I grew up with the story of Peter Johnson's skull and the tin pail in the front hall.

Going back a little in time, my father, wearing a sporty bowler of a shallow style, his expression a bit cocky, had edited in succession a number of amateur papers. Amateur journalism was then a favorite hobby of youth, its product small sheets published by boys and widely exchanged among the craft. Membership in the National Amateur Press Association represented a peak of ambition.

From *Our Endeavor* of May, 1884, I quote one of "Hough's Thoughts": "Grant wishes that every recruit would join the N.A.P.A. Though we feel that some time ago we ceased to be of the recruit element we think we can give a reason why many do not join the association. After the recruit has expended $2 for the printing of his paper and as much more for mailing, he looks with distrust at the $2 necessary for admission to the National."

The economics of the craft and the time supply also a measure of their innocence.

From scoring baseball games my father went directly into the employ of the *Morning Mercury* as a reporter, an aversion to Latin preventing him from entering college. One of his early assignments was on Christmas Day, when he rode a bicycle from the Wareham woods to Plainville, a considerable distance, inquiring whether anyone had seen the wagon of a murdered egg peddler. No one had. My father's Christmas dinner consisted of cheese and crackers eaten at the Head of the River, a place as bleak as it sounds.

He accepted the role of stakeholder for bets on a wrestling match between the city's champion and a mysterious "unknown," both wrestlers backed by saloonkeepers. The match took place on the bowling green at Dogfish Bar, later the site of a cotton mill. The "unknown" went to the mat in three swift falls, grabbed his clothes, vaulted a fence, and was gone. Confronted with so apparent a swindle, my father found himself in an awkward position. He was sued by one side or the other and was extricated from the difficulty only when his lawyer found that he was too young, legally, to be sued.

His newspaper career extended from 1885 through 1887 on the *Mercury*, then as telegraph editor and city editor of the *Standard* until 1909, and as managing editor of the *Standard* until his retirement in 1931. An interviewer then asked him what ideals he had followed in his profession, and he replied, "Crusading and raising hell."

Hell-raising had much to do with his three campaigns for a seat on the Board of Aldermen from Ward Two. He ran first on the ticket of an incumbent who was defeated by a handsome grocer and colorful politician, Charles S. Ashley. The mayor lost to Ashley by 506 votes, and my father won by 261. The lame-duck mayor wrote: "Dear Geo. — You said you could not contribute to the campaign fund. Did you mean that you could put in nothing or that you could not put in any great sum? Didn't know but you might like to give say $10. We are quite a little short."

I doubt that "Geo." dug down at all. I have a sample of his campaigning the next year, the script of a speech preserved in an envelope marked in his later years, "Political Claptrap of G.A.H."

The enemies who have tried to disrupt the Citizens' Party by intrigue with those who have been high in its councils have found that they cannot drive a party of 3500 voters out of existence, even though they have the influence of the most potent vehicle of corruption that has ever been inflicted upon us—a license board— behind them. Ever since Mayor Ashley repeated the words of Mr. Desmond that I was a slanderous mischief-making nuisance whose conduct has made me obnoxious to every intelligent citizen of New Bedford, I have been reaping the benefit. . . . To all those people who say they are going to vote for Ashley and Hough, I say I don't want their votes. . . . I want to be elected with Samuel E. Bentley. . . .

He said he didn't want Ashley votes and he got only nine, and by that margin ran better than Mr. Bentley, who was also defeated. Mr. Bentley wrote my mother in appreciation of her kindness in agreeing that my father should enter the campaign. I'm not sure that she had much choice. But she wanted what he wanted, and she also held strong opinions.

Once, at the dining table my father looked across at her and said, "You're a good hater, Louise."

"I don't see why you say that, George."

But her hatreds were the other aspect of her loyalties and therefore naturally intense. She took sides readily and held to them. Most Vineyard people were good side-takers in those days.

My father ran a third time for alderman in 1902, on a ticket with a handsome young Irishman, Andrew P. Doyle, who had a cowlick as flourishing as Charles S. Ashley's. The *Standard* didn't support Doyle, but nonetheless my father placed his name in nomination.

I have never underrated the mayor's ability, his remarkable personality, the corporate influences in his favor, or the powers of evil behind him as factors in New Bedford politics. Yet I have faith in an appeal to the common decency of manhood. . . .

We ought to unite now and nominate a candidate for mayor who will show some spark of manhood in checking the recruiting of young girls for a dive running full blast in arm's length of the third district courtroom in the prisoner's dock of which the procurer and proprietress ought long ago to have confronted justice.

I believe in advertising this evil, not in hiding its existence. If the procurer for Annie Rooney's entices girls who go to Lincoln Park from Fall River, what immunity from her wiles is given to the girls who go to innocent pleasure resorts in New Bedford?

Annie Rooney's is not the only openly conducted dive of the kind in New Bedford known to the police. . . . Down on the corner of William Street and Acushnet Avenue Jake Weihl, a broken down ball player and blackleg, has been running a roulette wheel openly.

Zeph Pease, of the *Morning Mercury*, my father's old friend, had been an Ashley supporter from the outset, and he wrote more urbanely than my father for the other side:

The testimony of a Fall River police officer whom Mr. Hough familiarly calls 'Bat' Shea as if the title were a guarantee of good faith, was to the effect, we believe, that a piano player met the girl at Lincoln Park and invited her to the New Bedford resort where she went willingly enough. . . . There is no pretense that the girl had hitherto been of good moral character, but we have no intention of defending the incident beyond saying that we have no idea, nor do we believe has any well-informed citizen, that there is any institution in New Bedford where young girls are procured for immorality as Mr. Hough insinuates.

I think my father's sources were better than Mr. Pease's. The story broke out in another quarter:

WINK AT SIN

The New Bedford Police
Condemned

Judge McDonough Frees His
Mind

Thinks It Is Too Bad for
State to Take a Hand

Fall River Girl Procured for
Houses of Shame

My father persisted:

**POLITICAL
JELLY-FISH**

So Mr. Hough Terms Five
Ashley Aldermen

At the Independent Rally in
City Hall

Candidate Doyle Touches Upon
the Issues

Perry Warns All Nationalities
Not to Sell Votes

Common Decency and High School
Plans

In the end Ashley defeated Doyle by a plurality of 1,912. My father's spirit did not seem affected. He rose from political defeat with as much fire as when, less often, he won. In early childhood George and I learned that winning could not be counted on as a usual thing and was not of first importance.

The next year it was proposed that my father run for mayor, but he declined. A friend wrote: "Dear George — Why didn't you let them shoot at you this year?"

My father's last political speech was delivered in the New Bedford Theatre, and there in front seats in the balcony sat my mother, my brother, and myself. I wish I could speak of the crowded theater, electric atmosphere, expectant hush, and loud applause, but I can bear witness only to the crowd and the applause. The impression is distant. I was too young.

Of what my father said as he stood at the center of the stage —and it seemed perfectly natural to me that he should be there —only one phrase is clear to me, and he may not have uttered it at all. I hear him refer to "this little minstrel show of mine," but the words do not appear in the full report in the *Morning Mercury*.

Ashley wasn't running that year. His candidate was John

McCullough, whose Irish flair, as I recall, was less than Andy Doyle's, but who had become known for his appearances in minstrels and amateur theatricals.

So my father characterized him: "Jovial John McCullough, the prince of interlocutors, fountain of oratory, exponent of Mark Antony and 'The Three Musketeers.' He has been endowed by Nature with the attributes of a great actor but not of a statesman. He has been both her dusky Demosthenes and bronze Adonis. And now is our idol of minstrelsy to be pulled from his pedestal to be a mere political puppet in the hands of Ashley and Abbott Smith?"

Then my father lit into Zeph Pease: "The Proteus of New Bedford politics. Like the hero of mythology he changes his form at will. He familiarly assumes three shapes—as editor of the Morning Mercury, New Bedford correspondent of the Boston Globe, and Ashley office-holder. . . ."

Thomas Thompson, a marble-cutter in white overalls, won that election, but Ashley came back the next year. So my brother and I, when you come down to it, grew up in a school of journalism and politics long before Joseph Pulitzer endowed the school at Columbia, and long before we ever supposed we would go to such an innovative academic-professional institution.

Many years later I wrote a newspaper novel, *Lament for a City*, which was not popular in New Bedford. It had a character based pretty much on my father, and Lawrence Winship of the Boston *Globe*, a friend of long standing, told me he had never known a newspaper editor like that, though he was willing to believe that there could have been one. My father had certain odds in his favor besides his force and commitment. He had grown up on the *Standard* under old Edmund Anthony, an owner who was also editor, a combination extinct in newspaper life today. When Edmund died, my father enjoyed some senior and professional advantage in his long relationship with Edmund's successor, the much younger B. H. Anthony, whose functions were on the business and production side.

It is remembered of Edmund Anthony that when McKinley was assassinated, the staff in the city room at a late hour decided not to get out an extra but to leave the story for the *Mercury* in the morning. Hearing of this at his home in Fairhaven, Edmund had his horses hitched and drove at a gallop over the bridge to New Bedford. The *Standard* got out an extra, and the story was not left for the *Mercury* the next morning.

My father's retirement from municipal campaigning was not the end of politics for us. We lived in an atmosphere of recurrent public interest, usually of partisanship, and he took George and me to all sorts of rallies. We went to Sharpshooter's Hall in the North End. We went to the Elm Rink, largest seating capacity in the center after the City Hall gave way to progress. We went to Odd Fellows Hall. We went to a smoky room over an English workingmen's club in the South End to hear the Socialist mayor of Milwaukee.

I made my own political debut at the age of nine when I ran through the streets with comrades of my own age yelling, "Are we in it? Yes we are. Tommy Thompson, rah, rah, rah!" I chased torchlight processions, walking beside the bands, picking up the sticks of spent red fire, relishing the excitement of crowds, yelling, and darkness, though how I happened to be let out at night I cannot now imagine.

In city politics I had no difficulty in deciding what side I was on, but a time came when I wanted to be a Democrat, and George said I couldn't be unless I believed in the principles of the party. Did I, for instance, believe in hides freely admitted from Canada, and free other things I have forgotten. This had to do with a protective tariff or tariff for revenue only. The question made no sense to me but I had to face it. Finally I said, squirming, "I don't see why they should pay."

"Then you're a Democrat," George said.

Luck was with me. My status was secure.

On Election night, George and I always went with my father to the *Standard* office to watch the returns. A projector

—we all called it a stereopticon then—was set up in the city room pointing through a window at a large screen atop a single-story building across the way. Crowds in the street could see the projected slides as the vote count proceeded—so many precincts or election districts give so many votes for this candidate and so many for that. Variety was provided by an occasional cartoon drawn by Ed Ashley.

In state and national elections New Bedford long carried that worn tag "safely Republican." There might be minor upsets, but in general the protective tariff was an issue that could be successfully exploited by the mill owners. A high tariff meant jobs. It was the only defense against destructive foreign competition. Some respectable socialism remained alive among textile operatives from Lancashire and elsewhere, but most people believed that socialism meant dividing everything up.

In 1904 a banner was strung across Pleasant Street by the Democrats, bearing the names of the party candidates, Alton B. Parker for president, Henry Gassaway Davis for vice president. Who else remembers the name of the man from West Virginia who was named by acclamation for second place on that ticket? "By acclamation"—that meant that everyone wanted him. I was greatly impressed.

Then came 1908, with Bryan against Taft, and my father said that if Bryan was elected he would take the family on a trip to Washington. This sounded interesting, but I don't think any of us much counted on seeing Washington right away. Bryan still loomed as a hero of the people then, not yet a tragic and comic figure. Francis Hackett wrote of him: "His brain told him practically nothing, but his hazel twig made him a water-finder in the desert."

The election year of 1912 turned everything around. After it was explained to me, as it had to be explained to almost everyone, I understood about Roosevelt's hat being in the ring, but I was baffled by the oratory of the campaign. Why would Roosevelt's election be the first step toward a dictatorship?

The Roosevelt split and the launching of a Progressive party ticket in Massachusetts made the state no longer "safe." Three presidential candidates made speeches in New Bedford—Roosevelt, Taft, and Debs. Only Woodrow Wilson stayed away, occupied in places where his candidacy could be more narrowly contested. My father, George, and I heard Roosevelt and Debs in rallies at the Elm Rink. My father noticed that only Gene Debs had his pants pressed. Nobody could have been more mussed than T.R., whose clothes hung slack or flung in a breeze, but this didn't matter—you looked only at his face, the famous Roosevelt grin, the teeth, and the black tape attached to his glasses.

I had joined the New Bedford High School cadets, unaware that I would be required to drill regularly and attend monthly dances and a semiannual ball, and so I marched with the two cadet companies in a parade with President Taft, from the Pearl Street depot to a speaking stand on the Common. Of course we had bands, escorting policemen, a following of small boys and girls and dogs, and the usual curbstone rows of staring adults. At the Common there was a sizable turnout, adequate to presidential dignity, and President Taft and his color guard were successfully delivered.

Taft's big figure made an interesting contour under his coat, sloping down over his policemanlike front. He wore a plug hat but took it off as he addressed the multitude. This was the year of the textile strike in Lawrence in which the Wobblies—the I.W.W., Industrial Workers of the World—brought fear to mill owners, capitalists in general, and the more timid of the middle class.

The newspapers reported dynamitings and other violence, and the flaming speeches of Big Bill Haywood, Joseph J. Ettor, Emma Goldman, and others. Come mobs, come sabotage, come revolution. But New Bedford labor began taking up collections to aid the Lawrence strikers, and sympathetic rallies were held with speakers from the I.W.W. movement.

At one rally in the Elm Rink a foreign-looking youth went through the aisles crying a pamphlet "written by Joseph J.

Ettor whilst he was in jail." Then Big Bill Haywood himself
was to address a meeting in Odd Fellows Hall, and there was a
lot of talk about the likelihood of violence, and should Big Bill
be allowed to speak in New Bedford? When we entered the
hall we saw policemen standing all the way across beside the
rear partition.

Presently Big Bill himself came in, looking—despite any
bombs he might have thrown or buildings he might have blown
up—as benign as any big man should look. Why not? He was
amused.

"Ladies, gentlemen, and policemen . . ." he began. Everyone, or almost everyone, laughed, and Big Bill had his audience.

He didn't say anything inflammatory in the way of violence,
but he denounced the mill owners of Lawrence and proclaimed
the rightful cause of the exploited operatives.

This was also the political hour of the High Cost of Living,
a phrase that became so familiar it was often contracted in
newspapers to "H. C. of L." Nobody talked of inflation, but
at one rally in the Elm Rink an orator slapped a thick steak on
the podium before him, still wrapped in butcher's paper, and
announced that it had cost some enormous price per pound. I
lost track of the exact figure long ago, but *Gazette* advertisements show that John Bent in Edgartown was selling the best
porterhouse for thirty-five cents a pound.

After a city election I went with my father sometimes to an
upstairs room downtown, usually a law office, where some of
the politicians were figuring out what had happened and why.
Of course this would be a smoke-filled room, usually crowded,
and one time the city solicitor, who had been castigated in the
Standard, made sure that I had a seat.

Whatever disrepute attached to reformers—usually a good
deal—made no apparent difference in my father's case. He was
a crusader but he was not a reformer type. He had warm
friendships among sporting characters of many kinds. He had
called Jake Weihl a "broken down ball player and blackleg,"
yet a dozen years later the *Standard* quoted Jake on the right

side in a campaign against the back rooms of saloons: "Jacob Weihl, proprietor of the Stag Hotel, which caters, as its name implies, exclusively to men, said yesterday, 'I haven't anything to say about the men who are running back rooms, only I'm sure I don't care for that kind of business. The drinking by women in a saloon never appealed to me. . . .' "

Not too many years later my father took me to dinner at Jake's restaurant, which served better food than other places downtown.

The *Standard*'s campaign against back rooms followed the shocking murder of a woman named Annie Walsh, who had been picked up in a saloon by the captain of the coal barge *Snipe* and hacked to death in the barge cabin. "Annie Walsh," the *Standard* said, "was simply one of a type—the girl of the back room. The back room is a place where men and women meet and drink together. It is, according to those who have visited it and know it well, a place where the underworld seeks its unhealthful and feverish pleasures."

Zeph Pease, in the *Morning Mercury*, agreed that back rooms were "sodden, through and through, heavy with the breaths of vulpines and drabs, noisy with chatter and oaths," but, he went on, "let us not be hysterical or hypocritical, or make one law for the prosperous and another for the down-and-out. If men and women may eat, drink and be merry in hotels, there is no reason why other classes of men and women should be deprived of the same opportunity at their places of resort."

A big *Standard* headline had just said: EVERY BACK ROOM MUST BE CLOSED: PROTEST ARISES ALL OVER THE CITY. Within ten days the New Bedford Retail Liquor Dealers' Association had voted that "giving reasonable time to warn decent people who want a glass of beer, we will absolutely cease to serve women in side or back rooms." CHURCHES REJOICE, said the next *Standard* headline.

George had already entered Columbia, so he wasn't around during this crusade, but I walked with my father through empty, shadowy night streets to see what was going on in the district below Purchase Street. We didn't see much, but once we caught sight of the tall, hefty figure of a minister stalking night life as we were doing ourselves. An old-timer named Latimer, then a reporter for the *Standard*, wrote the next day: "As the reporter turned north, the tall form of Evangelist Cunningham hove in the offing. He opened the door of Burke's saloon, took a brief look, then passed down Acushnet Avenue in front of the back room, studied the back room for a moment, and was soon hull down on the horizon."

My father commended this as good reporting, but when David MacGregor Cheney, who was brilliant and sometimes literary, got into print a philosophic comparison of streetwalkers passing the Merchants National Bank corner with those who frequented ancient Babylon and Rome, my father blew up.

One evening, not in this same year, my father and I were walking in the North End. He was hailed by a friend who, it turned out, was heading for the back room of a saloon. All three of us wound up there, welcomed by a congenial group, all male, occupied in eating cold boiled lobsters. One man showed concern lest I fail to dismember a lobster properly, but he quickly saw that I needed no instruction.

With the "best people," my father's associations were more formal, or perhaps it was when they were society people, squeamish about the rough and tumble of aggressive journalism. My father thought Daniel Ricketson, Thoreau's friend, was an "old fart." I don't think I heard him say one of the four-letter words more than half a dozen times in all the years I knew him, and he must have considered this a precise epithet. Yet in later years, finding Ricketson in Van Wyck Brooks's *Flowering of New England*, he remarked, "There must have been more to him than that."

At a time much earlier than that just accounted for, my father emerged from the front door of our Campbell Street house and found me playing in the gutter with a toy wheelbarrow and shovel. I wore a tam-o'-shanter, knitted leggings,

and one of the warm blue coats my mother ordered for George
and me each year from the Lilliputian Bazaar at Best's in New
York. My father asked if my mother knew I was playing in
the gutter, and I must have indicated that she did.

"Well, if your mother says so, I guess it's all right."

Of course it was all right, for Campbell Street belonged to
the era of water-bound macadam, from the surface of which
white dust washed gradually into the gutters at either side. Few
automobiles went past, and I knew well enough how to avoid
horse manure. At the curb stood a hitching post and a granite
mounting block. Three young maples had been planted in front
of our house by the city, a fact that seemed strange to me in
view of my father's war with Mayor Ashley.

And now, the Boer War in the news, he was denouncing the
English. He delivered an inflammatory speech in City Hall at a
meeting presided over by the same Thomas F. Desmond who
had called him a slanderous mischief-making nuisance. As chairman, Mr. Desmond was pretty hot stuff himself. "If I was an
Englishman, I should be an Englishman," he said, "but I am an
Irishman and I believe if I were an Englishman I should want
to drop dead." He ended with an eloquent reference to George
Washington, and introduced my father.

"This old hall has been the scene of many gatherings in the
past to espouse the cause of the weak against the strong," my
father said, "yet never has a more just cause been championed
within these walls than that of the struggling republics of South
Africa to whom tonight we extend our sympathy and heartfelt
wishes for victory. . . .

"The thought of the handful of Dutch farmers struggling
against a mighty monarchy is enough to send the Yankee blood
tingling through my veins. I believe the United States ought to
proffer its good offices to end this war. The nation ought to
say:

Who's for the under dog!
I'm for the under dog
Since the God of freedom led. . . ."

The meeting was under the auspices of the Irish societies of New Bedford. A week or so later a sort of ballad was circulated as a handbill with lines beginning:

> But wasn't ut foine av young idditer Hough
> To shpake for the Oirish, ah thot w's the stuff!
> Oi voted agin him f're aldherman wance
> But niver agin if he'll give me the chance.

Winston Churchill spoke from that same platform in City Hall during the Boer War, but whether earlier or later than my father I do not know. About a week after the Irish meeting, a gathering was presided over by the Reverend Elijah Humphries, who deplored all that had been said in behalf of the Boers. He particularly deplored the fact that the Sabbath had been broken, and that one speaker had "found it necessary to resort to the lowest kind of vituperation and balderdash." He then referred to my father by name.

The *Standard*'s report said that Hill's Band had struck up the tune of "Rule Britannia," notwithstanding the portrait of George Washington above the platform, and in an instant the audience was on its feet and "the words of the anthem rang through the hall." This wasn't surprising. The cotton mills had drawn from Lancashire its best skills and such surnames as Dewhurst, Ashworth, Ramsbottom, Walmsley, Drinkwater, Halliwell, and so on, a durable lot in spunk and loyalty. If there were any Boers in New Bedford, they were few.

My father had let Oom Paul Kruger off much too lightly, but the context then was of the Jameson Raid, Lord Roberts, Kitchener, the concentration camps, and Cecil Rhodes gazing north for conquest.

The City Hall and the great painting of George Washington were soon gone. My last memory of the stately auditorium is of a rally addressed by William J. Bullock, a ruddy-faced man of sturdy build who was running for mayor. George and I sat with my father in aisle seats near the middle. After Bullock finished speaking he walked down the aisle, probably heading for another rally, and when he saw my father he stopped, shook hands, and chatted for a minute or two while we were the objects of general attention. My feeling of importance lasted all evening.

Soon the City Hall was damaged by fire and rebuilt as a public library, with pretentious pillars, staircases, and wainscoting of imitation marble. People admired it. The former library building, across the street, was turned into a municipal building. What became of the busts of Shakespeare, Molière, and Goethe I don't recall.

On evenings at home we played dominoes or parchesi or Auction of Letters after supper. At times when my father had given up smoking, as occasionally he did, he would send one of us to Corson's drugstore for a bag of candy, or he would bring home big wooden boxes of peppermints, which went well on bookish evenings.

Alongside my father's far-ranging interests I would set down the equal importance of my mother, with her sewing, her work in the kitchen or in maintaining the atmosphere in living room and home entire for our family and occasional guests. In the early days she sometimes read to George and me, and that was how I first became totally attached to Huck Finn.

On Sunday mornings George and I often walked with her a great length of County Street to Grace Episcopal Church for the hour of service and sermon. We sat in a back pew and left before communion, since neither George nor I had been baptized. Neither of our parents believed in infant baptism, and I don't remember that the subject ever came up in later life except when Betty was afraid she and I wouldn't be allowed to get married in the church.

But I did think of becoming a minister. I loved the order of morning prayer and soon knew it by heart. I liked the Reverend Percy Gordon's voice, but during his sermons my attention strayed and I wondered whether it would be possible to climb to the church roof, using as handholds and footholds the projecting spikes that dotted the dull red groins and vaulted arches overhead.

My father dismissed the subject of church easily. He said he had gone so often during his growing up—at least twice every Sunday and once in midweek—that he had accumulated a surplus. He also said that church and religion were different things.

On Sunday evenings we were apt to pay a call on my grandmother on Elm Street, and at my Uncle Garry's on County Street, where we had four cousins, Dorris, Hilda, Katherine, and young Garry, who was about my age. Prominent in our walks was the companionship of whatever dog we had at the time. The first, an English bull named Jack, had been trained for the pit, but we had no occasion to test his fighting ability, though once he badly intimidated a Vineyard Haven barber who was trying to shave Uncle Ben.

Both George and I were devoted to Peter Pan, mostly tan, whiskered, and more or less a cocker spaniel. Peter died one rainy night at Fish Hook, and we were both bereft. We found him near the woods in the morning, and George wrote in the Fish Hook log:

> Blessed are the brides the sun shines on,
> Blessed are the dead the rain rains on.

Queequeg, an athletic cocker of good breeding, chocolate brown in color, lived to be eighteen, his years bridging ours, George's and mine, from high school to college. When we were walking on County Street he would run ahead for blocks at a time, because he liked to run, then full speed back to join us. Once, not at full speed but fast enough, he ran between the legs of a man unknown to us and sat him down neatly on the sidewalk. The man seemed annoyed. Queequeg was already far away, and we passed by as strangers.

The other evening I had fallen asleep in the living room and came slowly to half wakefulness when a soft brown head was thrust into my lap. Queequeg! I thought, for the muzzle was soft indeed. But of course it was Graham, and the odd thing was that no memory of Queequeg had been in my consciousness for years.

In our Campbell Street living room hung a gilt-framed and fairly enormous engraving from one of the Doré illustrations of *Paradise Lost*. Its shadowy vastness and dim-lit assemblage fascinated me, and I was fond of it, and learned the verses at the bottom, my first Milton:

> High on a throne of royal state which far
> Outshone the wealth of Ormus and of Ind . . .

For the poetry prescribed at school I had no regard whatever, but perhaps being exposed to "Marco Bozzaris," "Abou Ben Adhem," "What Constitutes a State," and Emerson's coy lines "The mountain and the squirrel had a quarrel . . ." was better than nothing.

4

It is hard for me to write about Martha's Vineyard—the Island. (We have always used the capital *I* in the *Vineyard Gazette*.) I knew the Vineyard so long ago, I have lived through many of its good years and now through the years of change—and I see the fate most people don't think of as a fate at all, for why shouldn't Martha's Vineyard be exactly like the rest of the United States or, worse still, the metropolitan eastern coast?

This morning the sun is warm, the elms are shaking a little in a mild September breeze, and Sheriff's Meadow Pond, not far beyond the window of the room where I sit at my typewriter, is bluer than the blue sky. Beyond lies John Butler's Mud Hole, which I can also see, a tidal pool between the pond and the open bay, which used to be the Eel Pond, and then Vineyard Sound, with Cape Cod on the other side. One would have thought the mainland sufficiently removed, and for some three centuries it was.

There is only one Island always for any Islander anywhere in the world, whether with palms and coral in the South Seas or with the sweet fern and bayberry and beach plum so well known to me. Even Pitt, in the Roaring Forties; Tristan da

Cunha, where it is seldom safe to land; Ascension, which with scant rainfall and little vegetation is remarkably healthful; Ponape, where a whaleman's grave was dug under a kuku tree; and Wrangel, where Stefansson found the Arctic to be friendly —all by insular character and mystery are both Robinson Crusoe's and Prospero's. Defoe knew the brotherhood of islands, for he was aware of Alexander Selkirk on Juan Fernandez but chose to put Crusoe on Tobago.

Martha's Vineyard was always particularly Prospero's in years past. John Brereton, gentleman adventurer and narrator of Bartholomew Gosnold's voyage of exploration in 1602, told of coming to anchor under a "faire island" and in the margin he put "Marthaes Vineyard," the first recording of the name.

The chiefest trees of this Island are Beeches and Cedars; the outward parts all overgrown with low bushie trees, three or foure foot in height, which bear some kind of fruits, as appeared by their blossoms; strawberries, red and white, as sweet and much bigger than ours in England, Rasberries, Gooseberries, Hurtleberries, and such; an incredible store of Vines, as well in the woodie part of the Island where they run upon every tree, as on the outward part, that we could not go for treading on them; also many springs of excellent sweet water, and a great standing lake of fresh water neere the sea side, an English mile in compasse, which is maintained with the springs running exceedingly pleasantly throw the woodie grounds which are very rockie.

And Shakespeare: "The isle is full of noises, sounds and sweet airs that give delight and hurt not." True. "How lush and lustie the grass looks, how green." We knew it so from the time we can first remember. "Ye Elves of hills, brooks, standing lakes, and groves." Yes, even the Elves we ourselves many times observed.

In the 1970's, though, came a change of idiom. The records in the Registry of Deeds attest in legal language that a dealer in 1972 bought 230 acres of land in West Tisbury for $20,000 and sold the same land within a few months to Benjamin Boldt, another dealer, for $232,000. Only a few years earlier two friends of ours, as much for sport as anything, had bought a large part of this identical land for a dollar an acre, selling it within a year or so for two dollars an acre.

To those who have known Martha's Vineyard through many years and seasons all the land is in some way special. That which Mr. Brine bought and sold, and Mr. Boldt bought and has sold or is selling in a gridiron lot pattern for "development," lies in Waldron's Bottom. The Bottoms—Quampeche, Willow Tree, Deep, and Waldron's—are grooves or troughs made by subglacial streams finding their way to the ocean as the glacial ice melted. Many of us liked to see them as we traveled the road between Edgartown and West Tisbury, the same road, once an Indian trail, that Charlie Brown and Beriah Hillman argued about in the *Gazette* long ago. Natural monuments need not always be bold or overpowering. Some geologists have studied the Bottoms with care, believing that the west banks are steeper because of the rotation of the earth, which they think deflected the subglacial streams.

The transaction of Mr. Brine and Mr. Boldt is one instance that typifies many. Gridiron and spider-web subdivisions multiplied in plans recorded at the Registry. Before long an 867-lot subdivision on 507 acres would be proposed for the slopes above Sengekontacket Pond, domain of the sachem whose daughter Alice Sesseton married Joseph Daggett, wheelwright and Quaker, in the year 1675 or thereabouts. The elves of hills, standing lakes, and groves were gone or going, exorcised by speculation, enterprise, growth, the fever of modern times. Prebuilt imported houses, the authentic stamp of the new America, began more and more to impose their pattern. But was it not written long ago that Prospero abjured his charms:

> . . . I'll break my staff,
> Bury it certain fathoms in the earth.
> And deeper than did ever plummet sound,
> I'll drown my book.

Martha's Vineyard, not so much as the Galapagos, but in its own island way, developed unique forms of life—for instance, the eastern prairie chicken or heath hen, Tympanuchus Cupido Cupido; a white-footed mouse, Peromypous; a white variety of the familiar wild rose; chickadees that sing with a different accent from those of the mainland. To be sure, heath hen and mouse are classed only as subspecies, but they were to be found nowhere else in the world. As to the heath hen, past tense is all. There are also the gray seals that breed only on nearby Muskeget. Similarly, the Vineyard induced in its inhabitants, generation by generation, subtle inflections of speech, manner, thought, and character. Naturalists speak of biotic communities differentiated by time and environmental influences, unique, and we had come to have on Martha's Vineyard the equivalent in human beings and their lives, day by day, year by year.

Winds and eddies from the mainland had not affected us much. The Islanders found not only curiosity but also respect in visitors and transplanted mainlanders through generations past. Outside influences passed over like summer storms, leaving residues to be lived away or absorbed, often usefully. Adopted Islanders became indistinguishable from the native born, whose ready example proved the best form of acclimatization.

Now has come the Age of Communication and Transportation, the cultural downgrading of the detached or separate, the smothering of differences that cannot be exploited. The age is an Instant Age. Competition admits of no pause, and why should it? Technology is more adjustable than nature and sooner put to practical use. Shove over! If you're not going anywhere, someone else is.

The age is an Age of Numbers, and with all possible respect to them, numbers dilute. Numbers overpower. Why should there be only 40,000 human beings on Martha's Vineyard when there can be 400,000? Martha's Vineyard has more area than Manhattan. Look, now! Be reasonable! Everyone in the United States has the legal right to visit Martha's Vineyard on the same day and at the same hour if he can get there. Let's do some figuring. How many can we fly in, on the average, per week, day, or hour, and at how much quick profit per head, including a percentage on concessions?

It is not precisely true that elves have gone out of fashion, but nowadays they must be Disneylike elves, caricatured in bright reds, greens, and yellows. Sophisticated elves, elves of common currency and tongue-in-cheek fantasy. A lot of them are kept in stock, or custom orders can be made up if you're willing to pay for overtime.

Only crazy environmentalists and elitists object to the modern system. An elitest is, by definition, someone you want to take something away from, first of all his privacy.

In my boyhood in New Bedford we used to walk to the steamboat pier under Johnnycake Hill to take the side-wheel steamer for the Vineyard. We walked down Union Street, leaving the shopping district behind and passing pawnshops, stores with shabby and cobwebby windows, a drinking fountain for horses at the foot of Bethel Street, where the corner building may have been Melville's Spouter Inn, then at the foot of the hill the wholesale grocery houses, warehouses with offices or counting rooms upstairs, the railroad tracks with rows of faded red freight cars.

In summer the boat train from Boston came down to the wharf from Pearl Street, and we, invariably early, watched the nicely dressed passengers disembark, get their boat tickets at the booth on the pier, and board by the after gangplank while George and I looked down from above. The forward gangplank was for freight. A swarm of deck hands, often on the run, wheeled barrels, crates, and sacks on hand trucks over the wharf planking and up the incline, and if they had to be stored in the boat's open bows they were covered with tarpaulins against the certainty of salt spray.

The cabin on the main deck was usually occupied by drummers, who played cards on overturned suitcases, and by equivalent personages such as Ben Blankenship, the horse dealer.

Other passengers settled in the cabin above, or occupied deck chairs outside in the open air.

George and I remember the *Uncatena* best, though we knew the *Gay Head*, the *Nantucket*, and the old *Martha's Vineyard*. We may even have taken passage on the *Monohansett* in her last days, she who had served Grant as a dispatch boat. The *Nantucket* wore gold and red on her paddle boxes.

"All ashore that's going ashore," and then the whistle sounded as we cleared the wharf and slipped into the stream, Fairhaven on the opposite shore, Palmer's Island and Butler's Flat Light ahead. Off Black Rock the course changed. The southwester and the seas kicked up by the southwester struck the boat on her forequarter and then amidships, and she rolled and wallowed. That was where I became seasick scores of times, hundreds of times.

At Vineyard Haven the passengers disembarked through the freight deck, and this meant that on the older side-wheelers one had to duck under the shaft that ran amidships from one paddle wheel to the other. I have a story from the time of the boats that antedated the *Uncatena*.

Alice Dexter called on Betty and me one evening. She ran the motion-picture shows in the town hall after her husband died, and was the first woman licensed as a motion-picture operator in Massachusetts. She had just come from the house of her father-in-law, the sheriff, and Mrs. Dexter. One was a Red Sox fan and the other wasn't, so that they needed two radios. Anyway, Alice said that Tom, the sheriff, had been reminiscing and had come to the subject of Charlie Osborn's wedding trip. Charlie and Tom, about of an age, were old friends. At the time of the wedding the boats stopped at Eastville, and it was there that Charlie got on with his bride, whom he had courted at the West Tisbury fair. He was wearing a beaver hat, and partly due to poor eyesight he failed to duck low enough under the shaft, which collapsed the beaver hat, accordion fashion, squarely down as far as his nose. He completed his wedding trip wearing a cap.

Tom had told this story to Alice just as his wife was coming in, and to promote good cheer Alice referred to it; but when Tom got as far as the first mention of the beaver hat, his wife interrupted.

"What was Charlie Osborn doing wearing a beaver hat?"

"Because he had just got married."

"You didn't wear a beaver hat when you got married."

Alice said, "The whaling captains wore beaver hats."

"Yes," said Mrs. Dexter, "but they were all old men, and Charlie Osborn wasn't an old man."

The sheriff surrendered and kept mum.

The *Uncatena* was the last of the side-wheelers. Robert Hillyer, the poet, had her in mind when he wrote a memorial poem:

> The paddlewheel boat with her walking beam
> Her churning wheels and her plume of steam
> Has paddled upstream, far, far upstream
> Beyond the wharves of the morning.

I have often been to the wharves of the morning, but not for a good while, and I have forgotten where they are.

My father was taken to Martha's Vineyard as a baby. His parents had a cottage in Cottage City, and he visited in Vineyard Haven, the old Holmes Hole. At a certain age he met Aunt Emma and remarked to Uncle Garry about her beauty.

"Yes," said Uncle Garry, "but wait until you've seen her sister Louise."

He did meet Louise, and they went driving in a livery-stable rig over a road that was long and leisurely then but isn't any more, to the up-Island region. One day they set out to visit Indian Hill, a summit with a view and a great boulder resting as gently on the top as if it had been placed by God in a tender moment.

I would guess that an hour must have passed before they had traversed Indian Hill Road, with its sandy horse path and wheel ruts, its ascents and declivities, and one sharp corner, and decided that they had reached the hill. They hitched their horse by the road and climbed to the top of one of the summits of the errant glacial ridge, from which they looked out upon a processional of schooners with white sails in the waterway of Vineyard Sound. Four-, five-, and six-masters were common then.

Across the Sound in primeval freshness lay the islands of the Elizabeth group, Naushon the largest of all, with glimpses of Buzzards Bay beyond, and against the far horizon a hazy profile of New Bedford. Robert Pitney wrote a poem mostly about Naushon:

> Along the liquid leash of islands
> The slumbering bourdon laps the beach
> Where sea breaks on the web of silence
> Breathing like peaceful beasts in sleep.

"Slumbering bourdon"—one is transported to an island domain with place names such as Tarpaulin Cove, Old French Watering Place, Black Woods, changeless as long as I have known. On the outlook hill itself were sumachs, wild roses, blackberry tangles, tussocks of native grass.

But my parents were not really on Indian Hill. They were on what is called Spyglass Hill, a few hundred yards to the eastward, and when they went back to the road their horse and rig were missing. The horse had been quartered for rest in a stone barn nearby by Colonel Albert S. Berry, of Kentucky, member of Congress, an early summer resident of North Tisbury, known to his constituents as "the Tall Sycamore of the Licking," the Licking being a river that runs from Magoffin County to the Ohio at Covington.

He had watered and fed the horse, and now invited my father and mother into his house for refreshment, the whole occasion afterward preserved brightly in family history.

Later, of course, we all knew Indian Hill well. On other expeditions, exploring the North Shore countryside, my parents came upon a hidden farmstead, its surroundings somewhat overgrown. Their full discovery comprised three gray-shingled houses, separated by fields and stone walls given over to the Island's favorite wild vines and thickets. At first my father bought one house, then a few years later a second, to be moved to the knoll to join the first, and finally the third, reuniting the ancient homestead property of a Vineyard tribe of Hillmans.

In 1898, when I was two years old, I was brought for the first time to the house which became a central spirit force in all my youthful years and hardly less thereafter. My father wanted a name for the place. His friend and fellow-worker Pete DeWolf, newspaper artist, held up a fish hook from a box of miscellany and said, "George, there's the name for your place. Call it Fish Hook."

My father said, no, no, it wouldn't do, but it did do. It took possession and both house and territory became Fish Hook and have remained so into the generation of my father's great-grandchildren.

Uncle Garry on his first visit said, "George, if you were looking for a place where nobody would ever find you, this is it." Aunt Addie kept her ideas to herself, except for dubious glances, but Aunt Ettie, conceding something, remarked nevertheless, "You can't live on view."

Well, almost you can. If you have the view, other essentials can be gathered around, and they need not be many. This sanctuary in the hills, this outlook over sea and woodland, this expanse of old neglected fields within lichened stone walls, this harmony of nature beloved alike in bleakness and sunny repose, many-sided in insular climate and character, possessed an entirety, an adequacy of its own. It was always old and always new.

There in the tall grass just below the knoll, which stood roundly to the eastward, exactly right for my father's flagpole, I see my mother, air and sky so vast about her, a shawl caressing her shoulders and accenting her slim figure, and in the grass my father comfortably lying, George and myself as small boys nearby, and Jack, our first dog, belonging with the rest of us.

We could command from our knoll, or from the house, a long vista of Vineyard Sound and the islands. If we climbed Mayhew G. Norton's hill, as countless times we did, we could look out over the outwash plain, with its scrub-oak cover, to the Atlantic beyond. Waiting for discovery in the woods that ran toward the shore were brooks, ravines, glades, swamp holes, and more stone walls, early built, when sheep-raising was a great pursuit. The shore itself had been strewn with glacial boulders, many of them glistening in the wash of the Sound, and on two sides of the road ending where Mr. Rogers's boathouse stood were bluffs of some ruggedness and height.

From my brother's bedroom at Fish Hook we could see the Gay Head Light flashing, three times yellow and one time red. George and I esteemed it a sign of good luck if we happened to look out at the moment when the red flash showed. This was a game of our own, but we often accosted the night sky, "Star light, star bright, first star seen tonight / Wish I may, Wish I might, have the wish I wish tonight." I never believed it made much difference what we wished, but it was important to see the first star. When I grew older I thought of Lorenzo and Jessica and the heavens "thick inlaid with patines of bright gold." I thought of Dido on the wild sea bank, but Carthage for me was transposed to Naushon Island.

Changes in Fish Hook came slowly. Mayhew G. Norton, our neighbor, who supplied us with milk, home-ground meal, and almost infinite good sense, built a new fireplace in the dining room. At my father's behest he shingled my brother's bedroom on the inside of the roof, the shingles looking down rather than up. This became, in Fish Hook usage, the "shingled chamber."

In the big living room downstairs, nearest the Sound view, we sat in the evenings around a table with a kerosene lamp, a fire on the hearth if the weather was cold, reading books or magazines, usually old ones. The walls were almost entirely occupied by built-in bookcases of simple boards, varnished.

Many of the books were my father's from his youth, volumes of the Seaside Library or the Franklin Square Library: *Valentine Vox, the Ventriloquist, Very Hard Cash*, detective tales by Anna Katherine Greene, novels by Harrison Ainsworth, *She* by Rider Haggard, *The Cloister and the Hearth, The Constable de Bourbon, The Phantom City* by Captain Marryat.

For going to bed we had candles that flickered and left a tang in the air when they were blown out, and the light of the stars or the moon began to come in.

The guest room downstairs had the most interesting big washbasin and pitcher. The room smelled always of Cashmere Bouquet soap, which we did not have in New Bedford and which went well with cool air and clean, cool sheets. In this room I experienced a childhood dream, more curious than frightening, of a whippoorwill monster that came toward me out of the distant sky. It combined the sound of the whippoorwill with the whiplike feelers of a red boiled lobster. I remember the dream after seventy years or so, but what it recalls most clearly is the walnut bedroom set, marble-topped bureau and washstand, and the night air refusing to be kept out by rattling windows. The stars were shining.

Family transport from Vineyard Haven was by horse and carriage over the white macadam road, which had signs along the way: "Do Not Drive in the Middle of the Road." The state had built the road and put up the signs. Trees arched overhead at several places, and there were stretches where the horse always walked, if, indeed, he didn't walk all the way. We allowed an hour and a quarter for the journey, which now takes little more than ten minutes.

The horse was generally tired, for we got him from Uncle Ben, who assigned him by way of respite from harder work. Uncle Ben Cromwell had married Aunt Emma, my mother's younger sister, when she was twenty-six years old in 1886. He was the son of a steamboat captain and himself a former master of the side-wheeler *Martha's Vineyard*. He had done some sea diving—for one place, on L'Homme Dieu Shoal, which he called

"El Hommadoo." His cheeks were round and ruddy, his white mustache generous, and his was a great charm when he did not show a bluff occupational side.

In the family it was always recognized that Uncle Ben would eat with his knife and nothing could be done about it. Didn't he know any better? Well, he knew as much as anyone else did and about many things much more, and what they did was well enough for them, but he knew nothing better for himself than eating with his knife, and he was very good at it.

My father, arriving for the weekend, would in the early days ride his bicycle from Vineyard Haven as far as Captain Kidder's house, on the Indian Hill Road, before the long, hard hills began. He would hike the rest of the way, and sometimes George and I would walk out to meet him. We used short-cuts when we walked to the North Tisbury post office on summer evenings and waited for the mail stage, the two horses galloping as they entered the village. The North Tisbury neighbors waited on the post office stoop, and some had their horses at the hitching rail close by. Lillian Adams was the postmaster, a thin, likable woman of old Island stock.

It was she who wrote about the pleasures of February on the Island, concluding:

> And at eve no word reveals
> Half the rapture that each feels
> As he skins his mess of eels.

After the Rural Free Delivery route was established in 1914, Miss Adams married Mr. Barlow and moved to Saskatchewan.

One of the North Tisbury characters was Calvin Tilton, white-bearded harness maker and prophet. He was the one who wrote on mailboxes and elsewhere in public view "Turn or Burn," and once he testified that he had reached a state of spiritual perfection and could not commit sin. Another neighbor, William B. Luce, turned his privy over in order to shingle it, and got the shingles nailed wrong end to, after which he was called "Butts Up." His son, Ed Lee, bullied the younger boys somewhat, and because of this and the fact that he had a flat nose he was called "Lord Pancake."

We walked home with our mail and often with a bag of jelly beans or a roll or two of Necco wafers, always over the summit of the Norton hill. That was a wonderful height overlooking both Fish Hook and Vineyard Sound with the lights of vessels passing through. George and I could find the path by the feeling of the ground under our feet, even on the blackest night.

In the very early summers my mother had a maid to help her, for she was alone with George and me all week, without a telephone, and no occupied house within sight. The household helper we were to remember best was Minnie Mahoney, who had only recently arrived in America. She played baseball with us, a queer game, since the base line ran in the wrong direction on account of the lie of the land. Minnie sang "Loch Lomond" or "Wait Till the Clouds Roll By" while she scrubbed the wash in one of the old and now forgotten red tubs that came before galvanized iron.

My mother cooked on a Glenwood range, burning wood because we had no coal. A copper wash boiler always stood on the back of the range with a supply of hot water. When the cistern gave out, as it often did in dry weather, we brought water in buckets from springs, as we called them, though they were really wells. One summer Minnie did the wash in a swampy hollow beside the Henry H. Norton spring, among the ferns and steeplebush. It wasn't long before she married Michael McCarthy in New Bedford and she came to Fish Hook no more.

Our nearest neighbors, Mr. and Mrs. George A. Rogers and their unmarried son and daughter, lived perhaps a quarter of a mile away, their house concealed from us by woods and hollows. Mayhew G. Norton and his son Charles, who became our lifelong friend, were a little more distant on their own high ridge.

Mr. Rogers had made three long whaling voyages before he married Ephraim Allen's daughter Margaret in 1884. Dr. Lane had advised him not to go to sea again, but a whaling voyage could have been no more rugged an ordeal than the life he followed of lobsterman and fisherman in the time of heavy boats dependent on wind and tide. He and Mrs. Rogers spent twenty-five Thanksgivings on the lonely island of No Mans Land for the codfishing season, his boat hauled out by oxen every night because of the shelterless coast. He was a Democrat, one of a few in the township of West Tisbury, and besides fishing he kept hens and a home garden. We got our eggs from him, and in my memory there is no cheerier person than Mrs. Rogers, though she was shut into a privacy of deafness.

My father liked to go over to the Rogers house of a summer evening, or on one of our visits at any season, and sit with Mr. Rogers, smoking their pipes, in a kitchen no larger than a ship's galley, talking fitfully, and occasionally spitting into the stove. After a long silence Mr. Rogers would repeat his last remark with a slight movement of his head or with a new emphasis, as if he had tested it and decided to let it stand. Early in their friendship they discussed the sinking of the bark *Kathleen* by a whale.

"Did you ever come up with a fighting whale?" my father asked.

"N-n-n-n-o," said Mr. Rogers, who stuttered somewhat. Then, thinking again, he called upon his memory. "That is, once we struck an angry whale."

This was a sperm whale which at first encounter had smashed the second mate's boat fore and aft. Then, turning belly up like a shark, the whale charged the boat in which Mr. Rogers stood with his harpoon. He rated as a boatheader, that special breed of which Melville wrote: "Now it needs a strong, nervous arm to strike the first iron into the fish; for often, in what is called a long dart, the heavy implement has to be flung to a distance of 20 or 30 feet . . . it is the harpooner who makes the voyage."

Mr. Rogers let go with his "strong, nervous" right arm, plunging the harpoon into the whale's throat, and by the sudden shock of the blow was himself propelled into the sea. He came up under the whale, stretched out his arm for a desperate shove to sink himself again, and this time surfaced clear of the whale and within reach of a rescuing whaleboat. What happened next he couldn't exactly remember.

He and my father sat for a few minutes, and then Mr. Rogers said, "I believe we got the whale." He let this remark stand as if giving it consideration, then repeated, "Yes, I'm quite sure we got the whale."

In his ears Mr. Rogers wore slender gold hoops, which to me were an inseparable part of his character, as much as his gaunt bronzed cheeks, blue eyes, iron-gray hair, and chin whiskers cut square, as if they had grown that way. Perhaps they mostly had. Always he addressed me as "Bub," an old form of usage for a cabin boy on shipboard.

He had been often to Talachuano, which he pronounced "Turkeanner," where, he told my father, the most beautiful women in the world could be seen; and he had been to Hakodate, Ponape, New Zealand, and Guam. What good neighbors they were, Mr. and Mrs. Rogers. How often we visited back and forth, and how often Mr. Rogers brought us a mess of lobsters or had fires blazing on Fish Hook hearths ready for our arrival for a holiday or a weekend.

But the prevailing wind of Mr. Rogers's mind made his view dark, sometimes despairing, sometimes strongly dissenting. Once I drove with him to the West Tisbury fair. As we approached the fair grounds I felt a surge of anticipation, but Mr. Rogers had sized up the crowd already—perhaps fifty or sixty persons—and found it too small.

"De-s-s-s-o-la-t-i-o-n!" he exclaimed. Yet in the course of years he seldom saw that many people together at one time.

When Calvin Tilton wrote one of his inscriptions on a roadside fence or rose in church to yell, "I say glory. What do you say?" Mr. Rogers always put him down with the muttered phrase, "D-d-e-v-i-lish fool!" "Devilish fool" was one of his favorite epithets.

Mrs. Rogers often had filled cookies in her buttery, and puckermouth pears and sassafras apples in summer, a red tablecloth, a warm kitchen, and the biggest, bluest hydrangea that could be imagined. Her flowerpots were ordinary tin cans wound with wallpaper, and she had many on her window sills. She found plenty to smile about and said she enjoyed washing dishes. I never knew any other woman who did.

When Mr. Rogers wanted Maggie to hear him, he spoke loudly, not holding back at all, in spite of his stutter. He said that any stranger passing by would suppose that he and Maggie were having a hell of a row. But strangers seldom went past.

George Hervey Luce drove his truck wagon on the road through the Rogers place, morning and evening, during the long summer season, bound to and from his boathouse near Salt Works Beach. It was under his father, Captain Hervey E. Luce, in the ship *Morning Light* that Mr. Rogers had sailed his long whaling voyages.

George Hervey, as he was always called to distinguish him from other Luces, drove past Fish Hook also, and whenever my mother wanted, he would leave a bluefish, bonito, squeteague, or perhaps a mess of butterfish or scup. We knew long ahead of time when George Hervey was approaching, for his wagon rattled loudly over the stony road, and the pace of his horse was slow.

As there were many Luces, so there were many Nortons, but only one Mayhew G., and it was not only his name that made him unique. He was tall, strongly muscled and boned, and as versatile as a New England year. I would name him a philosopher, too, though the term seems fancy for his unpretentious wisdom. When Senator Butler was buying up old farms at Lambert's Cove, Mayhew G. remarked dryly that the Senator wanted to own all that adjoined him.

I came to know Mayhew G. well because I went for the milk oftener than anyone else, George being occupied with caring for Molly, the horse we acquired around 1909. But of course we all knew him well, for we called on him and Charlie and they called on us often, and whenever we wanted anything built, repaired, trimmed, or brought into an accord with nature, Mayhew G. accomplished the purpose handily and directly.

My father kept a record of our Island life in the Fish Hook log, and this was the way of it at the turn of the century:

Sunday, Aug. 13, 1900. G.A.H. remained over. Had a fine afternoon's exercise at the woodpile. Hough family went after berries and butterflies and got both. Explored the Porter Clifford place. Afternoon G. A. H. and the boys went up on the hill. More exercise at the woodpile. Air heavy with smoke from fire on Nantucket. Mr. and Mrs. Rogers called in the evening. Breakfast, boiled lobster and johnnycake. Dinner pea soup and huckleberry pie. Supper, fried bonito and chocolate.

May 18, 1901. Arose about 8 a.m. Had a satisfying breakfast of fried bananas, scrambled eggs and chocolate. Hough family en masse went to beach at 10 a.m. and to Mr. Rogers' boathouse where they were presented with the finest mess of chicken lobsters in many a day. Called on Mrs. Rogers on the way home. Late dinner—hot lobsters. After dinner enjoyed calls from Mrs. Rogers and Carrie, and later from Mr. Rogers. In the evening had a pleasant neighborly call from Mayhew G. and Charles. Boiled lobsters at 10 p.m.

Sunday, July 28, 1901. Arose around 9 a.m. G.A.H. tackled woodpile. Family went up on hill with box kites. Saw the steamer City of Lawrence come down the Sound from Providence. Chicken chowder for dinner. Mr. and Mrs. H. paid a visit to the Henry H. Nortons and then to Mr. and Mrs. Rogers. Afterwards read Robinson Crusoe to George. A fine day at the outset but cloudy toward night, threatening northeast storm.

Henry H. Norton, who also lived on the North Shore ridge, was a stonecutter by profession. He told good stories and was not afraid of the improbable, the supernatural, or even the miraculous. He raised excellent melons, too. Often while walking through the countryside we came upon some boulder from which Henry H. had cut a slab or two to fashion into gravestones or doorsteps.

Oct. 5, 1901. . . . In the absence of the family Mr. Rogers raised the flag at Fish Hook at half staff in respect to the memory of President McKinley where it remained until after the funeral at Canton, Ohio, Sept. 19, 1901. . . .

Oct. 7, 1901. Wind died out early in the day and the sun gave warmth to an ideal Indian summer day. Went to the cranberry bog in the morning and picked something over a bushel of berries. Returned at 1 p.m. and after lemonade G.A.H. lounged in the hammock on the west side of the house until 2 p.m. After a chicken dinner the whole family went on an exploring expedition and finding a comfortable hilltop overlooking the Sound lounged there until 4 p.m. Upon return home A.L.H. and H.B.H. called on Mrs. Rogers and G.A.H. and G.A.H. Jr. supplied the fireplaces and watched the sunset. After supper G.A.H. Jr. rebelled against listening to Aladdin and His Wonderful Lamp on the ground that he would dream dreams. . . .

Tuesday, Oct. 8, 1901. Another splendid day—warm in the sun. Smoky sou'wester. After a late breakfast the family walked to Middletown. The boys drove home with Mr. Ephraim Allen, followed by Jack. A.L.H. encountered a three-foot blacksnake in the woods near the Methodist parsonage on the way back. Home about 1 p.m. G.A.H. occupied the hammock. After a dinner of green peppers stuffed with sea bass, sent up a box kite with a flag and moored it. Later sent up a Japanese lantern. Roasted corn and potatoes in the fireplace. After supper G.A.H. went over to smoke a pipe with Mr. Rogers. Read horror stories to Mrs. Hough on his return. Retired about 10 p.m.

My father's entries in the Fish Hook log in those early days speak often of the view of the Sound and what we saw. We saw squalls approaching across the water. We saw sometimes the stacks of tugboats and the topmasts of schooners moving above a white bank of fog that concealed the hulls; often in the afternoon of a muggy summer day we watched lowering thunderstorms, with their black lofty clouds known as double-headers, moving with the tide so that we could tell where they were bound. If the tide changed, making to the east instead of to the west, a thunderstorm would reverse itself and retreat whence it had come. Always at night we saw the light-houses of Gay Head, Tarpaulin Cove, and Nobska, unless the fog had closed in; and we could behold the Milky Way in August with shooting stars below, and Orion in the fall, and almost always the far-off lights of New Bedford.

Sometimes we had our own view of the world.

Monday, Aug. 25, 1902. Fine easterly weather. G.A.H. and A.L.H. spent the morning on the knoll and watched the return of the North Atlantic squadron of warships to Menemsha Bight. Four big vessels including the Kearsarge and Brooklyn steamed up the Sound followed by the dispatch boat Scorpion and numerous torpedo boats. A sharp squall struck on in the afternoon. A few claps of thunder and a rainbow and the sun was again shining brightly. Whole family visited Mr. and Mrs. Rogers, returning late. Mr. Rogers lit the way through the dark hole by the spring.

Tuesday, Sept. 8, 1903. The day was as near perfect as is likely to be found. The Hough family made its second annual pilgrimage to Prospect Hill. . . . Watched the cruisers and battleships at target practice in the Sound. Shot after shot and great shell ricocheted over the water, and the flashes of flame from the big guns, puffs of smoke, and reverberations like deafening thunder near at hand made a marvelous spectacle. At our feet in Menemsha Bight lay a fleet of large colliers with the supply for the warships. . . .

This was a holiday not only for us, but also for the Navy, in sign of which the vessels were painted white. The president in the White House now was Theodore Roosevelt. "Speak softly and carry a big stick," he said. "I wish to preach not the doctrine of ignoble ease but the doctrine of the strenuous life."

There are many pictures of T.R. in my birthday scrapbook of 1905—T.R., U.S.V., with the crossed swords of the cavalry on his collar and the Rough Rider hat on his head; T.R., wife, and five children against several backgrounds; T.R. hunting big game in the West; T.R. the new president with pince-nez glasses and cord, smiling his historic identifying smile.

Presently he would be telling the Berber pirates, "Perdicaris alive or Raisuli dead," and I would be wondering what he meant. He would be getting us the Panama Canal with the help of Goethals and others. He would be settling the Russo-Japanese War—my father had explained why we were on the side of the Japanese, and it wasn't until many years later that I learned Roosevelt's business reasons for wanting the war ended. And T.R. would be attacking race suicide and malefactors of great wealth, and coining the phrase "lunatic fringe."

Presently, too, T.R. would be sending the Great White Fleet on its excursion around the world on a mission of friendship and a demonstration of might. It was part of this fleet we had watched from the Vineyard hill as it engaged in target practice so conveniently offshore. Later the phrase was changed to "gunnery exercise," as more acceptable to the taxpayers.

All in all, those Fish Hook days and nights set one of the unfading bloodstream patterns in the life of a little boy growing up. H.B.H. never lost the look and feeling and whole strong thread of summers and holidays in the house at North Tisbury.

Someone said, "Shad Tilton has come back."

My mother said, "Oh, he's not worth bringing back."

Shadrach Tilton, Vineyard-born, had spent most of his years hunting bowhead whales in the Arctic. Aunt Addie, Aunt Ettie, and my mother remembered him as a boy in Holmes Hole.

Soon I saw him, the returned whaleman, big and hearty, blue eyes looking out of a face weathered to an Indian red, but not always seeing far. He had looked too much and too long at the glaring ice in the far north. The palms of his hands and fingers were worn smooth by ropes, spars, harpoon shafts, for like Mr. Rogers he had been a boatheader. He was credited with the scheme of timing oar strokes to a whale's breathing in order to come upon him unaware.

Shad's was still a Vineyard nature, and he began to take Aunt Ettie out driving, fancying horses, as some old whalemen did. He and Aunt Ettie went coasting along in late afternoon like some Flying Dutchman of the road; where they were going I don't suppose Shad half the time knew, and even the horse was in doubt.

Shad drove Aunt Ettie to Fish Hook, and my father pasted his picture in the log: "Shad Tilton, boatsteerer, bark Alice Knowles, a welcome visitor."

Nothing came of his attentions to Aunt Ettie except family smiles, and I did not see him for five or six years after he had become an inmate of that picturesquely named home of retirement for mariners, on Staten Island, Sailors' Snug Harbor. He greeted me cordially and of course we talked of the Vineyard. I went back again a few weeks later, but this time he wasn't allowed to see me. He had broken the rules to find an old whaleman's solace in a convenient bar. I should have liked to see Shad again.

In May, 1908, my brother suffered a serious illness, diagnosed after a long period of unconsciousness as cerebro-spinal meningitis. He made a good recovery, but it was late in the season when we reached Fish Hook for the summer, and our stay was therefore prolonged until almost the end of October to give him as much outdoor life as possible. He had a pony by way of recruitment.

He could be kept out of school for his health, but I was enrolled that fall in the one-room schoolhouse at Locust Grove on the Indian Hill Road. Each morning I joined the other school-age children of the North Shore hills—Elmer and Ruth Rogers, grandchildren of Mr. and Mrs. George A., and Roger Amidon, who lived with his mother in the Ephraim Allen house—and we walked over the crest of Indian Hill and down the other side, past the towering oak that produced sweet acorns. We took our lunches and stayed through the afternoon session before walking home.

The school had nineteen pupils, ranging in age from beginning five-year-olds to the prehigh eleven-year-olds and twelve-year-olds, all taught by Miss Lizzie N. Freeman, a competent New Englander of what seemed to be middle years.

When the smaller children were reciting and acting out their lessons—"Run with me to the tree" or "Rain, rain, go away, little Johnny wants to play, in the meadow on the hay" —at first slowly and bashfully, then with high spirit, I suppose the rest of us studied. We were supposed to study.

In warm days of September we ate our lunches under the trees beside a brook, then in cooler October days climbed to the top of a glacial esker and ate them in the sun. Once Gus and Johnny Erickson brought a watermelon from their farm on the North Road.

We older pupils—though "scholars" was then the favored word—were to recite some poem of our own selection. I thought I might luckily be gone before my turn came, but Miss Freeman managed otherwise. I delivered a poem about a storm in Vineyard Sound:

> Like a phantom pale the Gay Head Light
> 'Gainst the blackening veil of the squall stands out. . . .

My mother persuaded me to recite it also for Sea Coast Defence Chapter D.A.R. when she entertained the chapter at Fish Hook. I was missing when the moment for the recitation arrived, but I was found.

The climax of my Locust Grove career came with a party given by Miss Freeman in the house where she boarded. George was invited also, of course, and we walked over the hill under a starry sky. Miss Freeman led the usual parlor games, and someone played the piano while we sang "School Days, School Days, Good Old Golden Rule Days," "September," and "Papa's Going to Buy Me a Mocking Bird."

I suppose the countryside had no elation of its own when

we walked home, but it seemed to have, for our elation was
too abundant to be less than part of a heavenly whole. I wrote
in the Fish Hook log that I had never before had so good a
time. Presently we took the boat back to New Bedford, and
my boyhood invasion of the golden past was finished.

The New Bedford school system had adopted a plan of
midyear promotions which seems to me now like the splitting
up of shares of corporations. But I found myself in the first
February graduating class of the Parker Street Grammar
School in early 1911, and I entered the old brick high school,
with its small brick-covered yard. Later we moved to the
newly completed building of pale blond brick, and this was
where I stood on the platform and debated the merits of the
commission form of government.

It doesn't seem long now before I was moving closely
toward a February graduation, which would mean a delay
until September before I could enter college. This waste of
time ran counter to my father's activism, and he proposed that
I take the College Board examinations in June, letting the final
term and the diploma go hang.

The usual choice of a college for a New Bedford boy would
have been Harvard, but my father wanted his sons to experience a culture and an environment completely differentiated
from those in which they had been brought up. He plumped
for the brand-new, innovative, and exciting Pulitzer School of
Journalism at Columbia, and it came naturally to George. My
own destiny might have followed wherever I was dropped; I
experienced no "call." It was, rather, the line of least resistance
that led me to follow George to Columbia.

And so I stood on the front steps of the new New Bedford
High School on a June day in 1914 with Miss Tyna Hellman,
the Latin teacher with whom I was in love, discussing prospects. How fair the world was, how fresh the breeze from the
harbor, and how tranquil the glimpses of tree-shaded Fairhaven on the other side of the broad tidal river.

Classes were over, I was free, and Miss Hellman, now more friend than teacher—a new relationship that surprised and touched me as an unexpected step in coming of age—gave useful advice about the Latin examination I was about to take. The school administration had fallen in with my father's plan only grudgingly, but it had fallen in.

The College Boards were given in the school library under the supervision of a retired elderly teacher who clocked their beginning in the morning to a fraction of a minute. In Latin I did very well, I surprisingly passed easily in Intermediate German, and I must have got by in others, but in the last of the series, Advanced English, I managed to fail. I think I treated the final required composition flippantly, and maybe my handwriting by that time had become too offensive for an examiner to read.

I was not rebuked at home, but the failure presented a challenge. I lacked several credits to get into Columbia, and it was decided that I should prepare to take final examinations there in September.

We went to Fish Hook as usual, though my brother worked on the *Standard* most of the summer. He had advanced from a small pony to a real horse, Molly, who had a pony strain. She kept jumping fences, forcing gates, and running off to West Tisbury to join her horse friends at the Johnson Whiting farm. In George's absence it fell to me to pursue her. The Germans invaded Belgium, my mother contracted pleurisy, and in August my father engaged a tutor from Morningside, in New York, to give me a month's training, mostly in Advanced English as prescribed at Columbia.

Miss Kinney fitted into our extraordinary household at Fish Hook, tolerated my absences in pursuit of Molly, assisted my mother, and taught me a lot of perspectives and relationships beyond the trodden way of high-school instruction. Her interest in nature was great, she was a poet, and I catered to all this by applying blue, red, and yellow paint in blobs to mushrooms along the path to the beach, where I thought she would come upon them with wonder. By chance, my brother, back at Fish Hook for a weekend, discovered them first and carried them to the house with proper excitement, which, however, did not impress Miss Kinney.

In the war news the names Namur and Liège came and went. We were informed in headline and story each day that the German invasion had been halted. Excited by the war, I felt a little regret that so mighty a historical event should be closed off so soon. But somehow, in spite of all we were told, the Germans kept going ahead.

Between arrivals of the newspapers our routine went along as usual. I went for the milk each morning, and Mr. Rogers, sitting on the long stoop of his house, said, "Well, Henry, hard times!" I had been promoted from "Bub" to my own name. Mr. Rogers was not well and had almost given up fishing.

One morning Mrs. Rogers said to me brightly, "We had dry beans yesterday and we're having green beans today."

"Who in hell wants beans?" said Mr. Rogers, but not loudly enough for her to hear him.

Another morning I saw him with his suspenders trailing.

"I don't think I can do it, Maggie," he said. "I can't get up, Maggie. Don't believe I can do it. God!"

But he did do it, and Mrs. Rogers planted him firmly on a chair on the stoop. You could see almost the whole Sound from his stoop then.

A little later he said, "Want to go to the barn now, Maggie. Got to go to the barn."

"You'll have to have the barber next," she said.

"No, no! Be all gone before that. Be gone. Oh, my God! Too bad, too bad."

And so I witnessed the retreat of strength and the infinite sadness of the plight of the old.

The eggs in a diminutive nest of hummingbirds on an apple-tree limb in Mayhew G.'s orchard hatched out. The Germans had somehow got through Belgium into France. A man wrecked his car at the end of the Indian Hill Road. The water in the cistern gave out during the fine, rainless late August, and my father and George cleaned it. We all took turns lugging water from what was known as the Rogers spring. Aunt Addie and Aunt Ettie called. Aunt Emma called.

Such occurrences, mostly small, intervened day by day as if somehow planned to postpone my hour of departure. Duties of packing and getting ready came at last, against a final tomorrow morning. My father and I had our farewell talk on the beach, sitting on a driftwood timber. Polonius was not present, even in shadow or inflection. My father spoke casually, and what it all came to was wishing me well and telling me he knew I would get along all right.

The tide came halfway up the beach. The sand was hot from the rays of the sun. After a little while we walked up the hill together through the woods.

5

It was "Tipperary" they were singing, a row of youths walking on Broadway past the dormitory, Furnald Hall. I can hear them now.

> Good-by Piccadilly
> Farewell Leicester Square . . .

There must be many other ears in which the song and its identity with history will never die away, but for me it is accompanied by a gentle, sunny September warmth, the scent of a city fall, and the glow of my first days of independence and adventure at Columbia University, in the greatest city of the world. The present moment verged on ecstasy and the doom of war seemed far off.

In high school I had learned of the Triple Alliance and the Triple Entente, but I had also learned that there would be no more wars. Nations could not afford the cost. Civilization had gone beyond the battlefield to an Age of Enlightenment. The Balkan fighting, a tag end, would soon be over, and every prospect newly fair.

So I believed on the June day when I stood with Miss Tyna

Hellman on the steps of the high-school building, and I could hardly disbelieve it wholly even now. Not yet eighteen years old, I felt a surge of contentment.

Soon I explored, bought postcards of Columbia to mail to Aunt Addie and Aunt Ettie—it seemed important to acquaint them with the geography of the campus—and found the Journalism library, where the librarian, Miss Helen Rex Keller, introduced me to the first Journalism student of all those I would soon meet. He was Irwin Edman, of the class of 1917, shy, coloring a little, the flush showing in his unpigmented fairness. I don't know whether he remembered that meeting after he became a famous philosopher and teacher, but I never forgot. He also became a legendary absent-minded professor. Years later, at a gathering in the Faculty Club, he told me the same joke twice. It was about Mrs. Roosevelt, who at the time of much publicity about the loves of her son James was supposed to have said to him, "I do think you should have included *one* Negro."

But I was not yet accepted at Columbia. There were those entrance examinations, to be held in Earl Hall. Advanced English was the one that would make all the difference. I wrote a 600-word essay on "Edward III," a 600-word essay on "Addison, Pope, and Swift as Satirists," and a 200-word essay on "The Pathetic in Dickens." If it had not been for Miss Kinney, I could not have compared anything with anything else, since this sort of value judgment, as it would be called today, did not enter the high-school range.

I worried for a day or two after, and then walked into the office of Adam Leroy Jones, Director of Admissions, who rose from his chair, hand extended, and said, "Glad to see you, Mr. Hough. You're all right."

Only a teacher could inquire about the marking, and Miss Kinney inquired. Professor Baldwin, "who had the matter of Advanced English in charge," said that my mark was 85 and this was "almost unheard of for a student entering Columbia." He said they were exceedingly careful in marking entrance papers and that 35 and 40 were the more usual results. More-over, he had been ill, and a young assistant had put in several questions not covered in the prescribed study.

This I record for my father's memory and Miss Kinney's honor. I, who had let him down in New Bedford in June, had atoned on Morningside in September.

If New York was not then young, and even now it is hard for me to believe otherwise, I made it so through new love and discovery. I saw the city face to face as I walked in the streets. I gazed upward and saw it in the heights of lofty build-ings and loftier sky. I looked downward from the Journalism building and saw it slantwise, so many figures walking, cross-ing, standing, all engaged in enterprises of their own and all, like me, a part of the great collective enterprise of living in New York.

I soon knew the vistas from Morningside Heights: count-less rooftops and chimneys, the Pabst Beer sign over Harlem, the "L" at its highest, a glimpse of Hell Gate bridge in the hazy distance. I knew also the confrontation across the Hud-son from Riverside Park to the Palisades, Domino Sugar, Corn Products Refining, and Palisades Park lighted up at night.

Everything was new and good, but a little old, too, for I had read a great deal about New York in bound copies of *Harper's Weekly,* in Richard Harding Davis's Van Bibber stories, O. Henry as first published in *McClure's,* and so on and on. New York—busy but not too busy, high-spirited, humorous, important, concerned in odd ways of its own, aware of a long and mellow heritage.

I could remember two previous visits. The first was in the autumn of 1906, when I was nine, but almost ten. My father planned a vacation tour, the first for the entire family, and after a full day of travel our train waited at a small station at Lansingburg, just outside of Troy, which we would pass through to reach Albany. George and my father had stepped down to the ground, and I stood on the rear platform of the last car.

All three of us noticed a railroad brakeman with a red flag walking toward the curve around which we had come. He had hardly gone from view when a locomotive thundered around the curve hauling a train at high speed, its steam whistle shrilling.

"My God, she's on our track," yelled a man who was standing near my father.

"Jump, Henry, jump!" my father called to me, and I jumped. Then it was "Run!" and we all ran around a shed that stretched for some distance alongside the tracks.

A military special train carrying 400 horses and 350 men from Fort Ethan Allen to be embarked for Cuba had run into ours, telescoping our two rear cars and leaving my mother narrowly safe, her seat just above the cowcatcher of the troop train's locomotive. She was extricated through a window, and we reached Troy by a trolley line and Albany by a late train. Perhaps the most astonishing thing to me now is that my mother did not see a doctor, and I suppose that if one had shown up she would have said she didn't need him.

Five passengers were killed in the collision, and I recall a man beside the tracks holding out one arm, streaming blood, while it was bandaged. But all this left no residue of shock, and it became as dim as anything else in the dim past.

We even went sight-seeing in Albany the next day, for a guide pointed out a papier-mâché fireplace installed in the costly new capitol building by a dishonest contractor. Then we sailed down the Hudson on the Day Line, and I had my first experience of New York. We left the Day Line pier by horsecar, stayed at the Algonquin because it was across from the Hippodrome, and attended a performance of an extravaganza called *A Society Circus* there.

We lunched at Macy's. We stood on the sidewalk and watched the speeding presses in the basement of the *Herald* building. We saw the little time-striking bell ringers signal the hour on the *Herald* clock. We heard, saw, and smelled New York, and took the Fall River Line steamer for the voyage home.

My second visit to New York was arranged in 1913 after my brother had gone to Columbia and was supposedly settled there. He hadn't been allowed too much time to get settled, but he made a splendid host for his younger brother. I slept on a cot in his room in Furnald Hall, and on a stair landing I met Frank Scully and his magnificent smile.

George and I went to see Sothern and Marlowe in *Macbeth* at the huge Manhattan Opera House, and I assumed, with considerable disappointment, that all New York theaters were as vast and the players as far removed from observers like ourselves. During the performance it suddenly occurred to me that although I knew what my father and mother looked like, I could not readily visualize them when I shut my eyes. This worried me for a little while until the excitement of the city supervened.

We toured the city atop a double-decker bus, and when we were about to pass under an elevated structure the conductor came up and said, "Low bridge, look out for your heads." We went around Manhattan on a small excursion boat with a stack that leaned over to permit passage under the Harlem River bridges.

My father had arranged with a steamship man for us to be taken to Ellis Island, and the steamship man provided a full propaganda discourse on why contract labor should be admitted to this country to apply the tile in New York subway stations.

I was to voyage home by the Fall River Line, and I reached the pier at the foot of Fulton Street in the North River well ahead of departure time. From the hurricane deck of the grand old side-wheeler *Priscilla* I gazed up into the blue sky and, at the age of sixteen, beheld my first airplane. It might have been a fly or a mote, but I knew it was a genuine airplane. The newspapers had announced an air race around Manhattan, and I was watching the race, though how the pilots could know whether they were flying around anything at all seemed incomprehensible.

These two visits were in a glimmering past when I met the great city on my own new terms in that busy September warmth of 1914. I know it now as I knew it then, and I always will.

There came an interlude of waiting for classes to begin, and Miss Kinney helped me take advantage of free hours. We went on the subway to Spring Street and saw an Italian marionette show of Tasso's *Jerusalem Delivered*. Saracens and Crusaders battled until the stage was piled with the slain and there was no room for more. The manager later took us behind the scenes and, lest we miss the point, said, "Fight!" grinning with pleasure.

We went to see the street fete of Maria Sanctissima on the East Side, where for two long blocks colored lights were strung overhead and the streets utterly thronged. Chestnuts, peanuts, and cakes were sold, confetti showered, and an image of the Virgin in a shrine was carried all through the fiesta with a little girl marching proudly under it.

I went alone to hear *Carmen* from a seventy-five-cent seat in the balcony of the Century Theatre on Central Park West, walking down from Columbia and back. On the way I stopped at the Museum of Natural History and happened on an exhibit of Vineyard Haven Harbor, which had a painted scene of the town and encrusted spiles from Uncle Ben's marine railway, showing mosses, barnacles, and the boring of marine worms. I looked for the exhibit when I went back to the museum fifty years later, but it was gone and nobody remembered it.

I told a classmate, Carl Schaefer, that I had been to *Carmen*, and he hummed the "Toreador Song" and asked rhetorically if they had sung that. I didn't know whether they had or not, but I assumed they had.

The motion picture *Cabiria* was boldly new in the cinema,

and Miss Kinney invited me to see it, along with some other friends. We saw the eruption of Mount Aetna, with falling temples and pillars and flowing lava, and Hannibal crossing the Alps—"very pretty," I wrote home. Scipio and Archimedes were noble figures, but Hasdrubal and Fluvius Axilus shabby characters. The show was quite something for 1914, and advanced my notion of the movies.

I got back to Furnald Hall by midnight and was awakened at 4:00 A.M. by swearing in the next room and a voice that said, "You'll just hafta go to hell." I recognized an authentic note of college life.

The war, though distant, did have a way of creeping into almost everything. Miss Kinney would not condemn Germany, just as, to my annoyance, she insisted there was no longer much difference between Republicans and Democrats. She had been in Germany and knew and liked the Germans. But her older sister knew beyond argument that Krupp and the Kaiser had brought on the whole bloody business.

One evening Miss Kinney took me to a small apartment gathering where I met Randolph Bourne and heard him lead an animated discussion I did not understand. I didn't know of his importance then, or his radical views on education, or his pacifism, but I marveled at the fluency and composure of a man so cruelly deformed by an early accident.

Miss Kinney did not admire Grant's Tomb and had never been inside. She asked me what it was like, and I was just the one to tell her. I was making myself an authority on the sights of New York.

I ate most of my meals in the Columbia Lunch on Broadway, across from Furnald Hall, entering shyly at first, because I had never been in a restaurant by myself before. I did not know that one must take a check from the cashier's desk and have it punched at the counter. The blonde cashier looked at me pityingly, and I should recognize her instantly today if she were to appear, no matter where, as she was then.

Other meals I took at the Commons in University Hall,

where I was approached by an attractive youth who made conversation and invited me to his fraternity house for lunch. I did not know how to refuse. The fraternity brothers put me at my ease as much as they could, and I got along well enough. But I had no idea of joining any fraternity. The professionalism of the School of Journalism was to absorb me entirely, and my friendships were to be made there. My upbringing had also indicated to me strongly that fraternities were undemocratic.

Soon I was invited to another house, where I met, among others, a member of the Student Board who told with hilarity of a new necktie rush devised for combat between sophomores and freshmen. The beauty of the idea was that it would offer plenty of open-field scrapping for the entertainment of upper classes.

I thought this nonsporting and in any case an idiotic exercise, and was further put off from becoming a fraternity man. Soon I found in my box at Furnald Hall a note informing me that "one of our men" would call for me at a certain hour to take me to dinner at the house of my first acquaintance. I put the note back in the box as if I had not found it, and went elsewhere.

The issue persisted until at last I agreed guiltily to meet a fraternity man in front of Journalism at noon. When noon came I watched from an upper window until he got tired of waiting and went away. He happened to be a young faculty member of some account, as I learned later. But I would have been just as deeply ashamed in later life in any case. Why couldn't I just say "No"?

One Journalism classmate, John N. P. Cramer, came from Redondo Beach, California, and wore a Windsor tie and long hair. This did not indicate any lack of masculinity but, along with his height and bony figure, made him as conspicuous as Abe Lincoln would have been. The college sophomores caught him and made him deliver a speech from one of the fountains in front of Low Library. There was no water in the fountain at the time, and he didn't mind. Later, as by natural selection, he became our first class president.

His uncle was a friend of Melville E. Stone, eminent in journalism for many years as head of the Associated Press and spokesman for the profession. Cramer showed me a letter from Stone to his uncle saying that there was no future in journalism, and advising analytical chemistry as a life work instead.

Carl Schaefer and I got tickets from the Politics Department to hear Christabel Pankhurst lecture at Carnegie Hall. She talked not only about suffrage but also about the war, and Schaefer, who had relatives in Germany and who had taken the College Boards in Berlin, didn't like what she said. During the question period he asked her how about the secret treaty between England and Belgium. She said there was no such treaty, and not for many years did the world in general learn that it had been only an "oral understanding" with the force of a treaty. Walking back to Columbia, Schaefer insisted that he had stuck her.

Harry Mellamed, stocky, black-haired, and fond of strong cigars, had worked as a reporter for the Hartford *Times* and came with a good sense of what newspapers did and should do. He soon began clipping newspapers for a morgue of his own, as many of us were tempted to do, and his Furnald Hall room became rampant with clippings, most of them unfiled. I suppose eventually he must have thrown them all out.

He joined the staff of the *Dorms*, the dormitory weekly, and therefore so did I. There wasn't much to it except that we got free tickets for concerts and recitals, some at Carnegie but mostly at the old Aeolian Hall on Forty-second Street where Woolworth's was later. We heard Guiomar Novaes, Gabrilowitsch, Spalding, Claussen, and many others. In a primitive way I enjoyed them all.

Mellamed knew about the impending advent of the *New Republic,* but I didn't until he showed me the first issue. I did not yet know that Walter Lippmann only a year earlier had written *A Preface to Politics*. I lagged in fruitful use of my free time on Morningside, though I read Ernest Poole's *The Harbor* and some of H. G. Wells. I had missed the *Spoon River Anthology*, and noticed idly that someone in the class was endlessly reading *Jean Christophe*, of which I had never heard.

My brother's class, 1917 J, would be the first to go through all four years of the school, and hence was the first to move up from freshman to sophomore standing. So a new issue was introduced: what should be the relationship between 1917 and 1918? Should the two classes fall into the conventional college posture of confrontation and so on? The members of 1917 J decided not. Journalism as a professional school should remain indivisible in loyalties.

When the annual college tug of war was held between the under classes, Journalism took part, but its participants wore newspapers tied around their middles to show solidarity and some lined up with lettered placards around their necks intended to spell "Columbia Journalism." A photograph, though, showed the letters reversed by the camera, nullifying what was intended to be a historic record.

The print of the picture before me now is not a good one, but I plainly identify George Sokolsky and Frank Scully standing between the rows like team managers. Recognizable though almost incredibly young are the faces of Max Schuster, Merryle Rukeyser, Morrie Ryskind, my brother, Jim Marshall, and others who rose to distinction or fame.

We newcomers received invitations printed in the light-blue ink of Columbia, the same modest hue that decorates the 116th Street subway station: "The Class of 1917 cordially requests your presence at a reception in honor of the Class of 1918 J, to be held in Room 206, Journalism, Wednesday evening, Sept. 23, at 8 p.m."

Room 206 was the big, high-ceilinged typewriter room, a proper setting. Sokolsky, skinny, bushy-haired, and articulate, introduced my brother as "a man from safe, sound, conservative New England who is safe, sound, and conservative." Well, that was Sok's view at the time, probably a natural one for a loudly professed dissident and libertarian. I wrote home that George spoke for a few minutes and spoke well, as I am sure he did. He was conservative only in his respect for realism.

Sok liked to expound his revolutionary views, but they had no shock value for me. Ben Tucker, the American anarchist, who edited the *Radical Review* and *Liberty* in their time, was a New Bedford man, and a friend of my father's. He defined an anarchist as "an unterrified Jeffersonian Democrat," and what was there alarming about that?

Of the tradition-breaking Journalism reception, *Spectator*, the student daily, reported: "The last and most important of the speakers was Dr. Williams of Journalism, who congratulated the pupils on having broken down the familiar way of treating Freshmen and who expressed the hope that a spirit of service would actuate the future Sophomores in their relation with Freshmen." The *Spectator* headline read: "1917 Journalism Receives 1918—Denounce Rough Methods."

Dr. Talcott Williams stood before us with persuasive earnestness, eyes blue and bright under thick white eyebrows, white hair cresting a bit over his forehead. His mustache, also white, drooped in a fashion that suggested his nickname, "Weeping Walrus." A missionary style also invited the epithet. It wasn't that he failed to change timing, pace, and emphasis, for he had long studied a style of speaking, but even so his whole tone verged on the lachrymose. Lean, intense, and witty, he made an impressive figure, the green baize bag in which he carried books and papers around the campus marking him with the identity of a period as well as of a character.

His qualifications in journalism were clearly on record, yet he remained a man of the past century. He had been born in Turkey in 1849, a fact of which we were often reminded. Following early schooling in the Near East he was graduated from Amherst and worked first for the New York *World*, then successively for the *Sun*, the San Francisco *Chronicle*, the Springfield *Republican*, and the Philadelphia *Press*. This was a long journalistic journey, but in 1914 he seemed to have got back pretty much to the Near East, always allowing for a closeness in spirit and temper to the Ages—all of them, but without special emphasis on the modern.

Walter B. Pitkin stood out among the school's first faculty. When he wrote his autobiography, *On My Own*—dashed it off headlong, of course, as he did almost everything, in order to crowd as much into his life as possible—he treated Talcott Williams with some derision, referring to him repeatedly as the "Walrus."

Pitkin quickened me as few others have ever done. I am still, so to speak, galvanized by him. His current runs through me. I have looked him up, and he was thirty-six when he delivered his first lecture to the Class of 1918, rolling out sentences between lips that relished every clear transmission of thought into language. His keen intelligence had a neat, economical precision.

He wrote later that he had been supposed to cover "the history of philosophy, modern psychology, a dash of anthropology (say about one generation of it), the world's great ethical systems (by special request of Pulitzer), and an outline of logic which, if it accomplished nothing more, would at least aid a young reporter to smell a non-sequitur in the cross-examination of a witness at a murder trial. To cover all this ground I was allowed five hours a week or some thirty-two weeks, Total, 160 hours."

The wonder of it was that he did cover this ground, except that I don't much remember the logic, and assume it was woven in with the rest. The short allowance of time must have been partly responsible for Pitkin's pace and vividness, but he himself was responsible for the rest.

"I never enjoyed a task more than this one. It was, from the start, monstrously impossible. It was also fantastic. So it was the perfect sport."

To me it had a sustained excitement of discovery. Max Schuster said that Pitkin's course inspired him ten years later to publish *The Story of Philosophy*. Pitkin said many things that were useful, concise, and memorable. I don't expect too much credit for them in the context of the 1970's, but 1914 was younger and different.

"All transitions of energy toward normal are pleasant," Pitkin said. "Cultivate habitual reactions," he advised. "The human mind is not a simple bureau of truth. The working of it is colored by various things." "No individual can in any manner whatsoever discount his own biases in dealing with anything." "All views of the world which are products of individuals are grossly biased in some manner—all scientific conjectures, all religions, all philosophies." "Science is nothing but the attempt to face the problem of correcting individual judgments with respect to truth. . . . If science is to succeed, its investigations must in every stage be simultaneously developed by a lot of people, not by gifted individuals. In the long run their biases will cancel out. Scientific work is essentially public—publicity is at the bottom of all science."

"No moral rule that can be named is absolute." "Nietzsche is Kant combined with Schopenhauer." "Each individual is a center of action. The consequence of any chain affects many people." "Emotion is one kind of complex behavior. Intelligence is another kind of complex behavior. The difference is that emotion is an interference with, and intelligence is an adjustment of behavior. Emotion is the simple failure of adjustment in a biological sense." "Convention, etiquette, modesty, fear of disapproval, are simple social imitation."

Our first theme for Pitkin was on Jane Harrison's *Ancient Art and Ritual*, out of which he expected us to derive a starting line for every creative writer: "All art and all religion are the expression of unsatisfied desire." I wrote my theme as I would have written it in high school—words, words, words. I was good with words. Pitkin graded me a C minus: "You write glibly but without the slightest indication of having grasped what this is all about." I grew up overnight.

A boy named Crystal began his Jane Harrison theme:

"When we understand better what is Ancient Art and Ritual, the subject will become more comprehensible to us." Pitkin wrote on this: "Good news from the trenches," and posted it on the bulletin board. Once he wrote on a theme of Betty's: "This reads like an uneasy dream." But his breeziness quickly swept past any cruelty. He was leading us on and up, and we had to follow in a hurry.

Irvin S. Cobb, then at the top of his immense popularity as a humorist and short-story writer, spoke to the Pulitzer Press Club at the school, a student-organized and extracurricular group, scorning the notion that anyone could be taught to write. "Anyone who could write would be writing, not trying to teach," Cobb said. But Pitkin at the time was teaching story writing and selling short stories to the eagerly sought market of the *Saturday Evening Post* under the pseudonym Leavitt Ashley Knight. His fiction about the Philippines brought letters from people who thought they might have met him there, but he got most of his atmosphere out of one little red book.

Someone dug up a professional journal in which Pitkin was characterized by William James as one of the most promising of the younger philosophers.

Then there was Edwin E. Slosson, editor of the weekly journal the *Independent*, a rather stout, but not sloppily so, aphoristic, and charming teacher who rolled his eyes interestingly and made funny or astonishing statements with a disarming lack of facial expression. Dr. Slosson taught such elements of physics as might be most useful in the foundation of a newspaperman. He told us in 1914 that a piece of coal no larger than a pea could produce incalculable energy if the atom were ever to be split. He didn't say anything about radioactivity. He reported to us on the eclipse that bore out Einstein's special theory of relativity, and gave at least an overview of what Einstein signified.

We were in a posture of curiosity and waiting for many things, to see what would happen, or how they would turn out. The 1910 census reports would soon show that for the first time in history more people lived in the city than in the country—or was the balance just being clearly tilted at last?

Dr. Gerhard R. Lomer—Jerry Lomer—taught first-year English. He assigned us to report a talk by Columbia's President, Nicholas Murray Butler, on how the war in Europe came about. Dr. Butler had been on the scene. I compared his account to Victor Hugo's *History of a Crime*, which I had read in installments in the old bound volumes of *Harper's Weekly*. The comparison was apt enough, but I overdid it. Lomer gave me a C with the comment: "Avoid putting so much of your own that you spoil the proportion."

Politics we studied with Charles A. Beard, trenchant, wise, and challenging, but he was so thinly spread through the university that many of the lectures were given by assistants. One of these, Leon Fraser, 1913 J, had reported Sulzer's gubernatorial campaign for the *World* and could deliver a Sulzer speech verbatim. It was Fraser who said in class that Nicholas Murray would get cross-eyed trying to keep his eye on Columbia and the presidency at the same time. Dr. Butler had been a candidate for vice president, his name having replaced that of Taft's running mate, Sherman, who died after the nominating convention in 1912.

We were always close to the war. Beard brought us closer than anyone else. He quoted Bernard Shaw on diplomacy and approved President Wilson's neutrality message, especially its good sense in asking what we would be supposed to be fighting for. He thought that in Mexico and everywhere else the United States should let others stew in their own juice, staying firmly at home. The Philippines he saw as our only real problem, and we should give them their independence and get out as soon as possible.

This was isolationism but it did not have to be swallowed whole. Even Theodore Roosevelt had at first considered the invasion of Belgium an inevitable event and had switched tardily to belligerence. As for me, I was a pacifist to begin with, made so by reading and by the sense of world principles that Ben Franklin summarized when he wrote, "There never was a good war or a bad peace."

Talcott Williams taught courses in International Relations, the History of Journalism, and Critical Writing, all of which we reached in our final two years, the professional ones that followed the primarily academic. His notices on the bulletin board showed the hand of his secretary, Eliza McGill, a plump little woman of intense loyalty, who was not at home on any acropolis. For instance:

There will be a lecture on Wednesday afternoon, May 8, at 1:30. This will make the third lecture on account of the Director's absence in Chicago the week of March 18.

In the time of World War I Dr. Williams's mind returned to the Near East, the East, and the doctrine of extraterritoriality. He had long ago dealt with this, and he had also written a pamphlet, *Link Relations*, which concerned the uneasy ties of Europe and Asia in the tender region of Turkey.

Of course he did not avoid the current war. One of the items for a ten-minute quiz was this: "Name in order of time the cases of intervention cited by Lingelbach."

Lingelbach—where is he now? I have forgotten him. It was he who wrote: "Intervention, therefore, instead of being outside the pale of the law of nations and antagonistic to it, is an integral and essential part of it; an act of police apart from war for enforcing the rules of international law." This referred, of course, to intervention in the lands of backward nations; the Far East again.

Clara Sharpe, my future sister-in-law, took down literal excerpts from the Director's classroom lectures and sent many of them to me after I had gone to Washington. His language tumbled over itself a bit but usually did not conceal his wit and flicker:

When he was old he looked short, and when he was young he looked tall, and I don't know the reason for this except that when he was old he trimmed his hair very close, and when he was young he wore his hair in a pompadour. He was the only man I ever saw who seemed to be a pompadour all the way across.

The curious inspiration of newspaper life which leads us to work hard on half-pay in solitary confinement.

There is a line in Catullus in which he speaks of his wife as she walked across the room and the rafters creaked. The Romans did not believe in the sylphlike maiden. It is a beautiful line. If any of you have kept up your Latin it will be a passionate day when you discover the body of Catullus. This line is full of beauty and full of passion.

The best definition of the Cabinet that I know is when Theodore Roosevelt on Tuesday there was a republic in Panama, on Wednesday a revolution, on Friday the Cabinet met because they all knew it was going to happen, they all stood around, and he came in looking a trifle embarrassed because they had not been consulted, but it has sometimes been done, it happened a week ago Saturday, and Roosevelt said, 'You see by the newspapers what has happened, all I can say is that it happened.' Mr. Knox, who had the power of making people listen to him, and I wish that I had that power for often I know I have not, and Mr. Knox said, 'We are only clerks appointed by you, and you can do as you please, but the American people cherish a tradition and it will not be well for this tradition to be violated,' and Roosevelt blushed to the roots of his hair and said, 'Mr. Secretary, you are right. It won't happen again.' And there you are, and in the English Cabinet nothing is ever published and it is not considered a nice thing for a Cabinet officer to keep a diary which mentions meetings.

Some comments on important figures in American journalism:

Bennett, Greeley and Raymond—they are different not because they are different but because temperament leads men along different lines.

Bennett had no conscience. He started a demoralizing campaign of advertising which rendered until he was fined for publishing obscene matter. He passed his life with his hand against every man's hand. The way in which he was attacked passes all belief. He showed it was possible to run a newspaper without political support of any kind or another. He began the creation of pony expresses and the use of sailing craft to meet clipper ships and get the news.

The Herald has the most complete combination of editorial comment and facts about buildings.

I am inclined to think that a man must be totally detached from personal affairs if he is to be an editor.

Greeley—by no possibility could he ever look as though his clothes fit him. For some inscrutable reason he wore his trousers tucked into his boots. He lived outside New York, farming at great cost to himself, hardly ever making any money, which did not prevent him from writing about agriculture. He widened the editorial page to deal with the high death rate of children and the whole field of life.

When you get to his editorials I am afraid I have read more of them than any man alive today, for I read them as a boy. They are very dull; they reek with sentiment; they are full of vigor, using language which one hesitates to quote in this class—that he was fully capable of.

My knowledge of Mr. Dana consisted in a charming series of notes which he wrote at one time or another when I wrote something for which he cared in one way or another. When Dana reached the paper he was born in 1819 and was a man open to infection from any social microbe that is in the air. He was an omnivorous reader. It really seemed that he would go to bed with a grammar, woke up and bathed himself with a dictionary, and by night he had picked up the language.

Dana at this time had a great pressure for money—of course later when he made money he lived in great luxury, and collected books and was the only man I knew who really knew faience. He had an unfailing eye for it.

I have spoken of his language—when he was going to Russia he took up Russian and when he reached Russia he talked Russian and carried on conversations in it. Then he took up Icelandic offhand just because he would like to read it in the original. Now these were his various sides.

Raymond represented what you are—went to college—graduated at 16, came to New York, broke into print. He pushed through life with a sense of education.

Just as countries are dyed deep with their origin, just so, after everything is changed, after everyone is dead, buried and forgotten, there still remains something of the origin of a newspaper.

Dr. Williams spoke intimately of many figures of the stage. Some he remembered from the theatergoing of younger years, and others, including Julia Marlowe, E. H. Sothern, and Laurette Taylor, he knew well in our time.

You'll see the same thing in five or ten years. Some young woman will take the world by storm, and men seldom revive Shakespeare but Marlowe could have anything she pleased, and came and went to the Biltmore in her own car, and she got her $2,500 as soon as the performance was over—I was with her one night when she folded up the check, and I asked her if it felt good to be richer than she had been five minutes before, and she said it did feel good.

When Ellen Terry had passed her first fresh years and her waist had begun to threaten her face, she brought the Portia scene to a screaming comedy end, and made the audience look like thirty cents—pardon the slang.

There was for some reason I don't pretend to say a group of actresses together—Miss Neilson was so beautiful that a lawyer I know who always took his pleasures and wore his emotions in public, on meeting her he didn't know anyone could be so beautiful as to mold men, and he took his hat and left.

When Mary Anderson played Winter's Tale she called in Alma Tadema, the leading archaeologist of Europe and the British Museum, and these things all cost in one way or another what with the clothing and one thing and another, while Miss Taylor put on Over There and Happiness and one thing and another with little expense, and I don't quite know the reason for this.

I have seen almost every Shakespeare play that can be acted, almost without exception. I have seen twenty-seven Hamlets and survived.

And so the Director swept himself and his class into the past of relics and memories, and faced his students with as much of the present day as he could manage out of the restless, tumbling ferment of a vast accumulated knowledge. I can think of him now in the phrase he proposed to me as the definition of a critic—"like a priest at the altar, between the living and the dead." And he insisted to me a number of times that a dry sponge does not absorb, despite the familiar figure of speech implying that it does. A wet sponge is the one that absorbs.

Because of my background it was assumed at the school that I must have had previous professional experience. I think I assumed so myself, even until just now when I looked back from the vantage point of an April day in 1974 upon some of the Aprils long past. It was on April 19, 1920, that Betty and I together inspected the office of the *Vineyard Gazette* for the first time and found Mr. Marchant, the Old Editor, puttering at the type cases, a cigar stub in the corner of his mouth, faded purple sweater sagging, and an old straw hat on his head. The day was a legal holiday, Patriots' Day, and therefore he wasn't really working, and had lighted only a paper fire in the belly of the cast-iron stove.

I can see and feel the same day in April a year earlier, when the temperature soared under the noonday sun and Vineyard Sound looked so blue and inviting that Charlie Norton and I decided to go swimming on Fish Hook beach. The act was one of folly. I barely managed to submerge in the numbing water.

Longer ago still, in April, 1912, it occurred to my father to publish *Moby Dick* as a serial in the *Standard*, with illustrations by staff artists. The idea seems remarkable, for the Melville revival did not begin until Raymond Weaver's *Herman Melville, Mariner and Mystic* was published in 1921. The serial ran in the *Standard* and nobody paid any attention.

But the project led my father to take his family to see the Bethel on Johnnycake Hill, the Whaleman's Chapel of *Moby Dick*, and we read for ourselves the cenotaphs on the Bethel walls. The chaplain, the Reverend Charles Thurber, mentioned that in looking over a lot of books lately donated to the Mariners' Home he had been reminded of a book of his youth, *The Captive in Patagonia*, and felt a strong wish that he might read it again.

So my father gave me the first real assignment of my life, to find a copy of *The Captive in Patagonia*, talk with Chaplain Thurber about it, and then write a piece about the book and his memories. The book turned out to be an account by Benjamin F. Bourne, of New Bedford, mate of the schooner *John Allyne*, who had been cut off by natives near the mouth of the Straits of Magellan and had undergone a Melvillelike captivity. What I wrote was passable, and at the age of fifteen I had my first story published.

Now that I was in New York, my father moved to add further experience. Countering the economic squeeze of the war, the *Evening Sun* was sponsoring a Cotton Corner in Grand Central Palace, an exhibition place I came to know well. I found, as my father had expected, that most of the fine goods in the Cotton Corner had been made in New Bedford, beginning with Wamsutta sheets and going on to Djuma de Soie, Etolienne de Avignon, Voile Diaphane, and others as esoteric.

"Look," said the man in charge, indicating an elderly woman who was examining a swatch of Carvel cloth. "She thinks it's wool."

I had sense enough to write down what the man said, and this was good practice for a beginner. Write down what they say.

Later I was asked to do a feature about the Bourne Workshop for the Blind at the foot of Thirty-fifth Street in New York City. The timely interest came about because Miss Emily Bourne, of the old New Bedford whaling family, had given the Workshop and was now about to give a whaling museum to New Bedford.

I visited the Workshop and watched the blind men and women making brooms, but I lacked the courage or enterprise to talk with any of them, and ended with a feeble piece of description in which, to eke it out, I mentioned the fine view of the East River. My friend Carl Schaefer saved me from the stupidity of putting a view into a story about those who would never see it.

This slow growth was better than nothing for newspaper experience, and meantime Dr. Williams and Professor Pitkin had set about the innovation of teaching reporting by means of motion pictures. This was an advanced notion then. Some early industrial films—*Manufacture of Tubing, Cement Construction, Watch Making, Canadian Mining and Agriculture, Asphalt*—were shown with an accompanying talk by a representative of the industry. The asphalt man donated his $50 honorarium for a prize, and it was won by my brother. There was no excitement in any of this, but it gave a certain kind of practice.

On election night, Cramer, Schaefer, and I went down to Park Row to watch the returns in front of the *Tribune* building. Where would we have gone but to Park Row, the legendary and symbolic, the very Fleet Street of America? But this was an off-year election, and Charles S. Whitman, who had prosecuted Lieutenant Becker in the Rosenthal murder case, easily defeated Martin Glynn, successor to Bill Sulzer in his unexpired term as governor after Tammany threw him out.

Even as first-year men we were admitted to meetings of the Pulitzer Press Club to hear William P. Beazell, of the *World*, Herbert Bayard Swope, Rube Goldberg, Harris M. Crist, of the Brooklyn *Eagle*, and Charles M. Palmer, who praised the country newspaper. Heywood Broun came, bringing with him Alexander Woollcott, who made acidulous and amusing comment.

Arthur Brisbane, writer of short, moralistic, and simplistic editorials for the Hearst papers—one of them suggested that you discover what alcohol does to your stomach by putting some in your eye—lectured under the school's own auspices. He said we should never write "the horse ran down the street— and so on—and then that 'the equine' fell down." If this was what happened, say "The horse ran down the street . . . and the horse fell down." Forget about that "equine" stuff.

In December, Will Irwin was the Pulitzer Press Club speaker. Professor Franklin Matthews, formerly a *World, Sun,* and *Times* editor successively and now a mellow old-timer and faculty member, introduced Irwin as the premier reporter of the world, and Irwin had some claim to the title at the moment, for he was just back from Europe with a living account of the horror, magnitude, and dreadful impending hazards of the war.

Among other things, he described how the warring countries were molding public opinion through the press. In Germany, he said, censorship was accomplished with characteristic thoroughness and efficiency, in England it was being mishandled, and in France it was less efficient than in Germany. The English did well enough or even better, once they got their hand in.

In less than six months the *Lusitania* would be sunk and William Jennings Bryan, the most conspicuous symbol of official neutrality in the United States, would hand in his resignation as Wilson's Secretary of State, a portent as grave as any could be. But now the month was May, the air warm, and living with portents had become a matter of habit. That's how we are living now, I suppose, in the interlude before the next atomic bomb goes off.

Cramer, Schaefer, and I found a Hungarian restaurant on Manhattan Street, in the Harlem Valley, where we could have a full-course dinner for thirty cents and a five-cent tip, and we walked back along the river in pretwilight languor.

The final gym exam was held, and I made the mile run in 5.58, well within the permissible 6.30. The best part of it was that I felt fine. I flourished.

The college semester closed, and George and I went home, as usual, by the Fall River Line. In New Bedford I did more things for the *Standard*. I interviewed a bartender named Honest John Kelley, who had been the discoverer of a

popular fighter named Martin Canole. The sinking of the
submarine F-4 off Honolulu had given immediacy to the
subject of deep-sea diving, and I interviewed a trio of experienced divers, including Uncle Ben. One of them said that a
diver feels like a lobster looks, and this made my story, such
as it was.

Most of the summer, though, I spent off and on at Fish
Hook, mostly on, the nearest to a vacation summer I was ever
to have again. The world, far from the Island, might really
have been intact and safe. We did not even hear the big guns
in target practice; they were too far off, on business. I went
again to Mayhew G.'s for milk, stopping to talk to Mr. and
Mrs. Rogers, and did some gardening, and swam in Vineyard
Sound.

Max Schuster had entered Columbia in knee pants and had
been chased by college sophomores. Too young to be enrolled
in the School of Journalism, he had chosen a combination
College and Journalism course, so that although he was a
member of the class of 1917 he took some courses with 1918.
What impressed me at the beginning was that he used green
ink in his fountain pen and said "absolutely" instead of "yes."
But almost everyone did, and soon I was doing it myself.

Max wrote later that we "were lucky beyond words to be
at Morningside at a time packed tight with history in the
making. . . . Revolutions were a dime a dozen—revolutions in
politics, in nationalism, in science, in art, and in thought."
Did we know it then? In a way we did. At the bottom of
everything was the war. All had come loose, nothing remained
securely fastened.

Germans were singing *"Deutschland Uber Alles"* on Four-
teenth Street. Wrangling dragged on about "hyphenated
Americans." The Irish got into it, of course, and President
Wilson led in denouncing Jeremiah O'Leary. Plattsburgh was
in the news, the reserve officers' training camp unofficially
promoted because the government wouldn't do it openly.

German opera was on holiday for the duration. We were getting ready—for what? The issue loomed at Columbia.

Leon Fraser wrote to *Spectator* to deny that he or Professor Kendrick, of the School of Journalism, had retracted what they had said at a meeting opposed to the Plattsburgh idea. "I did not retract anything, and I will not retract anything."

David Starr Jordan spoke at Columbia and said of the United States: "This is the land where hatred dies." From the lips of that white-haired idealist I could almost believe it true, but not for long.

We—our side—soon figured in headlines in all the New York newspapers. This was in the *Sun*, which had most fun with the story:

FREEDOM OF SPEECH
WINS AT COLUMBIA

Ben Reitman and Frank Tannenbaum Help the
Students Adopt Resolutions

Stir over the Tolstoy Case

School of Journalism Accused of Being Hotbed
of Publicity Seekers

J. D. Prince, Professor of Slavonic Languages, had prevented the delivery of a lecture at Columbia by Count Ilya Tolstoy, and a protest meeting was held in a great room in Philosophy Hall. Those who couldn't get in through the doors were climbing through the windows.

A Law School graduate, Clark Getts, presided, but, as the *Sun* account said, "the principal rebel on the side of the students was George Sokolsky of the School of Journalism." "Professor Prince was afraid we were so unpatriotic that Tolstoy would turn us all into pacifists and traitors," Sokolsky said. He "sent an agent to Count Tolstoy threatening that something would happen to him if he tried to speak at Columbia. . . . Columbia should never become a third party with the Russian government in suppressing facts about Russia."

Frank Tannenbaum spoke, too. "Professors who prevent free discussion at Columbia keep Columbia from being the great University it should be," he said, a moderate enough statement. I met him many years later with Max Eastman in Edgartown, and it has been a lasting regret that I did not remember his part in the Tolstoy meeting.

Professor Dixon Ryan Fox, of the Economics Department, said the university should have somebody alert and authorized "to exclude a publicity seeker from Columbia" who would exploit the university's name.

When the moment came for the offering of a resolution, Sok noticed me and pushed through the crowd. He asked if I would read the resolution and move its adoption. Of course I would. The resolution called on President Butler to declare that freedom of thought and expression were not to be suppressed at Columbia, and asked that student organizations be permitted to hold such meetings on the campus as they deemed necessary. The resolution carried, with only a few straggling Noes.

The *Sun* report did not mention my name, but the Associated Press did, and it appeared on a bulletin board in front of the *Standard* office. I had wondered what my father would think. Of course he was pleased. The *Sun* went on to have its fun:

> The high altitudes of Philosophy Hall at Columbia University were somewhat disturbed yesterday when Frank Tannenbaum and Ben Reitman, the Anarchist supporter of Emma Goldman, and other shining lights of liberalism invaded those classic shades to say what they thought about the banishing from Columbia of Count Ilya Tolstoy, who didn't deliver a lecture on his father's works last Saturday because J. D. Prince, Professor of Slavonic Languages, objected. And Count Tolstoy says that Professor Prince speaks Russian very poorly.

Then at the end:

> And when the students, girls and boys, filed out through the corridor, there was Ben Reitman, Anarchist, giving out invitations

to attend lectures on birth control. He violently chewed gum and didn't seem to mind even if he was in a place where philosophy was dispensed for the young mind. He just handed out his circulars and chewed.

I had seen Ben standing against the wall, an oddly dressed, amused, comic figure. I recognized him because I had seen him only a little while back when I attended a lecture by Emma Goldman at a hall somewhere in Harlem, certainly not at the university. She had surprised me by her plainness and earnestness. Her sleeves were either short or rolled up. Her hair straggled over her forehead. She was real in a deeply human sense, and Ben Reitman was putting it on.

Nicholas Murray Butler paid no attention to the protest meeting or the resolution. He was then fifty-four years old but seemed to have been president of Columbia from time beyond counting, not just since 1906. He and his rhetoric were in a style of sounding words and scholastic authority. He denounced the newspapers, but Theodore Roosevelt had done that more or less when he lambasted the "muckrakers."

In one address Dr. Butler railed against the "inaccuracies and misstatements of the public press" and said that the fiction departments occupied the front pages of the newspapers. He said that the School of Journalism had not advanced far enough to reform the profession. But it was the School that made headlines he and the trustees didn't like, as when the class of 1917 J talked of striking against onerous assignments: "Duma at Pulitzer School in a Daze: George Sokolsky Fails to Get Fired but Revolution Proves a Flivver."

When the votes in the 1916 Student Board election were counted, it was found that Morrie Ryskind and Jim Danahy of 1917 J had been elected. In collegiate terms this was impossible. It upset the college and the fraternities. So the election was thrown out on the ground of "electioneering" in the School of Journalism.

His bitterness encouraged Morrie, as editor of the campus monthly, *Jester*, to write about "Nicholas Murray, the Butler," and to make fun of his "pink house on the hill." Morrie characterized Dr. Butler as disloyal for being warlike about Belgium when Woodrow Wilson was doing his best to avert war. Morrie also called Dr. Butler "Czar Nicholas." Morrie was fired, though he got his degree after he wrote *Of Thee I Sing* and won a Pulitzer Prize.

At the time, he made an amusing, irreverent, and knowing companion. He was agent for the Caroline laundry, and if I had saved them I would have quite a collection of slips from his firm saying "We consider this sock too badly torn to be mended." Nowadays, of course, Morrie is a confirmed right-wing columnist.

Our time at Columbia moved on. "World history was not an abstraction but an immediate experience," Max Schuster wrote later, "heightened by the realization that there were giants in those days on the Columbia University faculty. . . . My fellow students and contemporaries were also great teachers, many of them destined to become giants themselves in various creative fields. . . . To be young and sit at the feet of teachers who were true giants and to fraternize with fellow students who acted as a committee on new traditions . . . all this was for me the ultimate in life enhancement."

Max himself was of that *ad hoc* committee of the young. I, too, was glad that I was there.

In the spring of 1916 my field of experience broadened and I made the acquaintance of Lou Durlacher, Mike McNulty, Kewpie Ertle, and the Zulu Kid. Prize fighting had succeeded the sport of roller polo—a kind of hockey played on roller skates—in New Bedford, and Al Shubert, the city's bantam-weight whiz, had brought the fans to a state of high excitement. The matching of Shubert with Kewpie Ertle would be only one step from the biggest fight of all, Shubert—if he could beat Ertle—against Kid Williams, the champion.

I was sent to watch Kewpie Ertle fight Terry Martin at the Clermont A. C. in Brooklyn and report to the New

Bedford fans through the *Standard*. Mike McNulty was
Kewpie's manager, a man of quivery handshake because he
had been a rubber in a Turkish bath. He took me to a ring-
side seat identified by scribbled lines as often occupied by
W. O. McGeehan, sports writer for the *Tribune*, whom I
much admired. Kewpie clearly outboxed Martin, a lucky thing
for me, since I was not expert enough to judge any close
ones. Lou Durlacher, who was making the bout between
Ertle and Shubert, was naturally happy with my story and
the *Standard* headline: ERTLE ALL THE WAY.

I didn't report the New Bedford fight, though I saw it
because it was fought in the Washington's Birthday interval.
A month or so later I saw Kewpie fight the Zulu Kid in
Brooklyn, but already I was losing my enthusiasm for the
prize ring, such as it had been. A last flare-up was when Max
Schuster and I saw Dempsey beat Georges Carpentier at
Boyle's Thirty Acres, and Max wrote that the news was not
Dempsey's victory but Carpentier's loss. This was true, though
hardly anybody but Bernard Shaw had given Carpentier a
chance.

That summer of 1916 my brother toured for a while with
Barnum & Bailey, and I worked most of the time for the
Standard. I reported the high pontifical requiem mass for the
Reverend Hormisdas Deslaurier in the grandeur of St.
Anthony's Church, which he had built in the North End.

I joined a great number of clergy, impressively robed, in
the sacristy and looked out at the massive arches and colorful
splendor of the lofty church itself. My trepidation was mitigated by the presence of my father's old friend Father Pat
McGee, who had been the first resident priest on Martha's
Vineyard. Long before his death he became a monsignor, and
he and Bishop James E. Cassidy, a remarkable prelate and
human being, called at the *Gazette* office and then at Fish
Hook on no other errand than friendship and reminiscence.
In the sacristy that morning a reporter for a French-language
daily in New Bedford asked Father Pat if he could smoke.

Father Pat said, "No." Always and anywhere in the world there is always a reporter who asks if he can smoke.

Of the funeral, I wrote: "The ushers at the doors had difficulty in keeping the way clear. A woman tried to force her way in. A brief glance over the shoulders of the crowd and she slipped away. 'They have closed the coffin already,' she said." I was learning, though I had a long way to go.

Unexpectedly, three months later, I sat with a couple of other reporters at the press table in a Fall River courtroom where a hearing was held on a petition by the heirs of Father Deslaurier to contest his will. He had left a bequest to his housekeeper of many years, one Alvida Noel. I had to take down the rapid succession of questions and answers—"Q-A" stuff, Robert E. MacAlarney, city editor of the *Tribune* and Professor of Journalism, called it. . . . I never knew the outcome of the case. The judge reserved judgment, and soon I went back to Columbia. It's pretty much a lost trail now— so long ago.

A little later I helped report the case of the Commonwealth against Thomas H. Kearns, proprietor of the venerable Mansion House, once a leading hotel in New Bedford, which now stood bereft on the run-down slope of Union Street. Kearns was charged with keeping a liquor nuisance, a tenement for purposes of prostitution, and so on, the complaint based on evidence gathered by detectives of the Watch and Ward Society. Another reporter and I took down a running story in the courtroom, our pages fitting consecutively and handed to a messenger to be rushed to the *Standard* office.

Some of the personages involved were Shorty Foster, Pete the Iceman, and girls named Bessie, Mary, Violet, Blondie, and Emma, who, it was testified, sometimes went upstairs in the Mansion House with sailors. Some of these same girls may have been among those caught in a surprise raid and brought in the late evening to the Central Police Station, where I was waiting around for news. I was impressed that as the girls were brought in a policeman promptly drew down the window shades. One of the girls I thought was a beauty. None of them seemed depressed or even dimmed by having been arrested.

Tommy Kearns of the Mansion House was convicted, and later on he hired a detective to shadow my father. It is likely that the detective may have been mystified at the way we lived. He followed my father to the Vineyard and peered down at Fish Hook from the top of Mayhew G.'s hill.

That summer I went inexcusably wrong in reporting the death of young redheaded Tommy Hart, who had been a school friend. He worked in the composing room of the *Standard,* and Paul Murphy, who headed the union chapel, told me he had died from "mastoids on the brain." I knew no better, the copy desk apparently knew no better, and this cause of death appeared in print. No one complained, but this was a lesson to me; it takes more than silent consent or even unanimous agreement to make a story correct.

I also compared some rowdy occasion to "a Polish wedding." I meant no harm. "Polish wedding" was as current in New Bedford then as "Donnybrook" in many places. But a Polish priest rightly complained, and the *Standard* apologized.

As August yielded to September I was sent to the Vineyard to report the annual Governor's Day at the former Cottage City, now (since 1907) Oak Bluffs. Traditionally this event belonged to the Martha's Vineyard Camp Meeting Association, but the Association had to move over and make room also for the Chamber of Commerce. The governor was Samuel W. McCall, grandfather of Tom McCall, who long afterward became governor of Oregon. For a man of sixty-five, and not a spry sixty-five at that, the Governor's Day events amounted to an exacting ordeal.

Met at the wharf by a decorated automobile, Mr. McCall was escorted in "a monster automobile parade," which included "a simple but effective float of the woman suffragists." The parade wound up at Ocean Park, where the Governor crowned Belle Hudson, of Dorchester, as queen of the carnival, and "briefly addressed the assembled company."

He was then whisked off on a fast-moving tour of all the towns of the Island, his car "a traveling bunch of dust with something black in front of it." At Gay Head, twenty miles later, there was a stop for handshaking, especially with Edwin D. Vanderhoop, the first and only Indian to be elected to a seat in the Massachusetts legislature, and then the Governor was rushed off again.

"Thanks to the unusual speed," he reached Vineyard Haven an hour ahead of schedule, but there was nevertheless an adequate gathering at the Barnacle Club. Off again to Oak Bluffs and a baseball game at Waban Park, where the Governor borrowed fifty cents to put in a hat passed for contributions to help pay the expenses of the home team. Then it was six miles to Edgartown and a reception in the Home Club, where the Governor stood on the stairs and "addressed a few words to the gathering." Ice cream and cookies were pressed upon him.

Then back to Oak Bluffs, an inspection of the Country Club, a supper hour at the Wesley House, a brief rest, and a march to the Grand Illumination and the annual address in the Iron Tabernacle on the Camp Ground, to an audience of a couple of thousand.

"I have traveled and explored Martha's Vineyard until there is nothing left to the imagination," Governor McCall said. "It is a somewhat wearying process to see it all in one day."

He wasn't to be let off yet. There was still the traditional banquet at the Wesley House, but the Governor did not quite stick it out. He excused himself and went to bed while the band played "The End of a Perfect Day." The quotations, of course, are from my account of the occasion.

A year later I was again assigned to report Governor's Day, but Governor McCall did not show. Not for him again. He sent the redheaded Lieutenant Governor, Calvin Coolidge—to the disappointment of all concerned on the Island. One change, the country now being at war, was that Coolidge had "The Star-Spangled Banner" and the "Marseillaise" sung at him in the Home Club at Edgartown.

In the interval between supper and the march to the Camp Ground Mr. Coolidge took the air by himself on the Wesley House veranda. He noticed me at the other end, walked across, and asked agreeably, "Are you getting everything you want?" I said I was, and thanked him. This is a complete and true account of my private meeting with a future president of the United States.

That fall Woodrow Wilson was making his front-porch campaign for re-election to the presidency, speaking to multitudes at Shadow Lawn, New Jersey. Republican orators kept declaiming that he should be retired for good to the shadows of Shadow Lawn.

"Multitudes" is a word not misused here. I know, for John Cramer, Harry Mellamed, and I bought tickets on a special train the last day of September and rode out to Shadow Lawn, where a section of seats had been reserved for some purpose. No one interfered when we took possession of three of them a short distance from the porch where Wilson presently stood in profile. We were for him by conviction and by a kind of obsession with what we believed he meant to history.

"The whole spirit of militarism is abominable to me," he had written. In the Democratic platform, much as anyone might argue about how it got there, was the declaration: "In particular we commend to the American people the splendid diplomatic victories of our great President who has preserved the vital interests of our Government and its citizens, and kept us out of war."

He had kept us out of war despite Plattsburgh, General Leonard Wood, Theodore Roosevelt, the Republican press, the patrioteers, the Anglophiles, the militarists, the Merchants of Death. He had kept us out, and we were for him.

The presidential campaign was simplified because Progressivism, so charged with hope four years earlier, had been killed off. Theodore Roosevelt himself had killed it by backing the first Henry Cabot Lodge for the Republican nomination, leaving that particular field for Wilson's New Freedom, such as it was. I guess it was all right in its way, but the loss of Progressivism was the end of many high hopes. I wrote a Politics paper on "Progressivism and After" in which I said that after Progressivism there would be more Progressivism. I was wrong.

Meanwhile, William Jennings Bryan said that Wilson had gone off joy riding with the jingoes, and he was partly right. There was no doubting the lengths we had taken toward "preparedness," which was the shibboleth of the moment, and professors at Columbia were saying that what you prepare for you are going to get.

Tall John Cramer, now embarked on the study of law, decided it would help him prepare for courtroom practice if he went out street-corner speaking for Wilson. I thought the experience would do me no harm and would also be adventurously exciting. So we enrolled in the College Men's Wilson League.

Cramer had an excellent platform manner. I had none but I did have dedication. Evening after evening we set out from the Biltmore, where our League had its headquarters, in an automobile driven by a towheaded youth of Democratic persuasion. We usually had three speakers, the third one assigned by headquarters. I did have the qualification of debating experience in New Bedford High School, and I also remembered the advice of the old *Standard* reporter Latimer, "Don't start talking right away. Look 'em over. Make 'em wait. Show you're not afraid of them."

The gist of our story was: If you want war, vote for Hughes; if you want peace, vote for Wilson. We could say this in as many different ways as our vocabulary and resourcefulness permitted. We had been told that we must expect competition for good corners on which to hold meetings, and that the first to begin talking, not necessarily the first to arrive, could hold the spot.

When our towheaded friend halted alongside the curb in Columbus Circle, near the old Park Theatre, we could see that a short distance away an Indian was about to set up business in praise of a compound of Eucalyptus Oil. He had flowing robes and a good bit of theatrical atmosphere. We felt naked, by comparison, but one of us had to begin speaking in a hurry. I thought this should be the speaker from headquarters or, failing that, John Cramer. Cramer thought it should be I. He nudged me sharply and told me to get up and start things off. Obviously neither of them intended to make a move, so unwillingly I did.

Columbus Circle was quite an amphitheater then, if you wanted to put it to that use. Traffic was incredibly less than now, and the level of noise may be judged by the fact that my youthful voice was heard on the far side, in fact on as many sides as a circle can have. I knew it was being heard because people stopped and looked.

A young policeman strolled up to our car, was told that I had begun speaking first, and went on to send the Eucalyptus Oil Indian away. I can't say that I drew a considerable crowd, but almost anyone in those days would stop at least a few minutes to hear a curbstone talk. Cramer did better, and our third man wrapped everything up. We were blooded, and it was good to be out and around in the warm air of an autumn evening.

Sometimes we were heckled. A man on Broadway not far from Columbia didn't like the Clayton Act. He asked awkward questions about the effect upon American textiles, and Cramer, who was quite willing to carry on a debate in high economic terms, could not satisfy him.

One of Cramer's convictions was that since the Democratic platform had taken over so much from the Socialists it followed that good Socialists this time around should vote for Wilson. This was no philosophy to argue in the Bronx, where Socialism ran strong and suspicious doctrines were resented, but Cramer tried. We had a big crowd, the Bronx being always responsive to outdoor speaking. Cramer made his pitch for Socialist votes, and that is all I remember before the fighting broke out. The crowd eddied abruptly, arms lifting and falling, voices raising a fearful ruckus.

Cramer still thought that logic should prevail, and we had to pull him down as our towheaded driver got under way. The last we saw, a minor riot was progressing nicely, though probably it wasn't considered a riot in the Bronx. We didn't venture there again.

On an off-night Cramer and I went down to the National Democratic Club and heard talks by Samuel Seabury and William F. McComb, candidates for governor and United States senator. I went by myself to a meeting in the Gospel Tabernacle, a tent erected somewhere uptown from Columbia, and listened to a well-shaped address by Senator Thomas Pryor Gore, of Oklahoma, who held up, one by one, the fruits of a Democratic administration characterized by Mr. Hughes and Mr. Fairbanks as a failure—Federal Reserve, Clayton Act, Federal Trade Commission, and so on.

November arrived with chillier nights, and early on election evening Cramer and I settled into our headquarters in the Biltmore, and plush, agreeable headquarters they were. At the front of the large room stood an easel and display board on which the electoral votes were to be posted. The southern states were already credited to Wilson.

I knew from Boss Matthews at the School of Journalism that a Buffalo newspaper had once conceded a presidential election on the basis of a few votes in an upstate precinct in New York State that hardly anyone had ever heard of, but even now I was not fully aware of the political significance of New York.

Civilization hung in the balance—we knew that, at least: we were sure of it—and our faith did not waver as the returns

seemed unaccountably obstinate. They wouldn't come our
way. The headquarters had been crowded, but gradually the
crowd thinned out. After a while nobody attended the score-
board. Chairs were overturned. Floating cigarette smoke em-
phasized the fact of departure.

Cramer suggested that we go over to the headquarters of
the Democratic National Committee on Forty-second Street,
and we did. The place was crowded, and along with others
like ourselves, the real pros were there. We found seats next
to a man who looked like Josephus Daniels; he said he wasn't
the Secretary, he was the Secretary's brother. I can't say the
atmosphere was merry or hopeful, but it was taut and still
undefeated.

Before midnight the election of Hughes was announced by
lights on the Times Building, and extras were being cried on
the streets. Hughes, Hughes, Hughes. Mrs. Hughes had leaned
across a table to kiss the next President of the United States.
But where we were, the grim refusal to accept defeat hung
on. Minnesota was doubtful. I didn't even think of California
then, though I had read David Lawrence's prediction that
Wilson would be the winner there because Hughes had snubbed
California's own Hiram Johnson.

The early hours of Wednesday were already spent. Cramer
and I realized there wasn't likely to be anything final for a
good while, and around six o'clock we went back to Columbia.
I took a shower, had breakfast, and attended a nine o'clock
class. That was the first time I had ever stayed up all night.

The morning papers said the result of the election hung in
doubt; the *World* demanded editorially that the ballot boxes
be impounded to prevent the stealing of the presidency from
Wilson as it had been stolen from Tilden in the election of
1876. The first editions of the afternoon papers had nothing
more definite. My final class of the day was Politics, with
Professor Beard. Far in the back row I sat, fighting off the
drowsiness that at last succeeded the excitement of a night
and a day. I can't recall anything about Beard's lecture but

I can quote one thing he said. "Mr. Chew, will you please wake up the gentleman next to you." Through my sleepiness I heard this and the following general laughter, and Bill Chew didn't have to wake me up.

That evening Cramer and I went down to Democratic headquarters again, staying not too long, for I went to bed at ten, hardly making it through my sleepwalking condition. It was on Thursday evening that Bill Brown and I watched the conclusive bulletins at the Times Building. Bill was of the class of 1919 J, and once when he stood motionless all morning in front of the Journalism building he said he was mortifying the flesh. In later years he became the "B" of e. e. cummings in *The Enormous Room.*

We felt great. The bright promise seemed strengthened in December, and in January Wilson made his "peace without victory" speech. But on the last day of January Germany declared a renewal of unrestricted submarine warfare, and early in February Ambassador von Bernstorff was sent home. The "little group of wilful men" led by Fighting Bob La Follette prevented the arming of our cargo ships, but this was a final stand.

Within three months we were at war. Civilization had not been saved after all.

We covered assignments for our theoretical newspaper, "The Blot." Once I was tardy in arriving at the Biltmore for a banquet and, standing among racks and racks of tall silk hats, looked out from the high hotel windows over the purple city in its prelude to twilight while the lights came blinking on. Then I went inside the banquet hall, sat at the press table, and heard a corner-of-the-mouth East Side, politically wise address by Alfred E. Smith, then, I think, a candidate for the presidency of the Board of Aldermen. All he meant to me in my youth was Tammany.

I went to report a talk by Dr. George W. Crile, already a famous surgeon, who said that for the first time in history soldiers in war would not be dying for lack of adequate surgical knowledge and medical supplies. This was the lead in the morning newspapers but not in my story. I floundered among so much that Dr. Crile said.

I went to Mineola with a girl named Gladys La Fetra to report a day in the murder trial of Blanca de Saulles—or Blanquita, as the newspapers preferred to call her because she was so young and beautiful. That day in court was dull, but more than fifty years later in Edgartown I mentioned the case to Edith Blake, who writes and takes pictures for the *Gazette,* and it turned out that the murdered De Saulles was her great-uncle. As the story was told to Edie, her grandmother, whom she called "Appy" because of a childhood association, had taken a house on Long Island. Blanquita arrived at the front door to claim her child from her estranged husband, Appy's favorite brother. The door opened and—bang, bang, bang—Appy's brother died in her arms. Blanquita came of the best blood of Chile, where deeds of high passion or romance carry no stigma. But she had a good lawyer, too. She got off and went to live in Cuba. The lawyer's style impressed me greatly. I recognized him once afterward, walking through the Congressional Library, and I'm sorry I did not speak to him.

I astonished wholesale grocery executives in their cubicles at the top of dusty stairs, crowding them with questions about wartime food supplies and prices. At the press table in the banquet hall of the old brownstone Waldorf-Astoria I sat near that brilliant star of reporting Frank Ward O'Malley and listened to the beautiful Louise Homer as she stood in a gorgeous red dress a few yards away and sang operatic selections. Storms of applause swelled up when she was finished, but O'Malley applauded not at all—until the great Homer, descending from the platform, came abreast of him. Then he applauded, and she gave him a smile of warm, personal appreciation.

Dr. Williams wanted our class booked to see Shaw's *Misalli-*

ance, which was to open the new Broadhurst Theatre, but Eliza McGill, not finding the Broadhurst in the telephone book, reserved seats at the Broadway, where the attraction was a movie, *Rasputin the Black Monk.* The error was rectified in time. We saw Clare Kummer's play, *A Successful Calamity,* which Dr. Williams, that guardian of accuracy, referred to as "A Fortunate Disaster."

All through the Columbia years the theater was a great experience. Mrs. Fiske and Maude Adams, *Peter Ibbetson* with John and Lionel Barrymore, the Granville Barker production of *Androcles and the Lion,* Katharine Cornell at the Band Box and the Comedy. Maeterlinck seemed to be a favorite at the Band Box, and years later at Chappaquansett on the Vineyard I told Miss Cornell that I had not understood *The Death of Tantagil.* She smiled gently and said she wasn't sure she had understood it, either.

We went as often as possible to the Neighborhood Theatre on Grand Street and the Dunsany plays there. George and I saw John Galsworthy's *Justice,* with John Barrymore as Falder, the beginning of his new career in the theater. Lester Lonergan played the part of Hector Fromme, and it was he who proposed the lowering of lights in the courtroom to suggest not only a darkening afternoon but the dramatic shadows closing in upon society's victim.

Later Lonergan appeared in John Drew's production of *Major Pendennis,* a play based on the Thackeray novel. I interviewed him, and he said he had sooner be in New Bedford than New York—which was certainly partly true. He said his association with John Drew was pleasant. I did not then know that the elder John Drew had been paid $8 a week in Garry Hough's company in Troy in 1853. I interviewed Lonergan again when he played in *East Is West.* He talked of his hope that he could put on a translation of Felix Henri Bataille's *Les Flambeaux,* or *The Torches,* and in 1917 his chance came. The production wasn't a success, and I suspect it was ahead of its time.

Once again I saw Lester Lonergan, in Washington, where he was one of the Three Wise Fools in a sentimental play. I talked with him in his dressing room at the National Theatre and once again he reminisced about New Bedford.

Apropos of all this I look back to consider how gently I was eased into the ways and opportunities of newspaper work. Just the same, looking into the deeper past, I think of that early question asked by my Grandmother Hough, and I wonder what I might have wanted to do when I grew up. Not that it would have made any difference. Only in an occasional instance now and then does it, ever.

Among the events of April, 1917, two are reluctant to go away. On Monday, April 2, President Wilson addressed the Congress: "It is a fearful thing to lead this great and peaceful nation into war. . . ." And on Thursday, April 5, Columbia closed for the Easter holidays. When George and I reached Morningside again, the School of Journalism had undergone a wartime change.

Our classes had been canceled, and we of the third and fourth years were suddenly the staff of a new Division of Intelligence and Publicity, to work full time "gathering news and writing stories for the downtown newspapers on Columbia's part in the war, and also stories of general public interest and benefit during wartime."

The idea was Pitkin's, and in the absence of Dr. Williams on a speaking trip, he and a colleague, Roscoe C. E. Brown, recently assistant editor of the New York *Tribune*, had worked on President Butler and obtained his sanction. Dr. Butler would have agreed to anything that sounded patriotic.

The new division proved a sort of lark. My brother was head of the Intelligence end until relieved by Maria Sermolino, and Max Schuster ran the Publicity sector, until relieved by Merryle Rukeyser, when both George and Max, along with Lenoir Chambers, moved on to Washington with Pitkin in a more advanced development of his idea, the New Republic Washington News Service.

All I recall of my authorship was the writing of a series of articles on "What You Can Do to Win the War." They ran in the New York *Evening Globe*. I informed women that they should avoid waste, buy economically, and keep gardens. I explained the opportunities for youth in the Navy. There was so much good advice to give; there always is.

Our division also issued pamphlets written by faculty members, for instance one called *Enlistment for the Farm* by John Dewey. Some of us wrote essays intended for the series but they didn't get published. Morrie Werner, 1918 J, later a biographer of Barnum and Brigham Young, expressed indignation when he found he had made a definitive study of teeth in wartime for nothing.

Dr. Williams succeeded in sending half the third year men back to their classes, but I hung on with the division and had a good time mixing patriotism, disillusion, and the heady atmosphere of New York and the times. "About a week after the declaration of war," Professor Beard wrote afterward, "President Wilson organized a committee of public information for the purpose of 'selling the war' to America. At the head of this agency he placed George Creel, a versatile journalist of socialist affiliations, well fitted accordingly to reach critics and malcontents . . . never before had American citizens realized how thoroughly, how irresistibly a modern government could impose its ideas upon the whole nation and, under a barrage of publicity, stifle dissent with declarations, official versions, and reiteration. . . ."

Beard was right. We saw it happen. But Columbia remained in a ferment of disagreement and debate. In June President Butler felt free to speak as he had wanted to speak all along:

So long as national politics were in debate, we gave complete freedom, as is our wont, and as becomes a University, freedom of assembly, freedom of speech, and freedom of publication to all members of the University who in lawful and decent ways might wish to inform and guide public policy. Wrongheadedness and folly we might deplore, but we were bound to tolerate.

So soon, however, as the nation spoke by Congress and by the President, declaring that it would volunteer as one man for the protection and defense of civil liberty and self-government, conditions changed sharply. What had been wrongheadedness was now sedition. What had been folly was now treason.

This was the university's last and only word of warning to "any among us, if such there be, who are not with whole heart and mind and strength committed to fight with us to make the world safe for democracy."

Georg Brandes had written to Clemenceau in March, 1915: "The appalling thing about war is that it kills all love of truth." One expected nothing better of Dr. Butler's politics but much more should have been expected of his learning. Sometime in his scholarly career he should have read John Stuart Mill: "If all mankind minus one were of one opinion, mankind would be no more justified in silencing that one person than he, if he had the power, would be justified in silencing mankind."

Already three Columbia students, including one in Journalism, had been arrested as "anti-draft" plotters. The *Evening World* reported that "when arraigned before United States Commissioner Hitchcock, the three adopted an attitude of haughty silence, declaring that they were 'martyrs to the cause.'" But I, too, had joined the Columbia Anti-Militarism League.

It wasn't until fall that Professor J. McKeen Cattell, head of the Department of Psychology, and Henry Wadsworth Longfellow Dana, a mild teacher of English, were forced out of the university. Cattell had written to several congressmen on Columbia stationery urging them to vote against sending conscripts to France against their will. Dana had been a pacifist, but I think he was surprised by his sudden elevation as well as by the end of academic freedom.

Professor Beard resigned in October. Max Schuster had

turned his Boston *Transcript* duties over to me, and I sent the *Transcript* a story beginning: " 'Uncle Charlie' Beard has resigned. The man who was unquestionably one of the three or four best-loved teachers in Columbia University went through his lecture on party government in the United States as usual. When the bell sounded at 6 o'clock he made his first announcement to his class. 'My time is over,' he said. 'I regret to say this is the last lecture I shall deliver at Columbia.' "

The protest was not long in coming. Circulars blazed around the campus urging students to cut classes at eleven o'clock and meet in general assembly on the Low Library steps. A hundred or so responded to the call, including myself.

Gustav Davidson, 1919 J, not yet by many years secretary of the Poetry Society of America, introduced "Professor" Durant, who disclaimed being at the moment a faculty member of Columbia. But he said: "Professor Beard has taken his whole career in his hands and offered it up on the altar of free speech. . . ."

A few sentences more and Will Durant, the future author of all those volumes of "The History of Civilization," was pulled down by athletic and patriotic Columbia College students. Jack Hyde, captain of the 1916 swimming team, fought his way to a balustrade and said, "This whole affair is wrong. The fellows in back of it are not Columbia students. It does not reflect the spirit of Columbia and is not good for the college."

A young man named Weiner said that the proper course would be to draw up a dignified protest urging that Professors Cattell and Dana be asked to return, and that Professor Beard be asked to withdraw his resignation.

Maybe the demonstration would have gone better if Sokolsky had still been around.

That summer of 1917 I spent mostly in New Bedford, working for the *Standard* and not much liking it. The rest of the staff welcomed me with complete good nature but I felt uncomfortable in being so close to my father, then managing editor. Bill Tugman, a reporter at the time, wrote his memories of my father: "The day began with friendly feelings all around. By 10 o'clock Mr. Hough would begin to be nervous. By 12 o'clock he would be furious. By 2 o'clock (deadline) he would be raging up and down, ripping stories out of the old invisible Remingtons a sentence at a time. But if the day's paper turned out well, he would be enormously pleased and he might invite several of the youngsters to his home to share the New England bean pot."

I worked under the city editor, and the one thing I really enjoyed was telling the janitor what weather flag to fly on the staff on the roof. The forecast came in over the wire and required no exercise of judgment but gave a gratifying if minor authority.

New Bedford had been changing greatly, and now I could see the difference. Cotton textiles prospered with war orders that kept the mills operating around the clock, and the city was coming to be, if just for a little while, the third largest in the state, following only Boston and Worcester.

But if New Bedford, in Melville's words, "beat all Water Street and Wapping," it did so in new and less romantic terms than his. There were few if any "Feegeeans, Tongatibooars, Eeromananggoans, Pennangians and Brighggians," but the population was now about a third French Canadian, bred in a strongly nationalistic tradition of their own. There were Portuguese, Poles, Greeks, and in a region north of Pearl Street known as the "Holy Acre" a considerable colony of Italians. Here was, all in all, the largest foreign-born population among the cities of the United States.

I was sent down harbor on a tugboat to meet the arriving packet *Adelia T. Carleton*, forty-one days out of São Vicente, in the Cape Verdes, bringing 114 passengers, all of whom, the captain said, could read and write "except a possible twenty." No matter how miserable the voyage, New Bedford was the Cape Verder's city of promise.

I went to noonday lunch that hot summer in a crowded one-arm lunchroom operated by a chain, seldom seeing anyone I knew. Purchase Street had been widened at the cost of slicing off half the stone tower of the Reverend Frank E. Ramsdell's church. Hathaway's Theatre had been changed into a twenty-five-cent chain store, and Ike Sherman's livery stable had given way to a movie theater. County Street was regularly shorn of its trees, always of course for a convincing reason that corresponded with somebody's profit. Old residences now gave the street less character than did the occasional filling stations, funeral homes, and shabby makeshifts. Ashley Boulevard had been opened as a motor thoroughfare into and out of the city.

But Mayor Ashley had been defeated at last. The years had made him more conservative, and the growth at the ends of the city, the North End particularly, had produced a new electorate for new-style rabble-rousing. A wide-open city wasn't what it had been in the old days, but a candidate of easy ways was Ed Hathaway. A *Mercury* headline read:

**RACY STORIES AND
BEER THE FEATURES**

Ward Two Hathaway Club Organized — City Solicitor
Discusses Club After Getting Off His System a
Story with a "Little Edge" to It.

Every newspaperman's life is a history of journalism, his own and that of his times, and this is part of mine.

The Hathaway crowd promised "a hell of a good time" if he was elected. The *Standard* reported liquor-law violations at the Bristol House, a hotel in the center of the city. My father was involved in license board hearings in which the intention obviously was to put him on the defensive. He responded by swearing out a warrant for the arrest of the owner of the Bristol House, and thus brought the case before the district court. The other side then waived examination of the defendant and obtained a continuance until a session of the superior court after the election.

During the ensuing municipal campaign the Hathaway crowd discovered that a fine old house on the hillside, a traditional New Bedford dwelling, now decrepit, but still with good lines and an agreeable manner, inherited by my father from his Quaker mother, had become a whorehouse. The enemy was in a better position to know the true character of the tenant than my father was.

Ashley lost the election by 6,701 to 6,263, and the *Standard* said editorially, "Mr. Hathaway's election was accomplished by the most gross and brazen degree of corruption ever flaunted in the face of the public."

"You better wait to hear a laugh in the North End," one of the license commissioners had said. This was the laugh, and it was easy to trace a descent from the Ashley victories of years ago.

A historic occasion of the late summer came with the examination of draftees in the wardroom of the Willis Street police station. My father was appointed to a selective service board and Uncle Garry had volunteered to assist the examining physician. So, for several evenings while the examinations went on, I acted as clerk for the doctors, and wrote a story for the *Standard* next day.

The war was still so excitingly novel—such a break from the tedium of the familiar—that we thought we would always remember these evenings. But it turned out that we didn't. They soon became indistinguishable in the pall and succession of wartime events. But we remembered a phone call from a woman who asked that the shades of the wardroom be pulled down so that she wouldn't see all those naked men.

Back again at Columbia I found, not surprisingly, that the Division of Intelligence and Publicity had been disbanded. Pitkin's New Republic Washington News Bureau hadn't lasted long, either, and my brother had a job on the *World* of Herbert Bayard Swope at $20 a week. This was the champion job of the class of 1917 J.

The departure of this class made quite a difference. Sokolsky had kept up a club of his own, with dinner meetings and talks by professors or newspapermen. I never heard the group referred to in any way other than "Sok's Club." I got in on account of my brother. After commencement, Sok wrote to all the members, and I quote from the letter to me because of its youth and appealing desire to hold on to the past. Soon Sok had changed more completely and entered into the new times more ingeniously than anyone else. "Dear Beetle: The war has had the effect of breaking things up prematurely. . . . I feel that it is wise and necessary and profitable for us to retain the Club as a permanent institution. . . ."

Nostalgia for a fellowship already gone, and even from Sok himself. Soon he was bound for Moscow, his departure expedited, it was said, by the desire of a father of substance and society to break up an emerging friendship between Sok and his daughter. Pitkin was said to have managed the separation; at any rate, Pitkin laughed at the thought of Sokolsky walking up and down the Nevsky Prospekt. But Sok kept on going, across Russia to China, and when he came back many years later with a Chinese wife he was fat, his throat fairly jammed, froglike, into his collar, his beady eyes alone unchanged, except that they were more calculating.

He had become a right-wing propagandist, writer of a newspaper column admired by his old foes, the rich capitalists, and was taken seriously at fat-cat conferences and club meetings when he explained how President Roosevelt had brought the United States to the brink of a new World War in order to keep Justice Black on the Supreme Court.

We of 1918 were the fourth-year now, sitting under Robert E. MacAlarney, dapper, lean, and vibrant, who said, among other things, "You must know your Alice." We sat also under Talcott Williams, who for one assignment asked us to write a letter to Mrs. Mary Publisher, who had inherited a newspaper from her husband. Everything was new to her and she was hard pressed to make up her mind about the simplest issues. I had no trouble in setting her straight:

My dear Mary, your last question calls forth one final answer to all your troubles. You ask if every editor and manager must give up everything to his newspaper. Without hesitation my answer is in the affirmative.

You must make enemies. They will seem to outnumber your friends a hundredfold. But you must face the brutal situation and carry on without fear. . . . The general rule is never to suppress news. . . . Take the case of Mrs. Riskyrich. The fact that you desire to keep her friendship alters not by one jot or tittle the moral responsibility your newspaper bears to society. . . . No, Mary, you must keep on publishing news of her divorce case. . . .

I am glad that Mary Publisher, being mythical, never got to read my letter. It reminds me now of the high-school essays Betty and I found on the walnut editorial desk in the *Gazette* office. The essays dealt with the question "What is the harm in a glass of beer?" and the best one had taken a $5 prize from the W.C.T.U. It turned out that there was incalculable harm in a glass of beer. The W.C.T.U. had got what it wanted, and my letter to Mrs. Publisher gave Dr. Williams what he wanted.

Yet three years later Betty and I had begun to exemplify the advice in the first paragraph of my instruction; we had begun, though unknowingly, to give up practically everything for our newspaper, and so we went on for many years.

I was ardent also in carrying out other assignments for Dr. Williams. Of the Theory of Journalism I wrote: "Pedants may speak of 'yellow journalism.' Demagogues may flaunt the 'capitalistic press.' But newspapers are neither yellow nor capitalistic nor unintelligent nor Democratic nor Republican. They are all things. They are as infinitely varied as life itself because life is the thing they reflect, represent, and in all things follow close."

I had no misgivings. I was dedicated to verities. Nowadays an answer to the assignment would be simpler. Newspapers, as everyone knows, are part of a sinister monolith known as "the media," which they themselves have constantly instilled in the public mind.

Dr. Williams began having an affair with the National Security League, an organization that led in arch-militarism and right-wing patrioteering. One day he asked me if I could get up a list of groups that might be infiltrating into our country the propaganda of the Central Powers. If the National Security League didn't have such a list, I didn't know where I could get one, yet the naïveté of such leagues of professional patriots could never be overestimated. So I looked in the yellow pages of the classified telephone book and gleaned a pretty good list of organizations, most of them social or fraternal clubs, bearing German, Austrian, Italian, or hyphenated names. I gave this to Dr. Williams and heard no more of the matter.

In his International Relations course Dr. Williams had only now come to the Civil War and its foreign relevancies. Henry Clay Evans, who came from Tennessee, remarked, "If it hadn't been for Russia we would have won that war." Dr. Williams looked at him with glittering eyes, palms flat upon the table before him, and rejoined without hesitation, "Hereafter in this class, Mr. Evans, you may speak of the South as 'I' but not as 'we.' "

Professor Baker, in his history of the School of Journalism, wrote: "Their heroes were Lincoln Steffens, Walter Lippmann, Max Eastman, Art Young, and even John Reed." But of course. And why "even" John Reed? Wayne Wellman brought him to the school just before his departure for Russia, and I was one of the group who sat around a classroom table and listened with absorption to this gallant and magnetic figure. He spoke confidently and plainly. For one thing, he said that for the first time in history the warring nations would repudiate their war debts. In spite of Calvin Coolidge's "They hired the money, didn't they?," repudiation was about what it came to in the end.

Jim Danahy, of 1917 J, turned over to me his job as Columbia

correspondent of the New York *American,* and for a time I
also represented the *Christian Science Monitor.* Thinking that
the *Monitor* ought to be interested in what the opposition was
doing, I submitted a story about the costly expansion of the
Columbia Medical School. The *Monitor* was not interested.

I think we already had a sense of inhabiting the tag end of a
doomed world, a civilization at something more than the cross-
roads. As the war loomed closer our class eroded slowly, not
only because of enlistment or conscription, but also because of
a restless ebbing of interest, a doubt about what was worth
while. We felt all around us the total insistence on conformity
and unquestioning dedication to war. We read in the "Topics
of the Times" column of the New York *Times:* "Tuesday
must have been a gloomy day for the little group of pacifists
and pro-Germans that in times past made in and around
Columbia noises that occasionally alarmed well-wishers of that
great institution. . . . It was a noble speech that Dr. Butler
made, as he recalled what Columbia had done in other times
of national emergency, and the speech was nobly answered by
the young men who listened. . . ."

One was bound to wonder if he could oppose his own in-
stincts and his own young opinions against the judgment of the
noble, the profound and mighty—though not all of them. I
had gone to Hoboken to see the Peace Ship *Oscar II* pull away
from her pier, partly—I suppose—as an act of faith, and partly
because Charlie Phillips, of our class, was one of the diminished
group of missioners. Diminished because of ridicule in the press.
I didn't see Henry Ford scattering flowers or William Jennings
Bryan carrying a squirrel in a cage, but a man leaned over the
rail at the last moment to tell the crowd on the pier that he
was Mr. Amelia Bingham. Amelia was an actress of some fame.

History closed in rapidly over all such things, over the
hyphenated Americans, the peace meetings, the performances
of German opera. Pitkin told us that the Germans had block-
aded the port of New York, and this was the sort of thing
anyone was likely to tell anyone else.

Classes went on, though the heatless days came. Food and coal were immediate concerns; posters proclaimed "Food Will Win the War." Some of the school graduates came up to 116th Street on "Blot" night to help with instruction, among them Lester Markel, then and for so many years of the *Times*.

I spent an afternoon walking around midtown New York with Ernest Rorelstad, another class president, looking for a restaurant that would serve the best dollar dinner for the annual school banquet. It was well known that newspapermen and journalism students could afford no more than a dollar, and we had pride in our condition. This, too, proved a dying tradition of a tag-end world that teetered not toward a cross-road, but over a brink.

Presently Joseph Ashurst Jackson, of Kentucky and 1916 J, came to the school, as graduates so often did, and brought word that professionally qualified newspapermen were needed by the Office of Naval Intelligence in Washington. I don't think I saw Joe Jackson again, but after the war he was responsible for the John Barrymore film *The Man from Blankleys*. I had confidence in Joe, and in Wayne Wellman, who advised me to take up the chance in the O.N.I. I persuaded myself, also, because here was something that should not too much compromise my pacifist convictions and would also be a hedge against the chance that I was really wrong about this war.

So "Bishop" Beuick, of 1919 J, and I went down to Chambers Street and volunteered for general service, preparatory to being sent to Washington. "Bishop" seemed an appropriate nickname for Beuick, I'm not entirely sure why. It was to him that Slater Brown wrote some of the letters, intercepted by the French censors, that led to the detention of Brown and his friend e. e. cummings.

On my last night of "Blot" I was assigned to the telegraph desk and afterward some of us went to Lock Yin's Chinese restaurant at Broadway and 101st Street, where we had eaten many a dinner, and held what we called a wake.

6

On a morning early in March, 1918, I stepped down from a sleeper that had brought me from New York, and walked along the platform beside the train to a gate at the concourse of Union Station in Washington, where John Cramer met me. Cramer had enlisted some time before in the Quartermaster's Corps. He had a room in a red brick house at 226 East Capitol Street, opposite the Congressional Library, and he took me in.

Our landlady was Mrs. Araminta Carroll Calvert Chew, who almost but not quite embodied the Southern tradition. Cramer said he had once seen her and a gentleman caller sitting in the front room with their feet up and their shoes off.

I went a good deal to the Congressional Library at night, intending that the war should not blunt the intellectual side of my life, such as it was. I didn't read much, though, for I was too absorbed in the marble pillars, arches, statues, and inscriptions high in the great reading-room rotunda. Two inscriptions I still recall: "We taste the spices of Arabia yet never feel the scorching sun that brings them forth" and "One far off divine event toward which the whole creation moves."

Beuick had reached Washington before me and gave a

gloomy report about the O.N.I., a view I soon confirmed for myself. We were assigned to the operation of mimeograph machines in a white cardboard building, temporary, behind the Corcoran Art Gallery, and for that reason called Corcoran Court. Officially the Navy had us attached to the U.S.S. *Triton*, which I understood was a tugboat in the Potomac River but which neither of us ever saw; and I visited the Navy Yard only once, to pick up my uniforms and a copy of that outrageously dull book *The Bluejacket's Manual*.

Once in a while I caught a glimpse, usually at lunch, of the head man of the O.N.I., Captain Roger Welles, ruddy of complexion, white of hair, liberally gold-braided, and apparently a product of good living. Oftener but by no means regularly I saw Chief Yeoman Gail Thurman Judd, who was in charge of our section, G-2. Through the years I have met many knowledgeable people who seemed mysteriously to know what "G-2" signified, and to attach importance to it. I never knew what it meant or thought that it had the least importance.

If it had been possible to view the O.N.I. in Gilbert and Sullivan terms we would have felt better, but although there was little authentic seriousness, there was not quite enough light comedy. Beuick and I ran our mimeograph machines in a small room on the second floor, along with two or three other yeomen. A larger room was equipped with desks, typewriters, and a corps of girls—yeomen-F—brought down in a lot from New York and quartered in a big house on Rhode Island Avenue.

File folders of secret material—"classified" was the mystic word—were brought from the O.N.I. recesses and distributed among the girls, who were supposed to extract from them the names of suspicious persons to be incorporated in a master card file. The girls typed the names on stencils, and we ran off enough sets to satisfy the world demand. Sets were shipped to all our naval attachés, aides for Information, Allied Intelligence offices, and other appropriate co-operating agencies.

This soon became dull work, especially in the summer heat

of Washington. The girls managed to keep up their output, but the quality suffered: names, names, names—after a while any names would do. An erratic letter-writer in Toledo, Ohio, had written to inform upon Pope Leo XIII, as a baleful influence, notwithstanding that Pope Leo XIII had been many years dead. The letter had gone into the files, and the girls typed his name on a stencil. Our routine took care of the rest. A woman novelist complained about Cardinal O'Connell, of Boston, who was, indeed, implacably anti-English, and the Cardinal's name went out world-wide. Our cards contained nothing but names and addresses.

If Beuick hadn't caught it, President Wilson's name would have been distributed with all the rest, possibly to the confusion of our allies. The President had been mentioned in a document somehow or other, and a girl had fastened upon it. The card read: "Wilson, Woodrow" and, under the name, "President"—certainly no other address needed in this case. Usually Beuick and I didn't read the stencils; we weren't supposed to. But Beuick did show the President's name to Chief Judd, who didn't like to have such things called to his attention. A military routine should flow smoothly, no matter what, and no back talk.

I must speak up in defense of the yeoman-F, who had doubtless been lured to Washington by the same sort of fancy talk as used on Beuick and me. Some of them looked attractive in their uniforms, and uniforms must have been a bait; but they were so plentiful in Washington that nobody cared. A girl dreams of romance in the military, and where was it? Gail Thurman Judd could be written off, and no dashing ensigns or lieutenants came near us. Being shut up in a hot cardboard room with a typewriter and a lot of dull files was no better than office work in New York.

One yeoman-F deserted. No wonder another, trying to dream of cherry trees, the Potomac, and maybe Lieutenant Pinkerton, produced a stencil reading "Wilson, Woodrow, President."

Questions weren't asked. There was a war on. If the girls didn't know what they were doing, I'm not sure Beuick and I were much better off; but we operated at so low a level that no one needed to explain anything to us. After a while we didn't care a damn.

For that matter, if we made absurd errors, so did the efficient Germans. Dr. Heinrich Albert forgot his briefcase in an elevated car in New York City and some of its contents worked their way through to Lieutenant Hugh W. Robertson, 1915 J, in the O.N.I. in Washington. Robertson beckoned me into his room and showed me a name on a list Dr. Albert had compiled of persons who could be relied upon to circulate German propaganda. The name was that of Dr. Talcott Williams, of Columbia University and the National Security League.

I never knew what Robertson was doing in the O.N.I. Nobody knew what anyone else was doing, and this produced a militarily ideal situation.

At the end of each day the waste papers and spent stencils were taken to the Navy Building next door and burned in the furnace. But the building engineers didn't want their fires ruined, and they directed that the scrap paper be taken to the city dump.

Once outside Corcoran Court at the end of a day, we found wonderful compensations in the city of Washington. As soon as five o'clock came, Beuick and I were off to the Childs Restaurant next to the famous Occidental on Pennsylvania Avenue to fill up on wheat cakes, ham and eggs, or graham crackers with a bowl of half and half.

For a while we were ordered to drill one night a week in a back street, but as soon as the influenza epidemic became an overriding dread this drill was discontinued. So Beuick and I saw all the plays at the Belasco, National, and Poli's theaters, and there were many, for Washington had become a great tryout city. We went occasionally to Keith's Vaudeville, as President Wilson did, but we never saw him there. One night,

though, he and Mrs. Wilson occupied a box at the Belasco
while I was seated just above, in the front of the second balcony, looking down upon their upper ends: an unconventional
view.

This was my second glimpse of the President since Shadow
Lawn, for I had marched past him in his place on a reviewing
stand at the White House in one of those dreadful Preparedness parades. We were always aware of him. He was the nation's hope. Once, when Max Schuster and I walked past the
White House late at night and saw a Marine guard on duty,
Max said, "Guard well, young man." Outside the White House
on the Pennsylvania Avenue side, the suffragettes stood their
continuing vigil, usually with a bonfire against the chill.

In the men's room at Poli's Theatre I came face to face with
Professor Carleton J. H. Hayes, in Army captain's uniform,
just buttoning his pants. His eyes glowed with the old ironic
amusement, as if to say, "Imagine us being here. But here we
are."

Max Schuster, rejected for military duty because of his eyes,
had left a stint with the United Press to join the Bureau of
War Risk Insurance. He invited Beuick and me now and then
to dinner at the National Press Club, high up in the Riggs
Building.

Sooner or later, it seemed, everyone came to Washington.
Eliot Sanger, 1917 J, turned up, a chief yeoman. Clara Sharpe,
of 1918 J, had a job in the Department of Agriculture. Others
came, stayed a while, and left. We were all congenial and we
formed the Capital S. of J. Club and had our picture taken in a
paint-and-canvas submarine chaser in one of the photographic
studios on Pennsylvania Avenue.

We tried the different eating places of Washington, and
walked on Sundays along the towpath of the Chesapeake and
Potomac Canal, which had been reopened for wartime transport and along which we met canal boats, mules, and country
boys who stared at us as curiously as we stared at them. We

walked as far as Cabin John and Great Falls, and crossed Chain Bridge back and forth. One Sunday, Max, Eliot, Beuick, and I rode to Mount Vernon on a trolley, and then walked back as far as Alexandria, a distance of about eight miles—nothing to boast about, but an excellent outing, followed by a shower, steak dinner, and an evening at Loew's.

John Cramer was transferred outside of Washington, and I moved in with Beuick and another Columbia man, Alexander Cowles Glennie, who had a second-floor room in a red brick house at 307 C Street, N.W., opposite the red brick Arizona Hotel and near a church from which the bells played "Blessed Be the Tie that Binds" on Sunday mornings. I missed my morning walks past the mighty and magnificent building and national symbol, the Capitol, a walk-past that I think of now with excitement.

Our landlady on C Street was a neat and, to us, formidable Mrs. Nicklaus, whose establishment was patronized mostly by enlisted men like us. We washed our uniforms correctly in the bathroom. Some military lodgers thought it amusing to leave the bathroom door locked on the inside and to get out through a window that opened on a convenient roof. Once on a hot Washington night Beuick and I took our mattresses to this roof and slept there, as much as the mosquitoes would permit. Some of the Army lodgers followed our example without spreading newspapers under the mattresses, and Mrs. Nicklaus said we mustn't do it any more.

When I got back to C Street past midnight and found that I had forgotten my key, I thought it injudicious to ring the doorbell and arouse Mrs. Nicklaus, so I went around the corner to a telegraph office—Western Union was omnipresent in that remarkable era—and sent Beuick a telegram asking him to throw a key down to me in the street. I stood in front of the Arizona until the Western Union messenger arrived. I should have dashed across the street at this moment, but I was relying on Beuick, who, I found out later, was laughing so much he forgot

about the key. I slept in a church not far away that was kept
open for enlisted men, solaced by the eternal calm and musty
smell of a religious place.

In June I got leave to go to New York for commencement.
Anyone at Columbia who had enlisted during his senior year
would automatically get his degree. Not many of 1918 J were
present, just a scattering of survivors of our original forty-odd.
Of course my parents came on from New Bedford to see me,
and because of my Navy whites I made a conspicuous figure
in the academic procession.

Minna Lewinson and I had won the Pulitzer Prize for the
best "History of the Services Rendered to the Public by the
Press in 1917." This was one of the original Pulitzer Prizes,
but it was promptly dropped, not, I think, solely because of our
product. By definition, the public-service award invited praise
or even adulation, a kind of self-congratulation that didn't go
over well.

Hardly anyone nowadays can quite make out what it was
that Minna and I won. For a while the *World Almanac* put us
in a footnote, implying some illegitimacy, then dropped us
altogether. The *New York Times Almanac*, though, preserves
an accurate record, stating that 1918 was the only year in
which this particular award was given. I have a copy or two
of the *History* as it was published by the university but I favor
its suppression. What Minna and I recounted, as was inevitable
at the time, was mostly what the press had done for the War
Effort.

Minna and I divided the thousand dollars fifty-fifty and
received our Pulitzer Prize diplomas. Mine is still in the attic,
because I have never found a suitable place to display it without
feeling that it should be marked "advertising."

I invited my diminished 1918 J classmates to a dinner at
Healey's and a performance of the Ziegfeld Midnight Frolic
on the roof of the Amsterdam Theatre. I intended to pay for

this out of my prize money, but my father insisted on footing the bill, which came to about $75, showing the low cost of celebrations long ago. At the Frolic I had to be separated by a few inches from my comrades, because no liquor could be served at a table where a serviceman was seated. We took such good care of our men in uniform in those days! Not that I minded—I had not yet discovered the benefits of alcoholic intake. Most people hadn't, I think, or the country would have been spared the Prohibition agony.

I put my $500 prize money into Liberty bonds, which I later sold at a discount to pay *Gazette* paper bills. I think they brought something more than $80 for each $100 bond, which was the current market value of patriotism in the postwar years.

Those June days in New York—commencement, reunions, a round of pleasurable activity—remain enshrined in one of the rarest glows of my lifetime. I even showed a pretty girl how to tie a Navy bluejacket's neckerchief, my arms necessarily around her shoulders, and if I knew her number I should be tempted to call her up this morning, though necessarily out of a far past. I lived for a little while as the Student Prince of Heidelberg, my domain a small but sunnily vital part of Morningside Heights.

On the final afternoon I sat at my old desk in the Journalism city room and wrote a letter to Beuick on a sheet of copy paper, recounting some of the great events. But I was referring to my whole Columbia and New York career when I added with deep emotion, "It's all over. I shall never be so happy again."

I slept fitfully on the Federal Express that carried me to Providence, from where I proceeded to New Bedford and the Vineyard, ruminating on many things, not least on the fact that George and Clara were to be married. The next day, when the Vineyard boat changed course off Black Rock and exposed her quarter to a stiff southwester blowing across Buzzard's Bay, I leaned over the rail in the throes of an old familiar seasickness unbecoming to one in Navy uniform. My father often referred to the irony.

Two days at Fish Hook, Vineyard Sound still too cold for swimming, dinners of lobster and ginger ale, walks through the woods and over the hills, reunion with Queequeg, our aging cocker, and then back by the same route to Washington. Beuick said he had informed Captain Welles of my Columbia degree, and that Welles was "tickled pink." Maybe. But the mimeograph machine was where I had left it, and I resumed the familiar chore.

That June was hot even for Washington. I stood in front of a Weather Bureau kiosk on Pennsylvania Avenue and saw the thermometer registering 114. Rock Creek Park, where we had expected to take summer strolls, had become insufferable. In Corcoran Court an enterprising chief yeoman named Simpson hung wet sponges in front of the electric fans, only to see them dried instantly in the hot blasts.

One noon at lunchtime we were ordered out for a propaganda appearance by a group of French poilus, "Blue Devils," as they were called. They were just to be looked at, but an introduction was delivered in a morale-building talk by a handsome Assistant Secretary of the Navy whom I instantly disliked because of his style, Harvard accent, and manner, and the offensiveness of all this war propaganda. He was, of course, Franklin D. Roosevelt. When I next saw him—on crutches at the 1924 Democratic convention in the old, original Madison Square Garden—I had changed many of my ideas. I liked him.

As for the Blue Devils, they were amazed when they saw some of us taking cold showers at Liberty Hut, a wooden structure opposite Union Station which had been a Tabernacle of Billy Sunday, the evangelist. I had spent one night there, sleeping with my shoes on, lest they be stolen, a mistake I have never repeated. I felt about the cold showers as the Blue Devils did, and ducked in and out as quickly as I could.

With the heat came rumors. Someone had seen a contingent of gobs heading for Union Station with their sea bags, and it was reported that they were ordered to France to man big naval guns on the western front. Beuick and I got the idea that we ought to be doing something more for the War Effort than running mimeograph machines, which as likely as not were disseminating useless or false information, so we asked for a meeting with the personnel officer, who I think was a stove manufacturer in his civilian phase. We suggested that we might find women or girls to replace us in the O.N.I. so that we could be sent to sea.

This was a crazy idea, but Washington was a crazy place, and the war generated all sorts of crazy ideas. We discussed with Lieutenant Sard whether women could manage the operation of such technical marvels as mimeograph machines, leaving the matter in a condition of some doubt. Anyway, Beuick and I went around in our spare time for several days accosting strange females who might be inveigled into the O.N.I. We met with some encouragement on the part of a pretty girl in Huyler's who was impressed with our patriotism but thought there must be a catch in what we proposed. There was a catch in it. Huyler's was a far, far better place for a girl in wartime Washington than a hot enclosed space in Corcoran Court.

I can't suppose my heart was in our quest anyway, but it was a satisfaction to have tried and failed. Beuick and I continued our congenial theatergoing, and at the Gaiety Burlesque on Ninth Street admired the antics of a comedian called Al K. Hall, who sold Liberty bonds in the aisles during intermissions. There was another burlesque house on Pennsylvania near Harvey's Restaurant, where the chorus sang "K-k-k-Katie, Beautiful Katie," and I got so I could almost sing it myself, which would have been a triumph for burlesque.

For a week or so a selected group from the O.N.I. was ordered at night to the Government Printing Office for a mysterious special project. Beuick was included but I was let off, my competence being doubted. The project was, I learned later, the editing of our card files for publication of a giant book of names.

Beuick lived through this secret night assignment and was presently shipped off for sea duty on a tanker. This wasn't entirely because he called Judd's attention to errors, but also because Judd could see flaws in his Attitude. Beuick had a way of amusing the yeomen-F by entering their room in the characterization of a long-armed ape, knees bent, features assuming an apelike ferocity. Judd didn't catch him at this, but there was that observable something in Beuick's general behavior.

To replace Beuick at 307 C Street, I took in Lewis Levenson, of 1919 J, an Army private. And again in August I got leave to go to New York, to see my brother married to Clara Sharpe in a chapel of St. John the Divine. They went to Fish Hook for their honeymoon, after which George returned to Camp Upton and Clara to Washington.

Levenson had been shipped out, and I arrived back at 307 C Street to find a baby in my bed. I took this as evidence that Mrs. Nicklaus had meant what she said when she announced she couldn't let me keep the room by myself. This worked out well, for almost at once George was requisitioned from Upton by Herbert Bayard Swope, who had come to Washington as assistant to Bernard M. Baruch, whose post as chairman of the War Industries Board involved top wartime responsibilities. Swope assisted Baruch, and George assisted Swope. And I promptly moved into a room at the former Chinese Embassy on Iowa Circle, where George and Clara had found agreeable accommodations. My room had red wallpaper and sounds that came through a warm-air duct, but I heard no secret conversations.

The O.N.I. had also moved, abandoning Corcoran Court for one of the "temporary" buildings in Potomac Park, which were to stand dismally for forty or fifty years. Just at this time the Big Book of names was delivered by the Government Printing Office, at first a few copies, then quite a stack. They were handsome big books, a triumph for the G.P.O.

Soon, though, an order came through for us to tear out one page from all the copies on hand. This happened to be a page on which, under *B*, was listed the name of the Chairman of the War Industries Board. Unhappy accident! It must have been a tedious day when one of the yeomen-F came across that name in a secret file. A few days later another page had to be eliminated, and then another. Soon all the copies were rounded up and taken away. The entire beautiful edition was destroyed —by burning, I think.

We hadn't been in Potomac Park long when Admiral T. J. Cowie was named to direct the Liberty loan subscription drive in the Navy—all the world over. Somebody wrote him a letter equating his appointment to this post with that of Admiral Sims as commander of our naval forces overseas. I think this had already been Cowie's view.

He was short, stalky, erect, and red-haired. His chest stuck out and so did his red mustache. Max Schuster, along with the Navy's share of War Risk Insurance, had been under Cowie's bureau, and he now brought Max in to help run the Liberty loan campaign. Max got him to borrow me from the O.N.I., and he also borrowed or commandeered Eliot Sanger from somewhere, and there we were, the three of us, old companions from the School of Journalism.

Max had all the talents a publicity man or campaign director needed. The undertaking itself was a press agent's dream, for all Max had to do basically was to draft some ringing "Alnav" message and get Admiral Cowie's signature, and out it went to every Navy station, ship, and command in the world. And replies came in, reporting bond subscriptions, as duty-bound in the service.

But Max threw in his usual bubbling surplus of ideas. The artist Henry Reuterdahl had been commissioned in the Navy, and Max arranged for him to paint an enormous billboard in front of the Navy Building, depicting a destroyer dropping a depth bomb upon a German U-boat through a raging sea. The bomb was movable, and every Navy bond subscription sent it closer to its goal.

"Send that damn bomb down another notch!" Admiral Cowie would command as a telegram brought in a report of a big bond sale at Mare Island or Great Lakes.

A Washington newspaper misspelled Cowie's name in one of Max's releases, giving us a bad time until Max's ingenuity solved the difficulty. He corrected the error in pencil. When he showed the clipping to Admiral Cowie, the Admiral said, "I'm glad they caught that."

My labors were of the least importance but I was trusted to write a speech for Admiral Cowie to deliver from the steps of the State, War and Navy Building at a noontime rally. The speech went well until the Admiral, an old China hand, predicted our glorious entry into Pekin, instead of into Berlin. The crowd applauded loudly and the Marine Band, gaudy in dress uniform, swung into a stirring martial tune.

The war news day by day formed an accompaniment to our lives. We might have marched to it if it had had rhythm, but it didn't. Rhythm was lacking. It mixed importance with triviality, proportion with disproportion, and always conveyed the uncomfortable feeling that the public had to be played upon, and that victory was more than likely far, far off. Propaganda defeats itself. Russia's separate peace, of course, had been stunning. The business at Verdun—"They shall not pass!" —rang on and on in speeches and editorials. The engineers dropped their tools and picked up their guns at Château-Thierry—another dramatic and rousing patriotic scene. The Saint-Mihiel salient was wiped out, the first American battlefield triumph. But the mystique of power seemed to remain on the German side, imperfectly hidden in our torrents of words.

Even the false armistice report, after it was denied, left me no optimism. I never expected anything but more of the same.

Then at noontime on Nov. 11 I bought a jelly roll from a vender outside the Potomac Park buildings, intending it for a makeshift kind of lunch. I heard an approaching uproar, a storm, a moving power, which became visualized into a truck tearing along Constitution Avenue, a wide-eyed, yelling soldier atop the truck's cab holding the front page of a Washington newspaper spread as widely as his reach allowed. Black type across the page, filling half the space, read: GERMANY SURRENDERS. Two words. Two completely adequate words.

By some chance I walked alone that evening on Pennsylvania Avenue, adrift in the streaming parade of jubilant thousands, feeling no real emotion of victory. The war had gone on too long. What could one believe? Well, anyway, that there would be peace at last; though a friendly Marine in the Navy Building next day assured me: "There's one nation won't sign any peace treaty—Japan!" He was quite prepared to be shipped east for another war.

During all my time in Washington there had been a big biplane, a Handley-Page, they said, soaring over the city day after day, whether for guarding or training I never knew. Now, however, a host of small planes darted overhead, and the newspapers announced that Ruth Law, stunt aviatrix, would fly her plane through Pennsylvania Avenue in demonstration of the glory of our victory, and she did. I happened to be standing opposite the Post Office Building when she missed it comfortably and swept upward again into the sky.

My haste to get out of the Navy must be classed as on the order of a compulsion. I could have stayed on in Washington at an easy pace, going to the theater, the movies, the galleries, and walking along the towpath of the canal on Sundays. But I wanted what was over to be really over as soon and completely as possible.

Admiral Cowie, however, insisted that my services continued to be indispensable, so that it was necessary to get Uncle Billy Greene, our congressman, to use the political influence that had been unthinkable while the war was in progress. He got me out in no time, on the ground that I must finish my education. On the last night of 1918 Max Schuster and I occupied seats way down front at the Gaiety Burlesque for the midnight show. The audience ran strongly to soldiers and sailors, the chorus girls were nervous, and the show wasn't anything special —except that a sailor stood up at midnight and blew a bugle. The yelling died down, the girls on the stage escaped, and Max and I left the theater in the new year of 1919.

Since I had been released on educational grounds, I spent one more semester at Columbia, a replacement really for the one I had largely missed when I departed for Washington. Columbia had much familiarity and much strangeness, for the world itself, its ways, and the view of the world had hitched along by several long notches. There was no more Pulitzer Press Club. I joined in a committee of alumni with Merryle Rukeyser and others to discuss what speakers we could get for extracurricular sessions more or less like the old ones.

We got Colonel R. R. McCormick, of the Chicago *Tribune*. He drew a fair audience and gave a dull talk, partly because he found himself embarked on a story with sex in it and suddenly realized that there were women among his listeners. His face reddened and stayed reddened as he limped to a conclusion. After that we decided that no one short of Will Rogers would be attraction enough for the new generation of students, so the project was abandoned. The new generation had better things to do.

Pitkin had gone off on agriculture, and Talcott Williams seemed older and tamer. The most important thing that late winter and early spring was my growing friendship with Betty Bowie, of the class of 1919 J. The class was small and we did many things together, such as seeing John and Lionel Barrymore in *The Jest* and walking back to Columbia through Central Park after the play. I suppose we chose this route because of the fine night.

Dr. Williams took us to see a show of modern art at the Metropolitan, where Betty kept dropping things—a pencil, a glove, a handkerchief—and the Director was more agile than anyone else in picking them up. He speculated about the advantage of bending over backward and viewing the pictures between one's legs. After a while he led us out on a balcony overlooking Central Park, no small city loveliness in those days, and suggested that we "let the calm hand of nature soothe the hectic brow of art."

Betty and I had first become aware of each other's existence back in 1918, when I was about to take Marjory Adams to visit the Women's Night Court at Jefferson Market, supposedly important in showing New York's seamy side. It wasn't, but Betty and I both remembered one touch of enchanted evening in Ohlker's soda fountain. After 1918 I didn't see Marjory again for some forty years, but Betty and I were married in 1920.

I was to see Dr. Williams twice after that anticlimactic semester, once when I called at his house while he was waiting for a plumber to report to him why the hot water supply had failed. The plumber came downstairs and said the faucet on the third floor had been left running.

"Thank you," said Dr. Williams with a courtly expression. "Thank you for telling me what should have been so obvious."

I heard him speak at an expensive school dinner at the Commodore Hotel, the last I ever attended. He delivered a valedictory, eyes earnest, forehead shining under white hair, voice never more musically mournful, as he adjured us all when we came to the place where he no longer made one, not to turn down an empty glass but to raise a full glass. And he suited the adjuration to action by raising his full glass of water.

When June came it was settled, really as a gift to my mother, that I should spend the month at Fish Hook with her and then look for a job. That old question: What do you want to do? I had no idea what options there might be.

June proved to be a cool month and we had a fire on the hearth every night. The days swam past quickly, and at length my departure from Fish Hook was noted in the log in a marginal note by my father: "Exit H.B.H."

He saw me off on the New York boat at New Bedford with

the remark later that I reminded him of a Horatio Alger character off to seek his fortune. In New York I was at once recommended to Pendleton Dudley for a job with what was soon to become the Institute of American Meat Packers. It was Pen Dudley who had brought the packers together in a trade association at a time when they were under severe attack by the newspapers. The bigger ones were pilloried as a monopoly, and most of them feared a recurrence of the furor about "embalmed beef" that had followed the Spanish-American War; indeed, the government's wartime specifications for a stronger and heavier cure of meat than usual for the civilian market gave some ground for the apprehension.

When Mr. Dudley asked me if I knew the names of the "Big Five" meat packers figuring so sensationally in the news, I could name only Swift and Armour, flunking on Morris, Cudahy, and Wilson. I had gone down to 46 Cedar Street to his office, where he looked me over, and I didn't think I impressed him favorably. I certainly wasn't impressing myself favorably—I had never asked for a job before.

But I had been endorsed by Whitfield Woods, of 1915 J, whom he had already put in charge in Chicago, and he hired me and arranged for us to meet at the tube station the next day to board the Broadway Limited.

Chicago I didn't like, but Pen Dudley became one of the enduring influences in my life. He was a successful and innovative public-relations man with nothing slick about him, a manner habitually observant and thoughtful, an individuality of speech not noticeable enough to analyze, and a habit of candor. Soon in that summer of 1919 he was taking me to the pool at the University Club and then to dinner, and we rowed together in the lagoon at Jackson Park on Sunday. He usually came from New York for weekend visits.

He had recently undergone successful psychoanalysis and was ready with Freudian insights, which, however, I don't think he overstressed. When he was called before a grand jury in Chicago in some matter involving possible monopolistic practices of the packers, he spoke of that "good old autonomic relaxation" afterward, meaning that when the grand jury was through with him he had gone to the bathroom. An analyst I knew later said there was no such thing as an autonomic situation, but I don't think either the concepts or the idiom had been stabilized as far back as 1919. Anyway, Pen Dudley lived in an evolving world of changing motives and human sequences of cause and effect.

Whitfield and Dorothy Woods introduced me to the South Shore Hotel, where I was to spend my entire Chicago year, traveling by Illinois Central back and forth to the Loop. I didn't like Lake Michigan, which so continually invited unfavorable comparison with Vineyard Sound. I didn't like much of anything about Chicago, largely, I suppose, because I had become an exile there.

I didn't like the Chicago *Tribune*, self-styled "World's Greatest Newspaper." When Blasco-Ibáñez, author of *The Four Horsemen of the Apocalypse*, visited Chicago, a *Tribune* interviewer found him in his pajamas and compared him to an underworld character named Big Jim Colosimo. Foreign exchange was much in the news, and the *Tribune* referred to it in headlines as "Alien Cash." Upon the death of Cleofonte Campanini, conductor of the Chicago Opera, two of the city's newspapers began their obituaries, "The Maestro is dead." Pen Dudley said, "What is a Maestro?"

For cultural advancement, even now not having learned better, I attended a performance of *Aïda* at the Chicago Opera, but had the misfortune to sit next to a music lover who was saturated with garlic. I felt that garlic should have been included in the libretto.

My first duty for the meat packers was to write rejoinders to newspapers that were attacking the Big Five. The attacks occurred daily in city after city—hundreds of them—and to my desk came the clippings. Dudley schooled me in the art of reasonable reply, with facts, good temper, recognizing the point of view of the critics, assuming their good faith, considering broadly and humanely how to respond. The experience was important to me then and has been ever since—the art of living with people, of presenting a fair side to them no matter what side they might present to me and seemed to present to the world.

I looked on while the American Farm Bureau Federation was organized by delegates from the great producing regions, for the packers had been concerned as to whether the national organization would be radical or conservative. It was conservative, of course. Someone wanted to name it "Chamber of Agriculture," but a nicely literate delegate named Odell—he may have been a professor—said that the sanitary arrangements of farmers were now more modern.

I became familiar with the stockyards, but never went there from choice and never saw the slaughtering. Aside from the Lagoon, Jackson Park meant something to me, for I had pored over pictures of the World's Fair of 1893 in my father's compilations, and I looked eagerly at the structures of the White City of the Columbian Exposition that still stood.

On New Year's morning, 1920, Pen Dudley and I rode out on a train in zero weather to walk through the famous Indiana dunes, those lofty lake-shore sand hills that have so much majesty and character. We wound up at the Prairie Club, where we took shelter and cut wood with an axe to repay its hospitality. There I learned that one must never wear rubbers to keep one's feet warm. Rubbers make the feet cold. In the late evening we waited beside a bonfire for a trolley to take us back to Chicago.

Frank Bancroft, he who in 1887 had recommended my father for a job with the *National Baseball Gazette*, let me through the gate to see one of the 1919 World Series games. He now managed the Cincinnati Reds, but in intervening years he had managed the Adelphi skating rink in New Bedford and the Prospect House, a hotel overlooking the Lagoon on the Vineyard. I had no seat in the ball park, of course, but I saw the game, moving from place to place as a duty-bound policeman gave me the word. This was the year of the Black Sox scandal, but I thought the game well played.

A few times during my Chicago phase I made trips east and saw Betty, but the trips were brief and the partings by no means as sweet as such partings are supposed to be. It was by mail that we had to discuss and formulate our plans.

Wesley Hardenbergh, a good friend from 1918 Journalism, came out to join the staff of the Institute, and for a while we roomed together, a congeniality that if it had begun sooner might have reconciled me to Chicago. Might have—but I don't think so. He became president of the Institute and served brilliantly until his retirement.

7

Betty and I were married in a chapel of Grace Church at the corner of Broadway and Tenth Street on June 10, 1920, a day of blazing heat and summer. She was afraid my unbaptized condition might be a bar to marriage in the church, but it wasn't. She wanted no fuss, and only my parents and her brother and aunt were present.

Years later I came across the receipted bill of the Lake Mohonk Mountain House. "Were we at Mohonk only three days?" I asked Betty.

"I guess so," she said. "Do you remember how those women looked at me when I took my shoes off on the train?"

Mrs. Shepard, at first a summer visitor and then a year-round resident in the house next to the one we finally occupied on Winter Street, looked from her window, saw Betty and me hurrying to reach the *Gazette* office at a punctual 8:00 A.M., and said, "There go the lovers." She told us so long afterward.

In relating my father's part in our commitment to the *Vineyard Gazette* I have left out an important fact. We had corresponded with a newspaper broker or two and had learned about a weekly here and there that might be for sale, but we had no conceivable way of financing a purchase. We hadn't got around to thinking about that. So we really had no choice. It was the *Vineyard Gazette* or nothing.

Although too small for an ambitiously enterprising spirit, especially in the go-ahead year of 1920, the *Gazette* had the sort of smallness that could be compensated for by the labor of its editors and by slow accretion, rather than by a rush to fortune. Its field, moreover, which Talcott Williams called our "Island episcopate," had advantages of geography, tradition, and character that we were to prize more and more through long years, and which I mourn now that so much but the bare geography is passing.

The Island public wasn't being widely reached at the time, but it could be. Mr. Marchant said, "I always say we *print* 600 copies." A browned, cracked half-sheet of copy paper preserves the detailed circulation record: Edgartown, 192; Vineyard Haven, 154; Oak Bluffs, 125; R.F.D., 32; West Tisbury, 48; Chilmark, 20; Menemsha, 2; Gay Head, 5—a total of 578. At least it was well distributed.

This was a new time for us, yet no one could rightly call it a beginning. We came in upon something that had been going on for a long time, since 1846, in fact, and a lot of things we thought were new proved to be recurrences. Even small town journalism changed us as much as we changed it.

We had promotional ideas, or I did, which needed to be lived down. The *Gazette* was soon advocating a program of advancement for Martha's Vineyard which in today's context might be alarming, but having looked at it lately I do not think it nearly as bad as it might have been. We wanted to improve the Island's roads, so many of which were sandy then; to advertise its attractiveness to vacationers; to maintain good boat service with better facilities for carrying automobiles; to extend the vacation season in the fall, and so on. But we did want most of all to preserve the Island's natural resources. That was our No. 1 item, and it was there from the outset.

On the strength of this platform I was elected president of a new Edgartown board of trade. The organizational meeting was held at the courthouse. Dick Shute, of R. G. Shute & Co., was elected secretary. He had been a drummer boy in the Civil War and had been spoken to by President Lincoln, who, I think, had inquired whether the Army gave him enough to eat. He said it did. The rest of the Shute company was his sister Hattie, who headed the Wilmon W. Blackmar Woman's Relief Corps, played the organ in the Episcopal church, and relished corned beef and cabbage on the hottest days of summer.

There were a few other businessmen at the meeting, along with Dr. Worth, who represented the professions and had written a pamphlet, *Why Is the Vineyard Healthful?* The next day I heard that Jo King Silva, owner of the Main Street shoe store, would not become a member because he considered the annual fee of $5 excessive. My own spark of enthusiasm did not glow brightly or long, because, for one thing, the president was supposed to do all the work, and, for another, the *Gazette* required my full attention.

Betty and I had only a general division of responsibility. We shared one typewriter and did what seemed most to need doing as the days wore on. She reported the first big social event: "Gray Skies Fail to Mar Beauty of Eagleston-Judkins Wedding," and I set about getting advertising. The largest Main Street store was Captain Jethro Cottle's, which sold dry goods mostly, though he carried on a real-estate business, too. Behind the marred oaken counter familiar at the period, Eunie Ripley would be standing with her black sleeveguards on her forearms, whistling through her false teeth; and Captain Cottle, a lean, dry man, cackling a bit sometimes, would bite off the string as he wrapped up a corset or some spools of Coate's Cotton.

I knew of his past, for I had once interviewed him. He had sailed on the voyage of the bark *America* when a woman had shipped before the mast as a man. Many of the Island elders had pasts of adventure, and this was Jethro Cottle's. He advertised off and on, but it was slow going when I talked to him about monthly billing. He and Charlie Marchant had been accustomed to settling up once a year.

Will Mayhew, who kept the hardware and paint store on North Water Street, did so mainly because he wanted a place to go in the daytime and in the evening. It seemed too much trouble for him to take payment for a bill—at one period he couldn't get his safe open and all the accounts were inside—and he would often give a pocket knife to his caller and tell him to run along. Will was ready to advertise, though.

Captain Zebina Godfrey kept a men's clothing store on lower Main Street and contributed an account of his experiences to the *Gazette*. He tried to sell me a blue serge suit that had been on hand for a long time. He didn't ask me to come look at it; he brought it around to the house, wrapped in brown paper. I was tempted because I liked the Captain and had too little sales resistance, but Betty put her foot down. Our friend Howard P. Davis, the Methodist minister, finally bought the suit, as was proper. It was a ministerial suit.

At the courthouse I executed the documents by which we finally became owners of the *Gazette*. Beriah T. Hillman, Civil War patriarch, attorney at law, Register of Probate, and president of the Edgartown National Bank, took care of the legalities. He was also moderator of the Edgartown town meetings. I have told of his tilt with Charlie Brown over the West Tisbury road.

When the agreement was ready for me to sign, Mr. Hillman said, "Mary, come here." Miss Mary Wimpenney entered from the outer office to witness my signature. She was his clerk then, but she later became Register herself and served the greater part of a long lifetime, retiring only the other day. She represented past and present, all in one, and in her presence, for once, one didn't worry about the future.

Her father, Theodore S. Wimpenney, had sailed a whaling voyage in his youth and was now selectman, assessor, and crier in the sittings of Superior Court. When he had reached an age long past eighty, we saw him rise up in town meeting, eyes glittering, shaking his fist at an adversary contingent. But his was a nature of kindliness and settled compass course.

Also at the courthouse we met Jeff Norton, Register of Deeds then and now, holder of many offices through the years, honestly and rigorously competent, whose kindness to elderly people impressed Betty from the beginning, but who could give newspapermen a hard time. He was a handsome young man, and lived into so becoming an age that one missed the fact that age had entered into it at all.

Arthur W. Davis, a native Vineyarder who became an able lawyer and in turn clerk of courts, judge of the district court, and Judge of Probate, possessed a brilliant mind and more than a mite of oddity, for he talked to himself, wrote checks on scraps of meat paper, walked the streets of the town with his hands in his pockets, and might scratch his head or twist a pencil around in his ear at the moment of delivering an important opinion from the bench. He read widely, exhausted the resources of the public library in economics, and filled in with Dostoevski before more economics or politics or sociology came along.

The Civil War was the particular subject of Abner L. Braley, likewise an attorney, who became justice of the district court after Arthur Davis. His father was Judge Henry K. Braley, of the state's Supreme Judicial Court, who sat on the Sacco-Vanzetti appeal; we used to see him, seriously in thought, going about with his books and papers in a green baize bag. Abner could and did make Pickett's charge come alive at a Woman's Club meeting. He was young, but as Santayana said about someone else, age had come upon him early. It was he who, upon the centennial of the *Gazette*, presented us with a framed emblazonment of Judge Joseph Story's words: "Here shall the press the people's right maintain. . . ."

These were members of what was sometimes referred to as "the courthouse gang." Every county seat has one of a sort, but one like this? I don't think so.

The music that clung to the early 1920's as the morning smell lies over the harbor, reluctant to die on the air, was that of the wartime songs: "Keep the Home Fires Burning," "Smiles," "The Long Trail," and all the rest. The spirit of the community sing still hung over the Island, along with the impulses of wartime now aimless and bereft.

An invalid President still lived in the White House. Warren G. Harding had been nominated while Betty and I were at Mohonk, but he wasn't elected until that fall. Meantime, George White, of Ohio, became chairman of the Democratic National Committee, a good deal to his surprise, I thought, for he was summering in Edgartown and I interviewed him and took his picture. On election night Betty and I displayed returns on a bulletin board in front of the *Gazette* office. Only one man, a late-staying seasonal resident, stopped to watch them for a while. He expressed satisfaction in the victory of Harding and Coolidge, walked off along North Water Street, and was soon hull down on the horizon.

For Edgartown the election meant that Alfred Averill would succeed Henry Ripley as postmaster. Mr. Ripley, a Democrat, had worked in the Government Printing Office and knew the craft. He allowed us what was practically a charge account at the post office, sending the week's edition of the *Gazette* off in the mails and collecting postage early in the following week. The postage wasn't much and the arrangement was convenient.

The *Gazette* office, though situated at the famous "Four Corners," Edgartown's business center then and always, had not the slightest pretentiousness. It was upstairs over the Corner Market, reached by an outside staircase improvised to save space both above and below. We sometimes heard our visitors approaching on the stairs—Edwin Bryant Treat, proprietor of a tutoring school and author of historical outlines, whistling busily, or Lawyer Douglas, saying he was going to lick the editor.

The *Gazette* had a sanctum. Of course it did, a small room at the front, separated from the print shop by a portiere at the connecting door, and containing a beat-up walnut roll-top desk and an applewood table heaped with unopened junk mail.

The Old Editor, Mr. Marchant, was foreman and printer also. Two girl typesetters, one his daughter, sat on tall stools at the cases setting up or distributing type before or after the week's run. This wasn't a foreshadowing of women's lib, but a case of economic necessity. The shop contained a soapstone sink with paste pot, a cast-iron stove, a job press operated by foot power, a flat-bed Seth Adams press on which the paper had first been printed in 1846, and a Fairhaven newspaper press turned by a hand crank. A quarter of a ton of coal was piled in a rear corner, brought upstairs in baskets. More than a quarter ton might have dropped through the floor to the grocery store below.

The Fairhaven was sheet-fed, of course, and the printed sheet was carried by a butterfly delivery involving the precise opening and closing of two sets of grippers designed to catch, carry, and release the sheet. Many times the grippers would miss and let the sheet fall upon the forms and be ground up and wadded by the inking rollers. The crank had to be turned with a steady rhythm or the whole press might resort to acrobatics and throw itself apart. It was shimmed with pieces of wood and metal and held together here and there with string or wire.

Old proofs and posters decorated the walls, along with spatterings of ink and the blackening from long-gone whale-oil lamps, replaced now by droplights dangling under green shades. We found a place for our typewriter in the sanctum and began to function after a fashion in weekly journalism.

We suffered some from good advice because there was no way we could put it into practice. At the moment, the only way the paper could be produced, and then only with difficulty, was precisely as Mr. Marchant and the girls were doing. He looked at us expectantly from day to day as if waiting for a minor miracle to be passed; the girls asked for increases in their meager pay of $12 and $10; the landlord, who owned the grocery store below, raised the rent; and Chester E. Pease, wealthiest man in town, expressed it as his view that Betty and I had arrived "flush with money."

We did not live up to anyone's expectations, least of all our own, and that sort of thing is embarrassing and often puzzling to young people who began life, along with all else, exposed to class mottoes and the best instruction. We were not supremely happy, mostly because of recurring fatigue, but we did make a go of it. The trial period for anyone is often called the "time of struggle." Those early years of ours were years of effort but not of struggle; you have to struggle *against* something. Our lot was not cast among foes or demons but among changes and pressures and here and there possibly genuine but usually illusive opportunities.

We lived that first summer in a room in the Marchant house and ate breakfast sitting on the floor because of the convenience. It seemed odd to me to be in Edgartown, the Vineyard town I knew least of all, and I'm not sure my mother in her secret inwardness really approved. In generations past, "Old Town" had been held in contemptuous rivalry by Holmes Hole and the rechristened Vineyard Haven, which always threatened to get the courthouse away, to be relocated in its own center. The bank had been moved from Edgartown to Vineyard Haven in my boyhood, and I had heard people say they would get the newspaper, too. But Edgartown had retaliated by establishing a bank of its own.

Two newspapers had been published in Vineyard Haven, and one of them was still going. Harleigh Schultz, the editor, had nothing invested but his time, as Carey Luce, of the Martha's Vineyard National Bank, pointed out to us, and we bought out his paper for $500. Then we bought out the Martha's Vineyard *Herald* in Oak Bluffs for $1,000 and a swap of our job printing business. We borrowed the thousand dollars, largely on the reminder by Elmer E. Landers, the *Herald* publisher, that this would mean only $60 a year, six per cent then being the established interest rate. But $60 a year for how long? It seemed for ages.

I am writing mostly about Edgartown because this was where the *Gazette* was published and where the *Gazette* determined that we should live. But I did have Edgartown relatives, among them Miss Susan Beetle, a remarkable person in wisdom and old-fashioned graciousness, who combined two eras. She would not have thought of discarding the old in order to belong more comfortably to the new, but she made an exemplary pharmacist at the drugstore in an era of modernity, and had passed the state examination with rare high marks. We discussed our degree of kinship. Her Beetle line had split off from mine at the time of the second Christopher, who was born at Farm Neck in 1725 and died in 1820, but she could remember visiting Uncle Henry when she was a girl.

In the fall Betty and I moved to Winter Street, our house a rented one, built in the manner of a Greek temple, with fluted wooden pillars supporting a second-story pediment with Palladian windows. Whatever the architectural propriety, it was a beautiful house, ample, and hard to heat. We had the usual kitchen range, a parlor heater in the dining room, and a fireplace in the living room. Despite the absence of heat upstairs we managed easily the first winter, which happened to be mild.

Early in the second winter the cold set in with old-fashioned severity. We obtained the landlord's permission to cut a hole in the floor for the purpose of installing a register which we hoped would conduct the rising heat to our sleeping quarters above. It didn't. Either there was something the matter with kinetics that year or we were at odds with nature. We stood the bitter cold as long as we could and then moved our bed down to the parlor for the rest of the winter. We often had for "lights-out" music the strains of Victor Herbert's "Gipsy Love Song" played on Betty's old-model phonograph.

We had a telephone at the office but none at home, not really by choice but because telephones didn't come easily in those days. Anyway, it was a relief that we couldn't be reached on Sunday. Billy Mendence, in his tobacco and confectionary shop on Main Street, had what was called a public telephone, and he would send a messenger after anyone who might be wanted. There were usually idlers in his store who would go forth for a pittance.

This was part of our changing civilization, and there were others. Pigs were kept in a big barn slightly to the rear of the courthouse. Streets were surfaced with hard-packed ashes or scallop shells ground and bleached to a fine whiteness. Drays carried the freight. You saw them coming from the wharves, those low-slung, long and sturdy symbols of the horse-drawn generations. Roosters crowed at dawn. You heard them with the same habit of comfort with which you heard the town clock or the wheels of the milk wagon. When a blizzard struck on, John Donnelly, who was road surveyor at the time, handed out snow shovels to a gang of men, who dug out the great drift across the road abreast of Sengekontacket Farm.

Edgartown had four grocery stores and an A. & P. that closed during the noon hour for lunch. One store was that of Manuel Silva, Jr., in the rambling lower floor of a Victorian mansion built in 1866 for Samuel Osborn, Jr., who had soon become the largest owner of whaleships in the United States. The peaks of the house were high, as if defending the central cupola, and a use of Victorian ornamentation was repeated in the piazza that ran all along the front.

Manuel Silva, not more than five feet tall—"Good things come in small packages," he said—was born on Fayal and had shipped from there at the age of thirteen as a cabin boy on the whaleship *Linda Stewart* for a four-year voyage. Then he went hand-lining on the Grand Banks, mackerel fishing, and for a few seasons of coasting. At length he shipped on a revenue cutter, which brought him to Edgartown, where he stayed, first as fisherman, then as grocer.

Warmhearted he was, but with a gift of profanity it would have been a crime to suppress. His oaths came out as naturally as breathing, in conversation with his best summer-visitor customers as at any other time, and nobody took offense. Our first full-page advertisement was for a one-cent sale sponsored by the National Biscuit Company, and I can hear Manuel summoning the salesman from the far rear of his store—"Jones, Jonesy!"—with sea-born command.

John Bent, whose market was on Main Street, was born in Lisbon and came to the Island at the age of fourteen, working first on a farm owned by my Uncle Ben. John loomed, for he was tall and large of frame, widely enclosed in a marketman's white coat. In his spare time he carved or painted or produced some notion of his own in art or craft. He made an inlaid table with 250 pieces of different kinds of wood and carved the head of a steer, which hangs on a stair landing in the Harborside inn, which occupies the site where his store used to be.

One winter he filled a trench with a mixture of cement and sand—and some ashes—and sculptured from the resulting block the figure of a sea nymph blowing on a shell. After his death Marshall Shepard and I took possession of it for the Historical Society, but the Society threw it out long ago. In the frailty of his retirement after a long illness he made his own gravestone of cement. The lot is near the road, and I stop there sometimes to read the inscription that I saw him executing: "Pray for the Soul of John Bent." That and nothing more.

As we had our world outside and our world within, the *Gazette* could print an item concerning Antigonish or Pico or even Ponape and properly consider it local news.

The post office was in the Red Men's Building on Main Street and it was open from seven in the morning until eight at night, hours planned to accommodate the departure of the early steamer and the arrival of the late one. If you went downtown early you would see Herbert Pease, Assistant Postmaster, in his knee-length duster sweeping the sidewalk, not that this was one of his stated duties but because he liked to see what was going on and how the day was taking shape. More often than not, Morris Hall, of the department store next door, would join in the onlooking before business began and while the street was one of fresh shadows, greetings, and reports.

In the evening, with the post office lights shining out across sidewalk and street, Katherine Graham would most likely be at the wicket still open, while custom tapered off and the day brooded to an end. Miss Graham was born in Edgartown, daughter of Lieutenant J. E. N. Graham, an officer in the United States revenue marine service, and the town's own Florence M. Pease. Her paternal grandfather was a Scottish earl, and many who were fond of her liked to speak of her as Lady Katherine Graham. Young Thomas Dexter, who had a love of heraldry and so on, said the title was correct.

The drugstore would be open until late evening, also, and you could walk up to a glass-enclosed counter where chocolates were displayed in trays and order any assortment you liked, taking as much time as you liked: so many lime centers, so many caramels, so many nougats.

Down at the wharf there would always be a scattering of townspeople waiting for the arrival of the *Uncatena*, searchlights probing the darkness, paddles churning, as Captain Marshall allowed for the tide and brought her in for a gentle landing. When she was made fast with dripping hawsers he would come ashore, a proper steamboat captain, broad-shouldered, erect, uniform always neat.

There would be fewer on the wharf in the early morning, especially when a departure was scheduled at five or five-thirty, so coldly long before sunrise, but some would be on hand, bound for New Bedford or for Boston by way of Woods Hole. The flush of dawn, then the sun rising over Chappaquiddick, the coming of life to harbor and Sound, were worth the cost of the passage. A time came when the boat no longer steamed into Edgartown; so much could be saved by driving a car to Oak Bluffs or Vineyard Haven and shortening the distance and duration of the journey.

There were *chamaritas* in Red Men's Hall, danced to the same music as in Pico or São Jorge; the Congregational church devoted itself to Perpetuating the Faith of the Pilgrims; and the Edgartown Woman's Club had three divisions, Domestic Science, Tourist, and Literature. Flo Pease, of the Tourists, gave a paper about an island which had an elephant belonging to the mouse family. She kept a record of the refreshments served by various hostesses so that she could be guided in her attendance at meetings.

Mrs. Underhill, of the summer colony, lost her false teeth at the bathing beach, and Mr. Underhill dove for them. He was, at the time, president of the Underhill Society of America. For a winter dinner some would have eel stifle, built of layers of eels, potatoes, and onions; some would have kale soup, richly adrift with thin slices of linguica, that garlic-laden sausage of Portuguese origin and spirit; some would have beefsteak or haddock or chicken chowder, or, at the right season, fried scallops or scallop stew.

Change came slowly, but change was usually far from formidable. A new bakery was opened next to the post office where the scantly patronized bowling alley had been, and new fishing schooners were built for the deep-legged fleet. New teachers were hired for the school, and once in a while one of them found a different boarding place, though most stayed at Mrs. Mellen's.

Father Moriarty, of St. Elizabeth's, suggested a prize contest for the *Gazette*. Abner Braley brought to the *Gazette* office a man who planned a land development called "Hethern Heights" on the Lagoon, but he was some fifty years ahead of his time and missed making an easy fortune. The rumrunner *Arethusa* lay offshore to sell and discharge illicit liquor, and some fishing boats found a profitable side line. The steamer *John Dwight* was mysteriously sunk in Vineyard Sound, and double-crossing by some of the rumrunning vessels was suspected. Stills were installed here and there, and some were raided. Men who enjoyed beer learned to make their own and drank it with professed enjoyment.

We remained insular and set apart, not yet subjected to the

indignities of mass communication and mass transportation. One could look at the sky and see it clear, breath the air and be refreshed, look in any direction and not be offended. Lives were our own to be lived, no matter how queerly. Progress troubled us some but not much. Betty and I didn't listen for the music of any distant drummer, or claim to have heard it in those early years, but we did hear it later, more and more distant, until the sound was drowned out entirely by automobiles, airplanes, television, and the clamor of the age, so much louder and grosser than the barroom clamor of the century's youth.

The other day I drove with two companions to Wasque, the seaward land's end of Chappaquiddick, where bluff and beach meet the force of the Atlantic and are eaten away or reshaped almost day by day. The wind was easterly, and we all know that when the wind is easterly the land looms.

Across the long distance we saw Nantucket—to our surprise, because Nantucket lay below the horizon and was raised above it only through the trickery of reflected light and mirage. This does happen, but not too often. At first the island seemed a discoverable continent silhouetted against blue sky, and then the sun showed us colors and landmarks my companions could recognize. I couldn't, because this visit-by-mirage was my first to Nantucket since 1916, when I had spent a few minutes there.

Just so the image of the past rises from deep below the line of things within one's memory. I see the landmarks and colors of my mother's girlhood at Holmes Hole, when Aunt Addie and Uncle Press were living at Summer Hill and my grandfather was home from sea, sailing his customs boat, *Emma Louise*, around the harbor, and a sloping green lawn reached from Uncle Ben's house where the A. & P. and the blacktopped town parking lot now are.

And there is an opposite horizon, too, where the future rises by reflected or refracted light (I keep looking those words up but I'm still not sure of the difference) before one can behold its actuality. Raised against the sky are condominiums larger and more numerous than those built within the past few years, squatting prefabricated houses with colored roofs, Pizza Palaces, as the mainland calls them, Dairy Queens, bars, parking lots, fleets of automobiles, and everywhere the crowds, crowds, crowds.

Between these two distances, these two images, lies the span of our lives, Betty's and mine. Here are the starting and stopping places for this present documentation. We dropped in upon an Island and in a little while will both have dropped out, but the Island will not be the same even as it is now.

I found a note I had scrawled on a piece of paper some time ago and had forgotten: "It's a tragic thing when you see lives in all their completeness, especially your own. The unfinished state of life is the one thing that makes it bearable, the sense of more to come. Something always may turn up. There's still another chance even if it's a slim one. When the end is in sight one can feel only regret or chagrin or self-pity."

This was my mistaken notion of a passing hour. To survey a life completed is to experience at least the reward of rest, and that's a great thing. You may see where you went in, where you stayed, what you did, and you may pretty well guess where you will go out. If you are mistaken in thinking you acquired some wisdom, no one will know the difference. There is some wonder left in nature, and the follies of newer generations are worse than those of your own. All things may now be put off because the reckoning is likely not to come in your time.

Friends and strangers ask, "If you had your life to live over again, wouldn't you do the same thing?"

Sometimes I am truthful enough to say, "No." Anyone is a fool who would make the same choice when there is a different course to be tried. Where the real doubt comes is in whether there could be any choice. The roads of destiny lead to the same place even though Robert Frost's less traveled diverging way taken in the woods makes all the difference. Don't count on it.

Yet for Betty and me things turned out well enough. We never went to Paris or London, but that was all right, and we had neither need nor desire to go to Carcassonne. Nothing much came of our efforts—maybe a word of Betty's now and then (Ed Tyra was kind enough to say the other day, "Things haven't been the same around here since your wife died—she had a way of needling people, and they didn't like it at the time, but pretty often they came around and realized she was right"), censorship set back a little, a white lighthouse saved, some trees and grass kept green, the lot of a conscientious objector softened, and help gained for those stricken by hurricane or fire, and always support for the principle of human brotherhood. All transient things in the sense that they need to be fought for over and over again as long as the world lasts.

But I have a tendency to remember the wrong things—not so much opportunities missed and duties neglected, though there are plenty of those, but long hours of weariness, the emptiness of some days, the discouragement expressed in Betty's diaries, which I have only just read. I remember frictions and quarrels and telephone calls from those we hurt or offended, and the wrangles with those who wanted not to be hurt or offended. I wouldn't want to write a letter to Mrs. Mary Publisher now. I would know what to say but would hesitate to say it. Let her find out for herself, or, better still, take up a career in analytical chemistry, as Melville Stone advised my friend John Cramer to do.

Betty wrote in her diary at the end of a Monday in April:

One of the worst days so far as I was concerned, weather quite nice but *nothing* else. I went to Mr. Meikleham's poorly attended funeral. I accomplished just zero in everything I tried to do at the office and felt all washed out.

February could be bad, of course, an empty month of snow and bitter cold, even though Edward H. Pease always reported his crocuses in bloom on Washington's Birthday and also wrote about them to Observant Citizen in the Boston *Post*. As often as not we would have a blizzard of high proportions. Betty wrote:

Up at 6:30 with last minute stuff for the huge town meetings. Bitterly cold with worse forecast, blowing hard, the Sound a smother of white. Did some shopping in the afternoon and chatted with Jackie Litchfield and others. Sky beautiful, day wonderful—20 degrees too low, though. Fixed stuff for the Invitation Edition. H. took it into his head to take a trip to regional school meeting in savage cold while Dundee and I snoozed and waited.

Saturdays in winter had a wider margin:

Read Dylan Thomas 'Under Milk Wood' and loved it. A rough day; 1 below this morning, wind still raging, and Sheriff's Meadow Pond and Eel Pond both frozen. Sengekontacket too, I hear. I didn't go out until after lunch, then got a shot and did a little shopping. . . .

But on Monday:

Pleasant day as to mild weather. Old grind as to work and not much accomplished. Too much for me, and too much mess all over the place, Augean Stable style, but I struggled along somehow. . . .

Meantime:

Gentlemen:
Since your account now stands at the figure of $290.76 as of the end of August, we are writing to ask you to reduce this by at least $100 at your earliest convenience.
                    Very truly yours,
                    Vineyard Gazette (Mrs. Henry B. Hough)

Dear Mrs. ——
I am regretfully returning to you your article about Monte Carlo which I am afraid is a little too much out of our province. It is an illuminating article but, as you know, we don't often stray far from the Vineyard.
                              (Mrs. Henry B. Hough)

Dear Mr. ——
Please do not waste your time and ours by copying material that is sent in to you. If you are entitled to credit, just say so and add

it to your space. Will you kindly telephone us instead of our having to call you. Also, who wrote the report which constantly refers to "our hospital", "our" radio, etc., and will thus have to be rewritten. The entire report is little more than notes and making it usable will be a considerable task. . . .

Sincerely yours,

Mrs. Henry B. Hough

Dear Mr. ——

Our bookkeeper tells us that she has tried unsuccessfully to collect his bill from you. Of course legal advertising should be paid promptly and we shall expect to hear from you within a week.

Sincerely yours,

Vineyard Gazette (Mrs. H. B. Hough)

Dear Mrs. ——

Sorry the error occurred in your item. We have printed it correctly now, I hope, but to avoid another error I did not attempt a guess at the first letter of your middle name which we studied for some time without result.

Very truly yours,

(Mrs. H. B. Hough)

Dear Mr. ——

I did not write you on January 6 simply to pass the time of day, but to inform you of the situation concerning your two bills to the Gazette, of which we take a dim view. Please let us hear from you by the first of February or I shall take further steps.

Very truly yours,

(Mrs. H. B. Hough)

In one of her letters to a subscriber who was canceling a subscription after many years, Betty wrote: "We can understand your reasons for withdrawing. We probably would do the same if we could. As it is, I guess we must stick it out until the bitter end." I am sure Betty meant it at the moment—her lips pressed tightly together—but on a memorandum she wrote after the onset of her last illness, putting down as she liked to do the things she was going to discuss with her doctor, she included this phrase and underlined it: *"Retirement a horror."*

What we needed first was a Linotype. In order to install a Linotype we needed a new office, for there wasn't enough height between floor and ceiling in the old shop to accommodate one, and the floor couldn't be relied upon to support the weight. We also needed a press to replace the Fairhaven before the sum of its shims and makeshifts exceeded its original entirety. We needed to get rid of job printing, an incubus to the paper though traditionally an inseparable part of a small newspaper operation, and I have already told how we arranged a divorce. We needed a bookkeeper. We needed to know a lot and to forget a lot—perhaps more than we had still to learn.

The new office we acquired in a wasteful way, by degrees. The store on Main Street next to Ed Nichols, the Sanitary Barber, who occupied the corner, happened to be vacant. We leased it, with what, I cannot remember. We borrowed the $3,500 for a rebuilt Linotype and were an annoyance to the New Bedford bank for years and years. The Linotype arrived and was installed for us by Charlie Vinal, machinist of the New Bedford *Standard,* who delivered a homily as he wiped off each part and fitted it properly into the whole. His theme was that the Mergenthaler Company, though it considered itself next to God, was by no means perfect. He illustrated his theme by improving upon the assembly as he went along.

Still, most of the difficulties were of my making, though the Linotype was the only machine with which I had any degree of rapport whatever. Charlie Vinal went away and I was committed to become operator-machinist. I operated for many long hours for many long years and acquired good speed; I could "hang the elevator," as they said, which meant that a line of matrices would be waiting for casting while I had another line clicking into the assembly, but I never attained the smoothness and rhythm of a good operator. The fault was mainly one of temperament. I never relaxed. I was always in a hell of a hurry, and you can't hurry a Linotype. You've got to be in harmony with it.

One result of our temporary Main Street location, with the Model L in full view of passers-by, was that Win Smith dropped in to offer his help when he saw we were in trouble.

Win came of Vineyard stock and was already a skilled machinist with any sort of typesetting device. From that day on, all through the years, when he happened to be on the Island, we could count on Win; and now in his retirement, well along in his eighties, he is setting type for the *Gazette* with speed and accuracy beyond the range of most "swifts" among younger operators, because he would rather set type than subside into leisure.

I should speak of the Linotype, not just our Model L, in the past tense, for this epochal invention of Mergenthaler, which revolutionized the craft of typesetting and the industry of printing and publishing the world over and was a more significant contribution even than the movable types of Gutenberg, is no longer manufactured in the United States. Gutenberg's ascendancy lasted from about 1463 to 1884, a span of 421 years at least, and Mergenthaler's from 1884 until just the other day—say, about eighty-three years, of which our experience on the *Gazette* had a part in approximately half, though the *Gazette* has not yet conceded a victory to new processes.

William P. Bodfish, who owned the corner building, the onetime customs house and post office, wanted to sell it to us for $5,000. We couldn't have bought it if his price had been $500. The building is beautiful in its classical, Vineyard-oriented way, and I imagine it is now worth $500,000 or more —some vast amount, anyway. But the opportunities we lose are part of the story of growing America. Everyone can tell of them.

At length we moved everything into a former watch-repair shop on Summer Street opposite Manuel Silva, Jr.'s, grocery. The shop had been vacated in some haste by the jeweler and artisan who ran it because his condition required that he be "taken away." We had to fit ourselves into these new quarters among what was left of his possessions, though not among any clocks and watches, for these had also been taken away.

The shop was shaped more or less like a bowling alley, only sixteen feet wide on the street, somewhat wider when it turned into a shedlike structure at the rear, and running back more than halfway through the block.

We had no choice but to break up the old Fairhaven press with sledge hammers and to install a secondhand Whitlock press bought for $400, which accommodated a sheet at least twice as large and was more or less operable by electric motor. The Whitlock represented a major advance over the Fairhaven, and it had advanced troubles.

After a while a well-dressed stranger appeared and said he was administrator of the estate of the old jeweler and watch repairer. We asked what had become of the poor man.

"He has climbed the golden stairs," our visitor replied.

We had moved some cumbersome things out of the building into storage with Jump Spark Jim West, who at the time was restoring furniture upstairs over Ed Nichols, the Sanitary Barber, and who had ample room. Somehow these things could no longer be found, and our visitor changed from unctuousness to abuse. We didn't mind, but he upset our landlady.

She was Eunice Vincent, of whom we were fond and to whom we were always loyal. She was the wife of Horace H. Vincent, a carpenter of reliable skill, a town-dwelling member of the Vincent family, which had lived from time immemorial on the Great Plain. Every year when our lease was about to expire I made a ceremonial call on Mrs. Vincent and sat across from her in her living room while we talked about many town and Island things. My hope was to obtain a renewal of the lease at the rate of $15 a month, and Mrs. Vincent would have liked $20. She was a deliberate but not a hard bargainer and we paid $15 for quite a while.

Among the drawbacks in our new quarters was the fact that the press had to be stopped whenever the telephone rang. We still had the dreary occupation of feeding one sheet at a time, another erratic butterfly delivery, and then feeding the sheets again to print the other side. The two men who came from Boston to install the press were like the happy carpenters in the movies. They got it together all right, though delayed expensively through an extra day when the electric company shut down in order to clean its boilers. There were some parts left over, but I wasn't troubled by that until I found the press had no brake, and when the butterfly delivery let a sheet of paper drop to the forms, we had to watch its maceration among the inking rollers until lack of momentum allowed the gears to halt.

The installers offered to help me move the Linotype, and of course I needed help. But they took it apart so fast that I could hardly keep track of what came from where, and to get the machine together again proved a challenge. I accomplished this somehow on a memorable Sunday morning.

Mr. Marchant puffed contentedly on his cigar and went out and in, getting news and items; or sat at a table reading copy or proof. Betty went out and in, too, and she had little help from me, for I was pressed by circumstance into setting type, making up the pages, and feeding sheets into the Whitlock.

Bill Hamer, chief of the pressroom of the *Standard*, came to Edgartown to offer his advice and instruction. He talked us into using secondhand printer's ink for a while, ink that had been removed from the fountains of the big Hoe presses in New Bedford. Bill told me that having my hands in ink, as a printer must, would keep them as soft and mild as if I had been wooing cold cream; but I found that getting the ink washed off kept them in a state of constant erosion.

We managed to keep the office endurably warm by means of a P. P. Stewart stove and a newly purchased Heatrola, a stove with an outer jacket enameled to make it look like a phonograph. Once, overnight between Thursday and Friday, a sudden drop of temperature caused everything in the office to freeze. The banked fires were unequal to such a plummeting, and the forms were frozen to the imposing stones. I tried pouring on hot water, but the hot water froze at the moment of contact. Hours passed before we and nature accomplished a thaw.

For a long time we were a hybrid newspaper, with some hand-set type and as much Linotype composition as we could manage, along with a residue of boiler plate to eke out what we still needed. One winter we ran a boiler-plate serial, Louis Joseph Vance's novel *The Destroying Angel,* which had stirring scenes on No Mans Land, the solitary island of adventure lying four rough miles off Gay Head.

Archie Mellen, Main Street grocer and real-estate agent, said, "They've got more help at the *Gazette* than they ever had but they can't get the paper out on time." People waited at the post office for their *Gazette*s to be distributed, and they didn't like too much delay in this weekly appointment.

In 1922 Bill Roberts came to work on the *Gazette,* the beginning of an association that was to continue more than fifty years and was so full of friendship, understanding, remarkable competence, and loyalty that the memory will always be warm in the lives of those who worked with him. Not warm in heart and mind alone, but in the working out of days and years, the whole course of living to which he gave meaning. Nothing would have been the same without him. His was the organizing of the shop, his the undimmed will, his the long hours of close application and labor that brought about the production of the paper, no matter what.

At the Linotype he was one of the best of the "swifts"; at his ease in a comfortably inclined chair he moved his fingers deftly and evenly over the keyboard exactly as if they were responding with an initiative of their own. His operation was beautiful to see. He possessed also the informed pride of the expert printer who knew the history of his craft, its values, its standards of taste and appropriateness in typography. He would omit nothing that contributed to the clean, precise appearance of the printed page, no matter how much time and effort might be required.

Now the hand-set type was gone. No longer would Mr. Marchant or I or anyone in the *Gazette* office pick up a burnt match from the floor to jam into a loose line of type to make it hold. No more, either, would some green outsider be invited to look at type lice, which meant that the type he was looking at would be swiftly pushed together sending a squirt of water into his face. Hand-set type was wet with a sponge for easy handling, but our sponges were now gone.

Soon Everett Gale came to be Bill's assistant and staunch friend as well as the *Gazette*'s loyal, industrious employee. In boyhood he had been a state ward, brought up during most of the years he could remember by a sensible farm wife in western Massachusetts. Upon his public-school training he erected that memorable edifice, the education of an old-time newspaper shop, where skills were mixed, functions overlapping, and words and ideas a currency common to all.

Better years had come to the *Gazette* with Bill and Everett in the back shop, Betty and I in the front office, and all of us indistinguishably involved. It had been easy for me to tell Mrs. Mary Publisher what ought to be printed, but in a small town there is only a shadow line between privacy and public right, between the background of rumor or common supposition and the making of an accurate and appropriate news story. Nice judgments must be made, and we all acted as a sort of combined court and legislature on many an issue.

Everett Gale married and lived with his wife and two boys in a house he built with his own hands in spare time. One son found a career in commercial art, the other in broadcasting. Everett lived to run for selectman and got a respectable vote, to hold the office of constable, and to serve on the police force, all in his hours off from the *Gazette*.

How late they worked, Bill and Everett, side by side in the back shop that merged so well with the front office! The years were slow in making things easier, and with the years there was always more to do.

A time came when Everett, separated from the rest of us, stood near the silent Linotypes while we went on inserting and wrapping the week's *Gazettes*. His expression showed his sad apartness, his unwillingness to be excluded, even from added drudgery at the end of a week's labor. He was about to start for Boston to enter a hospital for tests that would show he had cancer of the lung. They treated him with mustard gas and he came back to work for the *Gazette* again, the latter part of the time with a cane to help him get around, and when he was forced to take to his bed and at last he knew the truth, he said, "Why didn't they tell me?"

Bill Roberts was of Welsh stock. His grandfather had worked in the coal mines as a boy but nevertheless lived to a graceful old age. Bill's father belonged to the aristocracy of textile operatives, the mulespinners, who epitomized a high kind of skill and achievement.

When he came to the *Gazette*, Bill was youthfully slender, his cheeks a healthy pink, his hair light. When he retired more than half a century later he had changed surprisingly little. His hair had darkened somewhat, he had become a bit stockier, and for a long time he had worn a neat, unobtrusive mustache. On the Vineyard he had earned respect and friendship. He served on the ration board in World War II, on the school committee, as a library trustee. He and his wife, Marion, possessor of much beauty of person and character, had acquired one of the fine old Edgartown houses and brought it to a state of comfort and loveliness.

But Bill said to Jon Sawyer, one of the boys he had trained in the printing craft, "I don't advise you to work as hard as I did. When I retired, the roof fell in."

Joe Allen came to the *Gazette* in 1924. He was born in a hilltop house just off the old North Road in Chilmark on the Vineyard, and as a boy had fished, sailed, and worked afloat and alongshore. Then he had traveled far, had served in the Army on the Mexican border, before heading back to New Bedford. On the night shift in a factory there, he listened to the rhythm of turning machinery and in his mind it became poetry of a sort, mostly reminiscent of the Vineyard, its people, and its past.

One of these poems he sent to the *Standard*, and my father published it; and then there were more Vineyard poems, and prose, too; and all this led Joe back to the Island and to the *Gazette*, with which he became the Wheelhouse Loafer, writer of fishing news, columnist of originality and humor sustained decade after decade without lapse, and doer of all newspaper things. He had and still has a limitless capacity for making friends and for being himself as an individual without either pose or self-consciousness. Joe lived in Vineyard Haven, and so widened the base of the *Gazette*'s support, but he worked as closely with Bill and the rest of us as if he lived next door. Nobody ever waited for Joe's copy, night or day, no matter what might be involved in getting it, writing it, and delivering it to the office.

This was how the close-knit crew of the *Gazette* came to be assembled, and to stick together in labor and companionship through long decades that at the last, because of this companionship, seemed to have passed quickly and lightly.

But Betty and I, because money after all was necessary, went back to New York for an interlude, though not to the New York we had known in college years. The working city was different. Betty became assistant editor of a journal then called the *Public Health Nurse* and I was hired for the publicity department of the Western Electric Company to deal with newspapers. Between us we were soon making $7,000 a year, a respectable sum in those days, but we had not restored our fallen fortunes, so we left gladly to get back to the Vineyard in time to see the apple trees bloom and to earn, between us, for quite a while, $25 a week.

From this New York experience I learned the ups and downs of elevators, morning, noon, and night, and, in between, buses, subways, the tired reek that did for air; and great offices filled with men and women working at desks in an ordered progression that might bring them promotion and might not. We participated both horizontally and vertically in the relationship of individual and mass in the urban society of business. It was like Chicago over again, but worse. Even the theater did not compensate, though that was when one could get cut-rate tickets at a downstairs counter in Gray's Drugstore in Times Square.

Return to the Vineyard could be identified as the correction of an error.

As evidence of how things went, I offer three examples of Joe Allen's intraoffice communications:

Dear Mrs. Hough: Our Mrs. —— died this morning (Sunday) following a considerable period of ill health. Her son, who is so slow that creeping paralysis would pass him in a cloud of dust, told me that if I would call him tomorrow, ye gods, he will let me know when I can see him for the dope for the obit! If it was the President I could get it before he was cold. Joe.

Dear, Dear Mrs. Hough: It is not that I give a damn personally, but the Vineyard Haven W.C.T.U. asks why the hell the discrimination. The national or state organization does not like to have husbands' names published and I have always tried to argue that it was the Gazette's policy to do it that way. Well, this time I was tripped, and badly, and the Vineyard Haven outfit says they will not allow the Gazette to report their activities any more. Now don't you feel badly? I am a total wreck over it. Good God, Mrs. Hough, you don't know what you have done to me. Joe.

Dear Comrade Elizabeth: I feel that you ought to be told how successfully you handled the ads last week. . . . Several of my regular clients remarked upon the perfectly swell job you did, under difficulties at times, and indicated in no uncertain manner that they felt that your light has been forcibly restrained under a strap-tub. Admiringly, Joe.

We didn't have formal apprenticeships on the *Gazette* but we always did have a boy whose duties were to make the paste, wash the press rollers, empty the wastebaskets, remelt Linotype metal and cast it into pigs for reuse, and to the extent possible learn what a career printer should know. Only a few of these boys wanted to stay on after they finished school or were allowed to drop out. This was not strange, for Vineyarders by tradition and inheritance preferred the outdoors, and hours regulated by seasons and tides and winds rather than by the clock; and the chief export of the Island has always been men and women.

So many worked in the shop for an interval that the roll has passed the limits of my memory, though I am easily reminded by this or that visitor of mature years of what happened and how things were when he used to carry out the ashes.

Bob McIntyre became a skilled union operator on a daily newspaper in Boston. He was an exception. I have always wished that we might have kept him. He still drops in at the office with his wife when he is on vacation, and laughs when someone reminds him how an umbrella was left in a *Gazette* wastebasket until it should finish dripping and he burned it with the scrap paper.

When Dick West worked for the *Gazette* he was hoping to win an appointment to West Point or Annapolis. Congressman Charles S. Gifford happened in to pay one of his occasional calls. We naturally called Dick from the back shop and presented him to the Congressman. Mr. Gifford represented an old school and knew how to behave with his constituents. He not only catechized Dick, but also made an examination of his teeth. . . . Although Dick didn't make either of the academies, he took a degree at Fordham, saw wartime duty at sea, and is now a food company vice president.

When we had been working through the *Gazette* to arrive at an effective countermeasure against wood ticks, Betty conceived what we called the Martha's Vineyard Wood Tick Project. It was carried on at Miss Katharine Foote's Animal Rescue League under the direction of Dr. Marshall Hertig, who made supervisory visits, with funds collected through Betty's *Gazette* stories. Congressman Gifford became interested to the point of arranging for the work to be taken over by the Department of Agriculture. He did this by adding the necessary amount to the total budget of the department when it was about to be voted upon. Only a well-liked legislator of considerable seniority could have managed this coup. The federal laboratory was established at Vineyard Haven and continued until the onset of World War II, when emergency work absorbed all funds.

After Mr. Gifford came Donald Nicholson, of Wareham, who moved on from Beacon Hill to Washington. He was a mellow cynic and the only politician I ever met who frankly admitted that he didn't care much of a damn. He expected to be elected because he was a Republican running in a Republican district, and he took it all as a matter of course but of no great concern.

In later years a new custom was introduced—the candidate would be touching down at the airport at such-and-such an hour to meet the press and those constituents who might accept his invitation to be on hand. Usually the weather was bad and the plane would be late, and sometimes it didn't arrive at all. Our present Congressman, Gerry Studds, a young Democrat who overthrew a long Republican succession, is of different mettle. He campaigns, he meets people, and he follows up on problems of importance.

Jim Curley visited the Island when he was both governor and out of jail. Joe Allen wrote quite a story about his evening visit to the Boston House in Oak Bluffs, during which he autographed a woman's shorts. The evening was a lively one. Calvin Coolidge visited the Island again as Vice President and maybe once as President, but without fanfare. Anyway, the *Gazette*'s Vineyard Haven correspondent, Lucinda Norton St. John, sent in with her weekly items a quotation from the state president of the W.C.T.U.: "We have three things to be proud of, Plymouth Rock, Bunker Hill, and Calvin Coolidge."

The Coolidge era went along easily. No one said, "Well, this is an interesting time to be living in," an observation that had been endemic in wartime and would recur whenever the country or the world slipped into trouble. Nobody wondered about so irrelevant a matter, though small-circulation magazines of social conscience ran articles about "This Amazing

Prosperity" in which the poverty of millions was contrasted with the parade of booming wealth.

The *Gazette* clung to its home character, determined to be an Island newspaper as it had always been, though with world awareness. We had no desire to be instructing Washington or counting the cats in Zanzibar. We were ringed around by mainland daily newspapers as well as by salt water, and everyone who took the *Gazette* was also a reader of one or more dailies, perhaps a news weekly, and eventually a listener to radio and a watcher of television. Circumstance as well as choice made us an Island newspaper and kept us so, and we didn't meddle editorially with national or state politics unless we saw them coming ashore at the steamboat wharf or approaching along the street.

But Betty and I were free to commit ourselves individually as we wished, and in 1928 we wished. Stanley Leaming, piano tuner and arborealist, imported some Al Smith campaign material, and we displayed a colorful placard in the rear window of our car. Somebody said the Houghs must be Catholics—and hadn't the Catholic church note headed the column in the *Gazette* that very week? But our Methodist minister friend, Howard Davis, said that anyone who went to church as rarely as we did couldn't well be Catholic.

In later years, when a birth-control referendum was to appear on the state ballot, Betty allowed her name to be used among the signatures on a political advertisement urging a "Yes" vote. She either was or wasn't denounced from the pulpit of Sacred Heart Church; Father Hurley says she wasn't, but her partisanship was noted along with disapproval of the advertisement.

How things went: Betty wrote to a necessary utility.

Cape & Vineyard Electric Co.
Gentlemen:
I am enclosing check for $35. I should greatly appreciate it if you would stop threatening to turn off my electricity. So far as I know we have never threatened your company when its adver-

tising bill reached a high point and was several months in arrears. Please return the courtesy.

To an earnest contributor.

Dear Mrs. ——
We are returning herewith your poem, MY DENTIST, and appreciate your thinking of us in connection with its publication. It is very cleverly done but we feel we cannot use it at the moment.

As we gradually reached more efficient production in the back shop, ambition set in like a spring tide. We wanted more versatile and better appearing headlines, machine-set, and more sophisticated typography all around. More sophisticated, but Bill chose such old reliable type faces as Caslon, Cheltenham, and Bodoni.

Bill Murray, the Linotype salesman, had convinced us that we needed a Model 14, with three magazines of matrices and type sizes up to 24-point, set from the keyboard, and that we could manage the purchase of a good rebuilt machine. This meant emancipation of welcome proportions, though troubles we would still have. There's no freedom from troubles in a small shop.

So we were grateful to Bill Murray, and we dealt with him for many years as a friend and expert adviser. One of the ways we became aware of the passing of time was through the gradual aging of the salesmen who called upon us. For many years they didn't change much, and then, seeing them once a year, we were aware of gray hair or more weight or other signs of "getting on." What they noticed in us I can only guess, but we still felt the same. At last others came in their places, and half the time I didn't know who they were because I had left so many years behind for good and all.

The decision to buy a real newspaper press was our own. We had considerable correspondence with manufacturers and, at the last, a call from an old-timer salesman who knew his business and gave us a lot of practical suggestions. The next step in advance from a two-revolution cylinder press would be a web perfecting press printing from type forms. The choice fell between a Goss Comet and a Duplex Model A. We favored the Duplex, but the Goss Comet came with an important-looking overhead brass plate stating that the press had been manufactured for us. The Duplex salesman said that if that was all that was keeping us apart, he would have a brass plate made for us. So he did, and it has been suspended over our Duplex press all these years.

The roll of newsprint went on the press at one end, the web was threaded through the various rollers, and at last was taken by tapes for final folding and delivery; no more butterfly nonsense, no more feeding of sheets by hand. During the operation, though, the web was held motionless in mid-transit just long enough for an impression to be made, four pages on the lower deck, four pages on the upper deck, with an equalizing device to take up the slack each time.

Since the tapes and rollers were dragging the web of paper through the press and back to the delivery end, and since the web must be stopped and released so accurately and quickly, the tension of the paper required careful attention. Too tight, the web would break. Too loose, it would tend to flap and tear. Adjustment lay entirely in the pressman's judgment, and he must know that conditions were different from day to day, depending on humidity and temperature. Of course we had web breaks, and the mess of cleaning tattered paper from inky rollers, but the breaks became fewer and fewer.

We could now print between 2,500 and 3,000 eight-page papers an hour—liberation! In the spring we signed the notes, and in the fall came the Wall Street debacle of 1929. So we met the Great Depression head on with a debt of more than $6,000, payable in precise installments, month by month.

When the bank holiday was declared, the Duplex Company sent a letter of some concern. We wrote them not to worry and not to lose confidence: the economy of America was basically sound.

8

Betty and I were fond of town meetings at the start and only a little less so as the years wore on. They changed as a new generation set in. Harry Tyler, the mordant tailor of Edgartown's Main Street, was no longer around to defend his aunt's beautiful shrub; Mike Keegan, of Oak Bluffs, had based his last argument on the principles of the Industrial Revolution; James Adams, of Chilmark, would not again oppose his own re-election to the school committee because he was against the employment of a music supervisor and objected to a poem printed in the town report that began "I am Music"; and Ben Collins, in Edgartown, would no longer take off his coat and descend from the moderator's post to the floor to oppose the extravagant payment of $25 a year for audit of the town's books by a state auditor.

Town meetings in the old years began in the morning, and while the first routine articles were being voted, the Vincents and others would be driving in from the Great Plain and hitching their horses comfortably. Gradually the town hall filled up, and by the time the moderator, who was then Beriah T.

Hillman, reached the controversial issues, all interested parties were on hand.

They were homely issues for the most part, small in scale, characteristic of the old Vineyard which would soon pass with the last of the soil-grown and sea-grown patriarchs. Progress, though, kept intruding in its peculiar way. At the 1921 Edgartown town meeting the women revolted, and it took three votes, one following the noon recess, to override Ben Collins and the finance committee in order to keep the streetlights burning all night.

The finance committee had pared down the appropriation for the police department to $720, providing for one man, who would serve as policeman in summer and as night watch in winter. Harry Tyler declared that an officer was needed at the bank corner to regulate traffic.

"The most I saw the officers doing there last summer was entertaining chickens," said Ben Collins. He was voted down, all the same.

Some years later came the historic meeting at which the Chappaquiddick ferry was advanced from the status of a skiff rowed from a ferry slip on the Edgartown side to Chappaquiddick Point by Jim Yates. Anonymous friends had presented Jim with a uniform cap inscribed "No. 47" which he wore as a matter of course.

When the new project came before town meeting, James E. Chadwick asked for details as to plans, the type of motorboat proposed. Arthur Hillman, for the selectmen, said he could go to the town office downstairs and get the plans.

"We've been waiting thirty years," said Mr. Chadwick. "I guess we can wait another thirty minutes."

The plans were produced and read, but all the voters couldn't very well inspect them. Mr. Chadwick then said, "I think we are very fortunately situated at the present hour. Our moderator is a graduate of Technology and I suggest that he give us an idea of the proposed piers."

"The subject of piers didn't happen to enter into the course as I studied it," said the moderator, "but at the estimated price I think you could put down a pretty substantial sort of pier."

Mr. Hillman suggested that Captain Antone King Silva, chairman of the finance committee, give some details, and Captain Silva did. Philip J. Norton said he had been told a man who built a pier on Chappaquiddick the previous year had to pay $45 a spile.

Captain Silva disclaimed any idea of using "$45 mahogany spiles—good oak would do very well." Mr. Chadwick brought up the question of the liability of the town. He said he had seen nine passengers in the present ferry. The ferryman had a bond of $1,000, and did this mean that if the nine passengers were drowned, each would get one-ninth of the $1,000?

Judge Arthur W. Davis said that the question might be raised as to whether this was not in fact a private ferry with a town subsidy and not a municipal ferry, and if it could be established that it was a private ferry, the town would not be liable.

Mr. Chadwick brought up the matter of equipment, which should include a life preserver for each passenger. "The present life preserver consists of a coal shovel," he said.

As finally adopted, the amended article provided for the leasing of the ferry at a dollar a year, the ferryman to keep the boat and scow in good repair, for which he was to be paid $366 a year, plus $75 to take care of a $10,000 bond he would be required to post.

And this was how, with so little sense of the momentous, the Chappaquiddick ferry entered the modern epoch.

It was a while before I participated in town-meeting debate, the occasion being a project for a new fire engine. This was defeated a time or two but finally won approval. Opponents doubted whether the town hydrant system would be adequate for a modern pumper, but Sheriff Dexter said briefly that there ought to be water enough between Edgartown and Nantucket.

Later on I argued for a platform or extended "widow's

walk" across the top of the reconstructed town wharf so that anyone could have a comfortable view of the whole harbor. I said the structure would be a poor-man's yacht club, a remark that led a friend to deplore my "setting class against class." It was suggested that I was a Communist, but my friend John MacKenty defended me—he said I was a Socialist.

Dr. Jim Wilson said that if the platform was built there would be lovemaking on it at night, and drunks would fall off, get hurt, and sue the town. Miss Christine Pease objected "to prettifying the wharf with flower gardens, sun dials, or penthouses," and a long-time summer resident, now a voter, asked, "Are we going to vote on the wharf or on the wharf with all the trimmings, flowers, catwalks, or whatever?" After this the opponents drummed away at the word "catwalk." They won the first time around, but the platform was voted later.

At an Oak Bluffs town meeting the selectmen were caught with having built an incinerator at the dump with firebrick laid edgewise instead of flatly, in the proper way. Naturally the incinerator had failed badly and would have to be abandoned or rebuilt. Mike Keegan rose to the defense of his board.

"Why do you people always look at the worst side of things? Do you realize that we have been paying tribute to Caesar for years when we needed sand, and that we now have a supply for 500 years in that dumping ground? Also the best of loam for your uses, too. I'll take the responsibility for the incinerator. I know that mistakes were made. The firebrick should not have been laid on edge, but good God, give us a little credit. We had everything to contend with and we tried to give the town service and save expense."

Mike was defeated for selectman in 1933, and the loss to town meeting was considerable. He had been born near Dublin but at the age of three had been taken by his family to Manchester, England, where he spent his boyhood and learned a lot of Manchester economics. He was taught singing and dancing, performing in music halls for pay. He finally came to America at the age of twenty-six, learned the trade of plastering, and was called to the Vineyard to help plaster the Harbor View hotel at Edgartown.

Our determination to report in the *Gazette* all public proceedings such as town meetings and court cases seemed innovative at first, but it wasn't. The oldest Old Editor of all, Edgar Marchant, great-uncle of our own Charles H. Marchant, had reported town-meeting debates almost word for word, notably in 1874 when it was proposed that Edgartown invest in a narrow-gauge railroad to bring excursionists from the camp meeting ground.

He reported court cases, too, and when Betty covered a district court proceeding in 1920 at the outset of our editorship, she resumed a long-ago continuity. The case involved the tall, eccentric figure of Dr. Charles F. Lane, who had established his own telephone company to serve himself and his patients. The Bell System had bought him out while I was a boy, but it was still legend how he used to shinny up a pole when necessary, wearing frock coat and plug hat. In the same costume I had seen him jump up and down in front of his drugstore with a fly swatter on a hot summer day.

He was the builder of the Lane Block in Vineyard Haven, the roof of which once caught fire. When the firemen arrived he was up there himself with a garden hose, and he exclaimed, "Oh dear! Oh dear! Everything was all right until you came."

Dr. Lane had now sued the American Express Company, alleging breach of contract resulting in the loss of four suits and two extra pairs of pants shipped to a New Bedford dry cleaner in a braided-straw suitcase. He had retained Charlie Brown to represent him, and Betty wrote that the doctor was "an ardent witness." He testified under cross examination that a letter in evidence was not written on the date set down in the superscription.

"Did you intentionally misdate it?" asked Mr. Pinkham, lawyer for the express company.

"I did not."

"Are you in the habit of purposely misdating your letters?"
"I'm not going to answer that unless you tell me to," Dr. Lane said to the court.

Advised that it would be best for him to answer, the doctor nevertheless declared, "I consider it an impertinent question and I won't answer it unless you order me to."

The court suggested that Mr. Pinkham not press for an answer, and Dr. Lane said to Mr. Pinkham, "You'd better not."

"Is that a threat?" asked Mr. Pinkham, but he didn't press for an answer to that question, either.

It was brought out that Dr. Lane, always impetuous, had not waited for an express company receipt when he shipped his braided-straw suitcase, but when it failed to reach its destination he did obtain a receipt, lost it, and then got another.

Mr. Pinkham argued that no testimony had been introduced to prove that the express company had failed in its duty as a common carrier, and that in any event the liability must be limited to $100.

Charlie Brown, in summation, said the issue was the old one of the fine print on the ticket, and since Dr. Lane had not taken a receipt at the time of shipment, it could not be shown that he had read the fine print on the back of the form. The court took the matter under advisement, later finding for the company and denying Lawyer Brown his innovative legal doctrine.

When Dr. Lane died, his will was found on file at the probate office, together with a self-written obituary which he directed was to be taken to the *Vineyard Gazette*. He directed also that there be no religious service at his funeral, but there was—his widow and her sisters were of a different persuasion. The *Gazette* regretfully omitted the doctor's prohibition against a religious service, inasmuch as his lifetime defiance seemed adequate, and he himself might have relented at last to allow the women of his family their principles and conventions as well as their tears.

That barrier beach, the narrow strip of sand separating Katama Bay from the Atlantic, concerned the *Gazette* almost from the time of our arrival. The problem typified the historic relationships of so much of Martha's Vineyard and so many of its people from times long past. The town of Edgartown had obtained a state grant of $2,500 and voted a minor sum itself, and put in the hands of Captain Antone King Silva the matter of securing a channel, bay to ocean, against the chances of wind, tide, and sea.

Tony King, as everyone called him, had been born on the island of São Jorge in the Azores but had been brought up Yankee style on the Vineyard. He had sailed in vessels out of Noank and Greenport, trawling in winter and hand-lining in summer. Eventually he acquired a schooner of his own, which ultimately was lost in a cruel blizzard, the Coast Guard rescuing him from the rigging after all his crew but one had been picked up from a dory.

Lately he had been fishing at Edgartown in a catboat, and he used to walk down Main Street followed by his brown dog, Joe, whose tail pointed almost straight out behind him. I have never known a rarer composure or serenity than Tony King's. It provided the background for a dry wit and many a crisp observation. He was also a handsome man, with regular features and excellent profile.

Many were skeptical as to his chances in the beach-opening project, for forty years earlier General G. K. Warren, of the Army Engineers, had spent a lot of government money and seen it buried in a wash of ocean rollers and sand. But he, whether or not from ill luck or failure of foresight, had made his final break-through into the teeth of a roaring southeaster. Betty wrote the stories about Tony King's undertaking:

A few minutes before 10 o'clock this morning an opening as narrow as a little girl's hair ribbon was driven across the beach, and the placid waters of Katama Bay began their exit to the ocean. Minute by minute the break widened, assisted by the efforts of four teams of horses dragging scoops, and the workers standing hip deep in water to loosen the sand.

An hour after the opening the channel was 20 and 30 feet wide, and the banks were caving rapidly. Where the fast-moving water from the bay met the breakers from the ocean there formed a sort of mill race which churned and sparkled in the mild spring sunlight.

Betty went to the beach in Captain George Studley's boat, which "chugged its way through one of the most beautiful of scenes the world around. The old fishing town nestled along the waterside, dazzling white in the sunshine. . . ." On the way home Captain Studley pointed out a gash in the beach, all that remained of General Warren's attempted opening and failure.

There were not many in 1921 whose memories went back across forty years to the time of General Warren, and I suppose there are few now who recall Tony King's opening of fifty-two years ago; but there are old-timers like myself who witnessed the opening project of 1932.

We were in the depression years, though many had thought the stock-market crash wouldn't much affect Martha's Vineyard, our world and its native elements being different and independent. At first it didn't, but nevertheless the President or the Governor or someone asked all towns to appoint unemployment committees. Of course they did, and I was named in Edgartown, along with Arthur Hillman and Tony King.

There wasn't much for us to do. At first only one unemployed client showed up, and his case posed no real difficulties. Arthur Hillman said that any able-bodied man could go out and dig himself a mess of clams any time, and this was true. But the underwater meadows of eel grass were afflicted about this time with a strange blight, not understood until two or three years later, when it was identified as the work of a parasite. As the eel grass disappeared, the scallop fishery diminished. Seed scallops in exposed waters had needed eel grass for protection; and the bottom now became shifting and restless with tides and storms. So the shellfishery was depressed along with almost all else.

Franklin D. Roosevelt had not yet been elevated to the White House when Edgartown undertook its first unemployment project, that of opening Katama Bay to the ocean once again, for improved circulation of water and nutrients, with prospective benefit to the bay shellfisheries, which included quahaugs as well as scallops. The town put up $4,000, quite a sum of money, and all the digging would be done with shovels, helped at the latter end by a horse and scoop or two. The unemployment committee met with the selectmen and approved a rate of pay—$2.50 for eight hours, with $5 for Tony King as director of the enterprise. This pay was based upon each man's contribution of a share of his labor for the general good.

Some eighty men were spread over the high dunes with their shovels. As the cut deepened, those below passed sand to shovelers above; and as the channel deepened still more, sand had to be relayed to a succession of levels. Not until the final moment, of course, was the big ditch to be cut through to the ocean. I drove often to the end of the road at Katama and walked the long stretch of beach to the scene of a homely enterprise that was a spectacle of its own kind. One wouldn't see the like of it afterward.

Sometimes the labor had to be suspended. The temperature fell to twenty degrees in a biting wind, and no shelter. That cold blast drawing through the dune gaps and the partly dug channel couldn't be withstood for long. When they could work, the diggers often sang, and called one another "the sewer-gang chorus," but the really apt comparison was with the chanteymen of the sea, especially since Willard Tilton had been a chanteyman with the best of them.

In late April the last sand was cleared except for a final barrier where the ditch reached the shelving beach; this final cut would be decisive. As soon as it was cleared, success would lie wholly with wind and tide. Tony King ordered the critical step begun, but weather signs changed, and the barrier was held. Another high tide in Katama Bay would come at two o'clock on a Sunday morning, and it would be a moon tide with favorable omens as to the wind. Everyone was ready to turn out at that hour.

Under an almost full moon which shone in a broad trail across the ocean and South Beach, Capt. Antone King Silva and his shovelers opened the long ditch. . . . The shovelers were silhouettes working in the moonlight. The lemony light cast its beauty over the whole scene—the sandy beach and its distances, the surf breaking with increasing force and threatening to undo the work of the diggers. During the day the ocean had been, as Captain Silva said, as smooth as a cat's back. . . .

I sat on the slope of a dune with Ed Vincent, stirred with the inner joy of all this—moonglade shimmering, crisp night air of new spring, ocean rollers making far out and gathering mass and movement as they fulfilled themselves to the climax of breaking into a surge of spray and foam. Ed and I looked on, and Ed began remembering.

He remembered how he had cut hay in a field way out where the breakers were rising; such in his time had been the loss of shore to the sea. He spoke of the old people, of the Money Light over the Katama woods which was said to have marked a treasure never found, of the life of the Great Plain, of long-ago feuds, and of the odd doing of Vineyard characters such as Leander Mayhew, who built a steamboat at Meshacket which was called *Bull of the Woods* because of the mighty effort to get it to a launching place.

When we went home at last the water of the bay still ran out, but the level had begun dropping, and the advantage was no longer with Tony King and his men. The slack was at hand, and then the ocean tide would run shoreward.

The digging had begun in mid-February and the final night of commitment and decision occurred in mid-May. Every Saturday, for convenience, we paid off at the *Gazette* office, and one Saturday I gave every digger a Durham-Duplex safety razor from a supply we had taken in an advertising trade. The new opening ran well enough at first, tide in and tide out, but before it had become secure an unseasonable run of onshore winds with high surf in late May bottled it up again.

"You can't sign any contracts with nature," Tony King said.

I went down one evening with him and Levi Jackson to inspect the sand-filled ditch, not an opening any more. Tony King wanted to see exactly what had happened, in order to put his experience to use another time.

That fall F.D.R. was elected. We got out an election extra, mostly for the fun of it, or the satisfaction, even though it meant working all night. We sold enough advertising to pay the cost, and arranged for a pony service from the United Press in Boston. The "basic cost" included nothing for labor; all the labor, front and back office, was contributed. In those days the daily newspapers did not reach the Island until early afternoon, and we could have our extra on the streets at seven in the morning.

The only thing that prevented us from achieving a historic success was that the election of Roosevelt was a certainty the night before. Our extra surprised nobody, but it did give the first printed account of many details. Martha's Vineyard went for Hoover, though not much of the rest of the country did. Our streamer headlines in 48-point had to be hand set with foundry type; this meant a lot of trial and error in completing three streamers without running out of necessary letters. Time had begun to turn against us and finally we had to be content with this third line: VINEYARD IS TRUE TO HOOVER.

Visiting newspapermen, including Charles Merz, then editorial-page editor of the New York *Times*, shook their heads at this, for they said it wasn't objective. We argued that it was precisely factual, any bias being in how you construed it.

Soon the new administration took charge—"the only thing we have to fear is fear itself"—and work projects came to the

Island as to all places, first the C.W.A., then the P.W.A. and the W.P.A. The look of Edgartown was changed forever when a W.P.A. project surfaced the streets with blacktop and there were no more thoroughfares of finely ground scallop shells bleached and white in any day's sun.

Eventually Tony King became distributor of surplus commodities, for he had been an indomitable Democrat through the lean years. When the next presidential campaign was coming along, I met him on the street. He said he had fallen in with Mrs. Orr, and she had said to him, "Now you know that giving away all those blankets and other things is bound to influence votes." He looked at me brightly but without other expression than the gleam in his eyes and said, "Shouldn't wonder if it did, Henry, shouldn't wonder if it did."

Ed Vincent, also an old-line Democrat, couldn't go along with F.D.R.—all the plowing under, and giving things away.

As to the Katama beach, history inched along as history does, and, the beach being closed, there is discussion of a new opening. But bulldozers are now commoner than horses used to be, and the Army Engineers have been brought into the argument. There are different calculations. The eel grass, after more than thirty years, has come back. The increased number of boats moored in Edgartown harbor in summer, almost as many as the harbor can hold, has brought a serious problem of pollution. Some observers say that for keeping the harbor and bay clean, a closed South Beach is best because the incoming tide runs into every little inlet and indentation with a scouring action, ebbing rapidly in turn. But some still say it is best to have an opening through which tides rush in and out of the bay on schedule. As to shellfishing, some believe the overshot of sand into the bay from the ocean is a conclusive argument against an opening.

Because the beach is low now, flattened by the hurricane of 1938, which swept those high dunes away. The town has had some success in rebuilding dunes through putting out brush and snow fence, but not enough. An appeal to the Army

Engineers for help has brought the counterproposal that the town apply for federal funds for a recreational project directed toward the dredging of the harbor and bay for larger mooring facilities, and use of the dredged material for building up South Beach. This ignores the pollution problem, but obviously what brings in federal funds most easily is the thing to do.

Way back there in the 1920's it was Bertha Beetle, daughter of Jo King Silva, and our neighbor on the other side of Winter Street, who suggested that we try to stir up interest in a county high school to take the place of the three separate high schools on the Island. The plan seemed so logical that it became our first major crusade.

Oliver Wendell Holmes said, "The mode in which the inevitable comes to pass is through effort." He was right, of course, but if we could discern the inevitable soon enough could we not save ourselves a lot of trouble?

Bertha Beetle, a beautiful woman with clear dark skin, bright dark eyes, and white teeth, taught school, tutored on the side, and beat Walter Nichols for election as the first town treasurer in Massachusetts. Later she served for many years as librarian of the public library. There was nothing the matter with woman's place in Edgartown even that long ago; Miss Susan Beetle, as I have reported, was a registered pharmacist, and Alice Dexter, after her husband's death, became the state's first licensed motion-picture operator, running the movies in the town hall.

When Bertha brought up the school matter there were 204 pupils in the three high schools, and the budgets of the major towns, Oak Bluffs, Tisbury, and Edgartown, came to some $65,000 every year.

"Those who argue in favor of one high school," I wrote editorially, "ask why three towns should burn coal and keep three furnaces going. . . . The united towns could develop a library, a gymnasium, in short every school essential, with small expense compared to the cost of a separate one in each town. . . ."

We queried leaders in different parts of the Island and all of them seemed to think a county high school would be a pretty good thing, though a few were choosy as to the location. Our endeavor got as far as a dialogue with the state Board of Education, which automatically favored new buildings, especially regional ones. The Island's union school committee, which administered the superintendency union, appointed a subcommittee to confer with our state representative as to enabling legislation.

The subcommittee report proved a damper: "It is not thought feasible to build at present on account of the high cost of material and labor, but it was thought best to make a start and be ready when the auspicious moment presented itself."

The auspicious moment, of course, never comes. The auspicious moment is the dark stranger passing by unrecognized on the other side of the street. But here, occupying the Methodist pulpit, was our young friend Howard Davis, the minister I have mentioned before. He was the son of an older minister, who had given him the soundest advice at the outset of his career: "Be sure to sift your ashes."

Howard had intensity, humor, and a lean and gallant sense of earthly good as well as of a remoter celestial excellence. Around his personality grew a men's club with membership from all over. With his leadership the club engendered a movement for a new school building in Edgartown to consolidate the existing North School and South School, bringing elementary and high-school grades together. Betty and I were in New York when the project went through, and its success seemed remarkable—although we noted that the crucial vote was taken when Ben Collins was in Boston.

The new Edgartown school was built of brick, a conventional monstrosity so far as appearance was concerned, but it had the first gymnasium on the Island and served its purpose well. And now, within a few years, the path of consolidation being blocked, both Oak Bluffs and Tisbury went ahead with buildings of their own. A generation intervened before economics and foresight could again justify regionalization.

Meantime I had been appointed to the school committee to fill a vacancy that had occurred in a characteristically small-town way. Raymond Walker, a member of the committee, turning from one enthusiasm to another, became involved in promoting boxing exhibitions, which is to say prize fights, in the roller-skating rink at Oak Bluffs. He borrowed some chairs from the school building, no harm to anyone, he thought; but the chairs belonged to the library, and Arthur Hillman, chairman of the library trustees, said that the chairs must be brought back. Raymond said that if they were to be brought back right away, it would be with his resignation from the school committee; but if they were brought back later, without his resignation. Arthur Hillman said, "Right away." So I was named to fill Raymond's place as school committeeman.

I served first with Mrs. Henrietta Hillman and Ed Vincent. Ed had been elected more or less on a platform of keeping the school budget below $30,000 a year, and I thought he might be pretty much on the conservative side. He wasn't. We got along fine. I learned that he had been one of the activists of years back, known as the Molly Maguires, who had brought about the installation of plumbing in the South School. He was good at confusing the finance committee about the budget and getting what we wanted.

Later I served with Stuart Avery, who had taken over Jethro Cottle's store and real-estate business, and we pushed ahead all we could in a progressive spirit. We even went up to Boston with Mr. Martin, the school superintendent, to interview teachers. That was actually a time of the world when a school appropriation had to be fought for. You even had to fight for money for roads, which seems even less credible.

The depression made things worse and worse, and the idea was abroad that $2,400 was a lot of money to pay a school principal, though he was expected to teach classes throughout the school day and somehow fit administration, interviews with parents, teachers' meetings, and so on and on into whatever time he could find. Chester E. Pease, reputed to be the wealthiest man in town, figured exactly what $2,400 a year came to by the hour, and it was more than the fishermen could earn.

I had hoped to influence the English curriculum, but we were stuck with Burke's *Conciliation* and Thackeray's *Henry Esmond*. There's nothing wrong with *Henry Esmond* that I know of, but I favored *Huckleberry Finn*. Mark Twain wasn't then permitted by the state Board of Education. It took about thirty years to get him into the schools, and by that time I had left the committee.

We bucked the coal company by chartering Captain Zeb Tilton's schooner *Alice S. Wentworth* to bring a load at a lower price from New Bedford. And we discussed disciplinary problems and got bids for the transporting of children from Chappaquiddick and the plain.

Mr. Martin, the superintendent, was an agreeable, blinking, and peaceable man, whom I liked, but his way through the years had been worn as smooth as he could manage. It did seem that the schools would benefit by a more modern and effective spirit. When we asked why he had not notified a teacher about some complaint, he said he had not found a favorable opportunity. Once when he and I were to face a meeting of probably disturbed parents at the courthouse, relative to smoking in the school building, I found at the last moment that he had gone to Cuttyhunk, that small island across Vineyard Sound, which was also within his jurisdiction. I rather think I paid him back by letting the parents believe everything was his fault.

When a change of superintendents was discussed at the annual union meeting, and a change seemed to meet strong approval, it was pointed out that Mr. Martin would be eligible for a pension in a couple of years. No one wanted to see him lose his pension, and we re-elected him on the understanding, as we believed, that he would resign as of the date the pension became secure. But we didn't get it in writing. I think this was my fault. Anyway, when the time came, Mr. Martin wouldn't budge. He most agreeably wouldn't budge, and now I think he was quite right, for this was a matter of politics, and politics is played as a game.

Nothing could be said against him, except that he practiced surveying at Gay Head when he should have been at the school. I don't know whether this was true, but it was certainly absurd to believe that he got a rake-off on the popcorn and soda consumed by groups of pupils when he escorted them to see Plymouth Rock or the New Bedford Whaling Museum, as he liked to do once a year.

In those days it was also possible to accuse the schools of being extravagant, a term no longer permissible in town-meeting debate. Someone always gets up and says, "The last place we should economize is at the expense of our children's education." Nobody ever got past that one. But in any case, a town meeting in Massachusetts cannot reduce the budget submitted by a school committee. It can, however, make a superintendent's life miserable. Hardly any superintendents in Massachusetts acquire tenure—they get shuffled too often.

Our new Regional High School came in at last upon this rising wave of the future, though only after a bitter, divisive struggle over a period of years. In 1948 subcommittees were appointed to look around at the existing school buildings—they had become old, older than anyone had realized—and to discuss plans for a regional district. Forming the district wasn't the hard part; that came about easily.

Whatever effect our *Gazette* editorials and reports may have had, they didn't convert a dedicated opposition, which included such respectable leadership as a retired bishop and a retired general. Four years after the formation of the district and after repeated town meetings, Tisbury was still holding out. If an indispensable unanimity was to be attained among the towns, something had to be done to resolve the stalemate.

This occurred within Tisbury itself when a diplomatic civic leader, Mrs. Wilfrid O. White, who was also wise and valorous, suggested an educational survey. The town assented, and a team of experts representing Tufts, Harvard, and Boston University brought in a report that occupied almost six full pages in the *Gazette*. We had never met so huge a production problem before. The report favored the regional plan without any ambiguity, and a majority of the Tisbury school committee now backed it.

A climactic town meeting was held to consider two articles: whether the town should withdraw from the regional district, and whether it would approve a bond issue in the amount of $1,075,000 for the construction of the proposed school. These were the two options, and at the town meeting they were well mixed. Someone moved from the floor to vote on the bond issue first. The debate, consisting of sharp exchanges, had to do with priorities, and on whether a two-thirds vote was required, and whether the moderator had figured two-thirds correctly; not a word about the merits of the school, for minds as to that had been long made up.

A selectman moved that discussion on either side be limited to fifteen minutes, and this was voted.

"It is now 8:30," said the moderator. "Whoever is on the floor at 9:00 will be shut off tight."

"May I start the discussion?" asked a voter.

"Yes," said the vocal selectman. "Let him."

"Then," said the voter, "let's vote right away without any discussion at all."

The ayes came out with 339 and the noes with 311 votes, and that was how, after years of bitterness and effort, effort, effort, the inevitable was brought to pass.

I wrote in the *Gazette* editorial:

Long beset by storm and disagreements the path has been, but the chances are that all will be forgotten more quickly than anyone thinks possible. From the tortured question of whether the Vineyard should have a school or not, and how much the school should cost, we advance now to the more vital issue. What can we put within the walls of the new building in the warmth and devotion of teaching, in the diligence and ambition of girls and boys? How much can it be made to help the rising generations?

After the first thirty years of the Regional High School I don't know the answers to such questions.

In 1933 the combined high-school enrollment was 266, and the aggregate school budget of the six Island towns was something like $300,000—not more. In 1973 the high-school enrollment had risen to about 500 and the assessed operating and capital expense of the Regional High School came to $933,604.98. It seems long ago and in some far country that I wrote: "Those who argue in favor of one high school for the Island ask why three towns should burn coal and keep three furnaces going. . . ."

My own view is that one of the major troubles with education is that the educators will not let it alone.

Our Regional High School is crowded, and one hears much talk of a new one. This time I think I can recognize the inevitable and will let others apply the mode of effort to accomplish its fulfillment.

When we moved into the Greek temple, Betty found a girl to cook and help her. This was a modest expense then. The girl's name was Virginia, and she was young, pretty, innocent, and incalculably knowing—as innocence can be. When Betty asked her why she drew a sharp knife toward her when she was cutting—and had just wounded herself—she replied, "It's a little way I have, Mrs. Hough."

Once when we were having lunch, sounds of a feminine altercation came from the kitchen. Virginia was having words with another girl, or vice versa. Betty called her from the kitchen, apprehension on her face. "Do you need any help?" Betty asked, and that was that.

In the evening Virginia often sat in the kitchen with an attentive young man who was an oiler on one of the steamboats. He kept a flatiron handy to aim at the rats when they came into the open. And once Virginia and our first collie, Rikki-tikki-tavi, had a free ride to Woods Hole and back.

Betty and I went often to the movies in Lee Colter's new Elm Theatre on Main Street. Mrs. Colter, the always lovely and friendly Jessie, played the piano, nicely suiting the music to the moods that passed on the screen. You not only saw Momba, the elephant, shuffling off into the jungle, but you were alerted and excited to the quality of Momba's big moment. Between reels, a slide was shown: "One Moment Please." Between reels, also, advertising slides could be shown.

Some of the younger seasonal visitors were much enamored of a girl named Betty, or thought they were, and now and then she let one of them take her to the movies. One of the ingenious ones persuaded Lee Colter or his operator to flash on the screen this message: "Will Whit Griswold, Bill Potts, Jack Swords and Hastings Hickok please go home. Their mothers want them."

It was not much later that Whit Griswold became the *Gazette*'s first columnist, writing his observations of the current scene over the pseudonym "Sancho Panza." Quite a lot later he became the president of Yale.

Betty and I saw Mary Miles Minter; William S. Hart in *The Cradle of Courage; The Saphead*, featuring Buster Keaton; and comedies with Charlie Chaplin or Fatty Arbuckle. We saw Alice Brady in *The Fear Market*, Ethel Clayton in *Sails Adrift*, and so on, through a roll of names mostly lost. Who else remembers Wallace Reid, Lois Wilson, and Theodore Roberts? Well, a good many probably do, but we are fewer in number as the days pass. Often we would go to the movies with a bag of old-fashioned chocolate creams purchased at

Bill Cottle's on the corner. It was Mr. Marchant who put us in the way of doing this.

The Edgartown Library was pretty good, and Betty read a lot. I hardly kept up.

I don't know why we delayed so long, but it was a year before we got Rikki, our first collie—not Betty's first, for she had owned Philadelphia, who was almost a collie, and Danny Deever, who was wholly one. It was hard to persuade Rikki to come indoors on summer nights, and I tossed chestnut coal at him until he got into the Buick, which was parked in the side yard, and we let him spend the night there.

We needed no special variety in the evening, for we had plenty of that all day at the office or circulating around town. Suspense built up all week until the pangs of publication and the letdown of relief.

I have mentioned Mrs. Shepard, our next-door neighbor. Her son Marshall, somewhat older than either of us, called at the house often and became a lifelong friend. He had come to Edgartown as a boy in a summer family and had later studied at the Art Students League, and finally settled on the Island year-round. He and Theodore Wimpenney had invented a new type of mooring, which they patented, and Marshall had become an authority on Vineyard history, an even better one than Charlie Brown, and a principal founder of the Dukes County Historical Society.

Betty and I went to Fish Hook weekends, not always, but often. Fish Hook remained the same but its relevance had subtly changed. By moving to the Island I had yielded to the principle of hostage-giving. I no longer crossed water to get to it. The associations of childhood and youth were closed off by the widening experience now intervening, and by the necessity of making a living. Accessibility from Edgartown might be even less in the end than the old means of the *Uncatena* and Uncle Ben's tired farm horse. And now a family past had to be joined to the particular future Betty and I were making. The junction could not be entirely smooth and even.

Nevertheless, sanctuary was still sanctuary, though in different measure. The beauty of the woods throughout the seasons could not be less; soon for the first time I would see the North Shore deeply covered and molded with winter ice, and the surf pounding before the chilliest northeasters; and always the old places were where we had last seen them, ready to be revisited. Sometimes, not often, Betty and I were at Fish Hook alone, using the house as a headquarters from which to set out upon explorations.

On our first Vineyard New Year's we drove up-Island to call on Mayhew G. Norton in his wonderful old house, unchanged and unchangeable, houses being capable of more reliability than people. He was glad to see us. We sat in the sunshine that poured through the small panes of the old windows and across the clean, painted floors with the rugs of a comfortably old and self-reliant Island. In my recollection, New Year's Day on the Vineyard has almost always been a day of mildness, proof against the change marked in the calendar; and almost always on that day I have seen a robin.

Our year was marked off. The Washington's Birthday blizzard, yet the first crocuses in the nearby yard of Flo and Eddie Pease. Arrival of the advance guard of male redwings at the end of the month or in the first days of March, and the welcome sound of "Kree-ee-ee" coming from around Sheriff's Meadow Pond. Those last few white frosts and the blooming of the myrtle or periwinkle, blue among glossy green leaves. The spring peepers, traditionally known on the Island as pinkletinks, raising their evening chorus to herald April and spring.

The daffodils, in old dooryards and in old fields to which they had escaped, not later than Patriot's Day, the commemoration of Paul Revere, Lexington, and Concord. The dependable spring beauty of trailing arbutus first found on southerly slopes along the roadsides; the shadbush or wild pear, and then the craggy black beach-plum bushes bursting into white prodigality of bloom, a combination of oriental design and New England hardihood. Then the little spring flowers, bluets, star flowers, cinquefoil, and soon around Fish Hook but not everywhere, the robin's plantain. Lilacs for Memorial Day, a host of them, purple and white, blooming separately or in tall hedges, in town and in the countryside.

Summer, with its erratic mixtures of dripping fog, bright sunshine, and sweet-smelling rain, and always the southwester blowing, blowing. August with hot, moist days, and occasional days also of crisp dry northeasterly or northwesterly weather, and ground fogs where the road across the plains dipped into glacial hollows.

The first chill of the northeasters with driving rain, summer people taking fright. The embarkation of Labor Day, golden September, and still more golden October, the year's best month, welcome for brisk late swimming, a grand reprise of warmth by day and easy coolness by night. The bright limb-torches of the swamp maples as they turn to reds, oranges, and yellows along with persisting summer green. The deep red of the tupelos, the massed ruddiness of sumacs and huckleberry thickets on the hills.

November and the opening of the scallop season; catboats going early out of the harbor, bleaker northeasters and warning drops of temperatures, but not yet a killing frost—not before Thanksgiving, anyway. Then, of all marvelous things, true Indian summer, thoughtful, tender, and wistful weather smoldering with the haze of Indian campfires of long ago and with the thoughts of youth.

At last the early darkness and lighted streets and shop windows and houses away on the hills or bluffs; the snow-feeling but no real snow yet, only perhaps a brief dusting; cold night air under the bright, bright stars, and Christmas.

New Year's and anyone's guess as to the first hard freeze, the blizzard, the January thaw. Perhaps skating on the ponds for a little while, or even iceboating in an occasional year. In the old era in which we still lived, the cutting of pond ice and storing it in vast gray-shingled icehouses. Town meetings, entertainment gotten up by schools, churches, clubs, or other community groups. And again the Washington's Birthday blizzard.

Now again March and April, days of spring offered and snatched away, the season advancing, retreating, all fits and starts, spring fever and sniffles, then raking, painting, and cleaning up, the redwings around the pond, the blue myrtle flowering.

We were travelers on an annual round of experience, making the same ports, never without a freshening sense of adventure shared by town and Island. We saw each season many times, reflected in the faces of fishermen and carpenters and the shopkeepers of Main Street.

Betty and I built our own house in 1928, when we were advised we shouldn't, what with building costs at an all-time high, and the widely recognized inferiority of materials. You couldn't depend on anything. We had planned to spend $10,000 on a seven-room house copied after the white Greek Revival dwellings of Edgartown, but the final cost came to about $13,000 after all possible economies. We borrowed $8,000 from the Co-operative Bank and still owed a great part of it after the original twelve-year term had passed.

But our plan had been to pay for the house by renting it in the summer season. Rentals were high in 1928 and 1929, and a house like ours would bring, say, $1,700 or $1,800 for a three-month season; or not even three months—just as likely only ten weeks all told. Our expenses in some small, modest, rented place, would be a fraction of that.

But lifting ourselves by our bootstraps didn't work out even in the distorted economy of the late 1920's. First there were the niggling details of work and the increasing inconvenience of moving out and in, the unexpected costs of housekeeping and care at both ends and even in the middle, and at last the depression arriving without grace. Summer rentals dropped, and many houses were not rented at all.

Still, we had our white house, sitting sidewise in its field for the sake of a southern exposure in winter and a northerly view of pond and Sound all year; and time, we hoped, would take care of the debt. We faced upon a rural way called Pierce Avenue, after Dr. John Pierce, who had lived in the big square house at the upper end; after the way was widened and surfaced with blacktop it became Pierce Lane. An irony here suggested to me the design of a novel, *The Road*, which embodied variations on the theme of road widenings and surfacings, our own experience thrown in.

Our postern entrance was on Sheriff's Lane, so named long ago for Sheriff Isaiah D. Pease, who owned the outlying acres, the ice pond, and a segment of John Butler's Mud Hole. When we settled here the property had descended to Louis H. Pease, dealer in fish and ice, also a nurseryman, a slight, dependable man of good nature and old-time firmness. He had said to himself in youth that what another man could do he could do; and so he built a chimney when he needed one, and made no bones about it.

On any winter morning we looked out and saw him walking across the brown fields to the pond to measure the thickness of the ice. In most winters the temperature did not fall low enough or stay down long enough to freeze marketable ice, but he had another icehouse on Edgartown Great Pond, where freezes were harder and more dependable.

Sheriff's Meadow Pond would have been a marsh but for a dike, anciently built, which impounded a respectable body of water. The overflow was discharged into John Butler's Mud Hole, a tidal basin in the marsh where herons, egrets, and otters fished, and thence into the Eel Pond, which gave upon the Sound. These waters had their own colorations and seasonal changes one could observe better than any calculated art or pageant.

After the death of Louis Pease, the ice and fish business

was managed by a daughter, Grace Ward, who had built a house near us and near the pond. The last time she cut ice on the pond was at night after a succession of bitter February days. She made regular calls to Mr. Rideout, a weather broadcaster from Boston at the time, and he kept her directly informed of the prospects. At length he warned of a quick thaw ahead, and she turned out a force of townsmen under floodlights strung from long cables and wires, and the plowing and sawing went on as efficiently as if these processes were done every day.

Then the cakes were piked to the inclined hoist which took them to the proper tier of the great weathered icehouse. I imagine the cutting and harvesting of ice would always have been done this way, for I don't know how it could have been further mechanized. But electrical refrigeration was at hand, and within a few years Mrs. Ward tore down the icehouse, and the timbers in it were used to build a dwelling house not far away.

Mrs. Ward lived alone, and we agreed upon a signal by which Betty and I would know if she needed any sort of assistance. She would draw a certain window shade up or down, but neither she nor we could remember which position indicated distress and which didn't. Once or twice I thought distress indicated and went quickly to her door, but she was doing very well indeed. Another time, with the roads blocked, I waded through deep snowdrifts to learn if she needed anything from the stores downtown. She was surprised to see me. There was nothing she needed.

Hers was a long-lived family, and she continued as our neighbor for many years. Eventually Betty negotiated with her for the purchase of the pond and the land around it, a narrow border except for a knoll on the far side. Betty always said that the purchase price of $7,500 came from the sale for that amount of magazine rights to my second newspaper book, *Once More the Thunderer*, and in a sense this was true, for the $7,500 did pay off existing debts and provide a start for the complex and ingenious financial operation Betty contrived, an operation I never felt I fully understood. Anyway, it worked, and we owned the pond and whatever of Sheriff's Meadow went with it.

In view of our circumstances, we agreed that we would sell off the knoll on the far side and recoup as much of the purchase price as possible. Of course we never did sell it off. The whole beautiful and primitive domain was too important to us, as it was to the muskrats and great blue herons.

We even borrowed $7,000 later on to acquire additional acreage, part of the former Sheriff's Meadow estate, which extended the preserve as far as Planting Field Way. This was a sort of blue-sky speculation on our part, for it was based on Sterling North's sanguine prediction about the sales of *Great Days of Whaling*, which he asked me to write for his North Star series of juveniles. The book never did supply any sizable fraction of the $7,000, but we retired the notes in fewer years than at one time seemed likely. By this time World War II had ended, and the first wave of postwar inflation was immensely helpful to us and others like us. Money was really circulating! We had forgotten that in any practical sense it ever could.

Owning Sheriff's Meadow Pond and its neighboring land, and having no aim for it now except the dear aim of preservation, we consulted naturalists and conservationists about what we should do next. We learned, of course, that neither an Audubon Society nor any other nature or conservation group could be responsible for a lot of small sanctuaries, no matter how desirable. If we wanted to give Sheriff's Meadow Pond away, we would have to give an endowment along with it. This was true even though everyone who saw the pond, John Butler's Mud Hole, and the waters beyond, strongly urged the importance of such an estuarial region, an importance out of all proportion to its size.

So Betty and I thought for a while and talked for a while, and then established the Sheriff's Meadow Foundation, presenting to it the pond, the knoll, and every natural prospect. Our good friend Arthur W. Davis at the courthouse submitted his bill for the legal expenses: "To services forming charitable corporation, $75; to services writing deed, $10; to services recording deed, $15. Total, $90." I suppose this is a minor landmark, but nevertheless a remarkable one in the history of conservation in America; where else was such a foundation ever set up for $90? But there was never another Arthur Davis. "Ecology" was a new word then, and Arthur, Betty, and I discussed its meaning, Arthur probing deeply into the subject, as his habit always directed.

The Foundation's charter was issued on April 2, 1959, and its notice of tax-exempt status was dated Sept. 27, 1961.

The purposes: "To preserve, administer, and maintain natural habitats for wild life on Martha's Vineyard for educational purposes and in the interests of conservation; to acquire, receive, and protect such natural areas so that they may serve as living museums and as means of assuring to the future generations a knowledge of the natural endowment of the Island of Martha's Vineyard and of similar terrain in New England; and to co-operate with other agencies in the field of education and conservation to further their aims as much as possible in the public interest."

It hadn't occurred to Betty and me that the scope of the Foundation would grow, but it did. Sheriff's Meadow neighbors, Ferris and Marion Angevin, Alida Gulick, and the Morton Feareys extended the sanctuary boundaries so that it included more marginal land, the whole of John Butler's Mud Hole, and two beautiful acres of sequestered swamp bordering the Fearey place. Other natural areas were given, until at the close of 1973 the Foundation held title to a pattern or system of open spaces representing many different aspects of Island character—upland, shore, woodland, marsh, and traversing brooks—with a total area of more than 750 acres.

The popularity of this remains in question, despite the

support and enthusiasm of environmentalists. It was expected that assessors might grumble a bit over removal of property from the tax rolls, even though surrounding valuations were increased. But we learned that as nature abhors a vacuum, so people abhor empty and unused nature. The Island's able and energetic representative in the General Court said to the Rod & Gun Club, "Nothing makes me madder than people who put birds, deer, and other animals ahead of the pleasures of people."

I think Terry would be less likely to advance this view in serious argument than most of the others who hold it, and certainly he did not speak as a villain, but expressed what I am sure is the voice of the age in America at large, as on the Vineyard.

"Service" and "price" are the concepts that have meaning today. What offense can be greater than to have land used for *nothing?*

Betty and I had not aspired to philanthropy, but I think now that any approach to philanthropy had best be avoided by people of moderate means. Think carefully before you give anything away, especially land; you may be in for a hard time, and what trouble others do not think of will surely be carried to your mailbox or door, year after year, by the Internal Revenue Service.

Bill Brine, one of the Island's most active land-dealing entrepreneurs, warned me on the telephone the other day that if "we" keep on "stockpiling land" it will wind up sometime as garbage and rubbish dumps.

Betty was all for planting trees, exercising foresight I wouldn't have been up to. My range was more on the scale of tomato plants, such annuals as snapdragons and verbenas, and perhaps early peas and Golden Bantam corn. I didn't even go for roses until she goaded me into what became an addiction. For years afterward our place was abloom early and late, rose beds in front and at the side, climbing roses wherever a place could be found for them.

As to trees, Betty said that people should not stop planting elms. I said, "Where shall I plant them?" She said, "Well, we don't want the house too much shaded. How about there and there and there?" I planted as she suggested, and her offhandedness soon turned out wonderfully.

In early 1974 I went out to measure the girth of the greatest elm, a towering giant planted as a slender pole not more than six feet high in 1934. I wound a string around the trunk at a height of three feet above the ground, and the measurement came out nine feet, four inches. An experienced tree man came by a year or so ago, looked at the elms, and asked, "Do you fertilize them?" "No," I said, "do you think we should?" "Heavens, no!" he exclaimed.

But all our trees have had recourse to lawn and garden fertilizing and watering through all the summers. Betty's advocacy of elms was typical of her acts of faith, and an act of faith is always blind. How will it turn out? If you could know that ahead of time you could well dispense with the faith.

Dutch elm disease reached the Island years ago, but it stayed away from Pierce Lane until last summer, when a great branch of one tree began to wilt. Dick Mansfield came around and administered a new fungicide by injection. Wonder of wonders, the elm, minus one infected branch, which Dick removed, kept its health for weeks. Just as we began to feel safe, another telltale wilt appeared. Dick tried the fungicide under pressure, and the tree appeared to recover. The following spring, which happens to be now, its leaf buds are swelling. We shall see, and meantime I must have some of Betty's faith.

What with the heavy shade of all the trees—elms, red maple, lindens, tall oak, white fringe tree, dogwoods, and so on—and an ancient mulberry at the gate which pioneers planted in the hope of raising silkworms—our premises drifted into a shady, lazy aspect. A gardener, standing outside the fence looking in, remarked, "This must have been a beautiful place once."

A *Gazette* innovation of our early years was a column of observation or comment or anything timely or lively which could be run under the heading "Things Insular." This column continued to be a favorite of Betty's as long as she lived, and much of her love, humor, awareness, and sometimes bitterness, went into it.

"Things Insular" comes from "A Ballade of Islands," written by Lucy C. Bull, of whose further identity we knew nothing. Her Ballade begins:

> I would I had been Island-born.
> I dearly love things insular.

That was at the beginning and has continued through all the years. Other things kept coming up.

During a period when fights were held in the rink at Oak Bluffs, and prior even to a later time when women wrestlers were imported, we learned that the fight promoters—Mike Keegan was one—had been told that their featured bout couldn't be held, yet had gone ahead selling tickets anyway. We reported the imposture, as we considered it, and I thought we were serving the public pretty well.

After the paper was out, I went into the barbershop on Main Street and mentioned the matter to Ed Gentle to learn what he would say.

"Oh, those fellers done the best they could," he remarked, and I detected an accent of reproof.

Many a long year later, during the Ervin committee hearings, I witnessed a television session during which the man named Barker was asked why, since he had found no document in the category he had been instructed to photograph, he went ahead and took pictures anyway.

"Well," he said, "I did the best I could."

It was while I was writing this that I read Howard F. Stein's essay in the *American Scholar* on "The Silent Complicity of Watergate." "Not moral absolutism but moral mendicancy in leadership is what an equivocating electorate needs to maintain the stability of its way of life." The larger public must have it both ways, an outward profession of rectitude and a tacit need to keep open all ways of profit. There's always the marketplace voice, often raised by the best people, too: "Oh, lay off the poor son of a bitch—he done the best he could."

I have heard Scotty Reston say he believes in the goodness of people. I suppose it's there if you dig for it, and if the occasion is right, but I would never lay any money on it, especially on the sort of goodness that requires commitment.

Ahead of goodness comes selfishness or cupidity or whatever you wish to call it, even if it is only protection of the fortress "I"; and then weakness, the avoidance of commitment—"let someone else stick his neck out"; and then sentimentality that evokes a festival of sympathy for a run-over cat or boy but does not respond to the slaughtering of millions or the ravaging of distant lands by devilishly ingenious means of warfare. Even a Lieutenant Calley stirs pleas to the White House, and the White House responds with gestures of palliation.

We do not now live in an age of goodness. There is a lot less of it around than when I was a boy.

It didn't really matter about those fight tickets, though, and Mike Keegan's feelings were only slightly hurt by our story in the *Gazette*. There was a good attendance at the fight, minus the feature bout, and nobody asked for any money back.

In the late 1920's, times being pretty good in New Bedford a little longer, and the education of his sons having been paid for, my father began the custom of going on winter cruises with my mother. He had earned that freedom in his long career with the *Standard*, and a voyage on a freighter was no more expensive than staying at home during the cold months. They didn't go to London or Paris or Naples, but they did go to the South Seas, the Indies, twice to Australia, to New Zealand, once around the world, and once they were slightly shipwrecked in the Black Sea.

For New Bedford, though, even a moderate prosperity was running out, and a depression of the city's own struck before the Great Depression of the world outside. Climate was no longer a unique advantage, and the better wage scale at last won for the textile operatives became an incentive for the mills to move south for cheaper help.

Long ago I had heard my father discussing with my mother the implications of the word "nepotism." This came about because nepotism was one of the ills of the New Bedford cotton mills—the descent of control and management by favor of family relationships, a practice carried over from whaling days. Most New Bedford cloth, too, was sold as "gray goods" to be finished by converters and specialty houses, to be retailed under their own trade names. Only Wamsutta sheets and Beacon blankets had an identity in the marketplace. I went through the Butler Mills with Max Schuster and he asked why the mills themselves didn't reach through to the buying public.

"We don't need to" was the answer, and Jim Adams, the mill superintendent, went on to show us a new fiber, rayon, which would melt in your mouth but would give gloss and appeal to newly mixed cotton cloth.

The largest cotton mill in the world stood in the North End, fully equipped but silent. Its machinery had never turned. It had been built for the manufacture of fabric for automobile tires, but meantime cord tires had come in. Tire fabric was out of date. When I wrote the history of the Wamsutta Mills for their hundredth anniversary in 1946, also the centennial year of the *Vineyard Gazette*, I mentioned to Ted Broughton, under whose leadership Wamsutta was still great, this anomaly of the idle mill. He took out his pipe, smiled gently, and spoke of that rare quality "foresight."

So New Bedford lost its textile industry as it had lost its whaling prosperity. But there were other reasons for a crisis in the affairs of the *Standard* than the woes of a declining city in a nationwide depression. New generations had grown up, replacing an old culture with what was less a culture than idiom of the commonplace, an attitude, a drift in the faceless age of technology. Differences were subsiding among cities as among people.

The fountain room in the New Bedford hotel, later the taproom, following the repeal of Prohibition, might be called the "Spouter Inn" after Melville, but the hotel was a perfect mate for countless others built in the same mode in city after city. There might be a project for a "Moby Dick Shopping Mall," but John Avery Parker, Abe Howland, Joe Grinnell, and Melville himself were just as effectively forgotten. The old brownstone post office on William Street, with a brownstone owl on one corner, had been peculiar to New Bedford; but the modern pillared granite post office on Pleasant Street was common to any city in the land.

Aside from all else to be contended with, a strongly independent and individual newspaper could not quickly adapt and retrench with the times, cutting salaries, laying off old employees, changing method, proportion, and perhaps principles. So the paper into which so much of my father's life had gone was now at the disposal of bankers and such, the money men. They arranged a sale to Basil Brewer, whose business credentials and successful management in Michigan commended him.

My father and mother were at sea at the time, and Zeph Pease wrote to him an account which may well stand as representing many another newspaper scene during the era of suspensions, failures, consolidations, and extensions of chain ownership:

For the first few weeks nothing happened. No activity in the business department where everybody appeared serene and untroubled. Then last week came the dramatic time. . . . We were all summoned to Ben's room, George and Gaw and I and Jim and Miss Chace and Beriah and others, and Ben in a broken voice, very white and trembling, looking as if he might collapse, introduced Mr. Brewer as the new publisher and manager. Ben had only been told by the directors five minutes before. . . . The expressions on the faces of Murray and Miss Chace, the latter as white as this paper, was tragic, and so was Ben's. It was pretty hard on Jim to break the news to him in the presence of the entire company. Jim sought out Mr. Brewer a little later and asked his standing but did not get much satisfaction. He told me it meant he and Miss Chace would go, but he hung on until yesterday when he cleared out his desk and went.

If anyone wants to know how to kill the soul of a newspaper, this is the way it's done. "Ben," of course, was the son of old Edmund, who had dashed across the Fairhaven bridge to get out an extra the night McKinley died, and grandson of the founder. With him a chapter of journalism was closed for good. Now it was all up to the money men.

When my father reached New Bedford he did not go back to his old desk but made as much haste as he could to get to Fish Hook, where he entered upon a vigorous retirement. My brother, meantime, had moved from the *World* to the *Standard* when Bill Devoll, city editor during my work there, died of influenza. The wear and tear of New York life, subway riding and all the rest, had been an accumulating horror for George, and a return to New Bedford couldn't be resisted.

Now, as an earnest of the future, he acquired the Falmouth *Enterprise,* on Cape Cod, a weekly in a town that was to become increasingly prosperous without sacrifice of identity and attractiveness. This did not dilute the energies George put into the *Standard,* but I believe it was made the principal cause of a break between him and Mr. Brewer. Hanging over all, of course, was the drive during this new day which could be satisfied only by complete centralization of power.

With little regret at the time and none at all through later years, George and Clara and their two young sons, both born in New Bedford, moved to Falmouth and developed one of the best weekly newspapers in the country.

In no great while Zeph Pease died, his tradition dying with him, and Brewer suspended publication of the *Morning Mercury* for good. We had an obituary in the *Gazette*, and I quote part of it as a sort of landmark in my own history of journalism:

The "Morning Mercury" died this week. This is hardly important to most Vineyarders because few of them took the "Mercury," which was a neglected, run-down newspaper under a sprightly, imaginative old name, published in New Bedford by a corporation that did not care for it. Those who wrote for the "Mercury" and edited it cared for the paper, but nobody else did. The publishers said it had outlived its time, which is an easy thing to say.

The "Morning Mercury" first appeared in 1807, carrying a new proclamation by Thomas Jefferson in the initial edition. It reported the rise of the whaling industry and was read in their time by such men of New Bedford as Abraham Howland, great gun of the Barn-Burner Whigs; Honorable Joe Grinnell; Gideon Allen, a whale oil millionaire, William R. Rodman, a go-ahead sort of man who owned a sheep farm in Australia, had whalers out of Le Havre and business everywhere in the world; William W. Swain, martyr to gout but a hero in investments; shrewd and industrious Pardon Tillinghast; and other Howlands, George, James and John, Quakers all. It is a pageant of old New Bedford, and there are no such men on the banks of the Acushnet any more, or the "Morning Mercury" would still be read. . . .

But now it is dead, and to be buried without honor or ceremony in the city it served for so many generations. It is not fitting for a fine old newspaper to pass in this way, and so we honor the "Morning Mercury" here, and the memory of Zeph Pease and Arthur Luce and others who made it so well worth remembering.

Another one-newspaper city was added to the growing number, for Brewer soon brought about a consolidation of the *Standard* and its competitor, the *Times*. This was the new formula for success, and although some might still speak of the "calling" of journalism, as Talcott Williams did, they must mean it in a changed sense.

The *Standard-Times* moved to the extreme right under Brewer control, and there came to be considerable national significance here. Taft aspired to the Republican nomination for the presidency, and Brewer emerged as one of his most dedicated supporters. When Henry Cabot Lodge promoted the candidacy of Eisenhower and took so influential a part in elevating Eisenhower politically at the expense of Taft, Brewer's bitterness against Lodge mounted to a backlash thirst for revenge. He put the *Standard-Times* behind young John F. Kennedy in Kennedy's contest with Lodge for United States senator, and Kennedy carried New Bedford. This may have been the pivotal city—some astute politicians assert that it was—for Kennedy did defeat Lodge to go on his way to the presidency, still with Brewer support.

An aftermath of this, not too indirect, was the construction of a hurricane dike across the entrance to New Bedford harbor at a cost to the federal government of many millions. The avowed purpose was to protect the New Bedford fishing fleet if the conditions of the 1938 hurricane were ever to be repeated. They never have been.

New Bedford had become the foremost sea-scalloping port. The fleet could hardly be protected unless it had remained in port awaiting a hurricane. With improved warning systems, this might be practicable, though, if forewarned, the vessels might not need the dike at all. Meantime, some said, with a good deal of authority, that the Acushnet River and harbor above the dike had been turned into a sewer, and a New Bedford mayor spoke, not too strongly, in view of the financial situation, of a second opening through the dike to provide more effective flushing by successive tides.

My father, so long an activist, had become pretty much an onlooker, but an ardent one. One evening at Fish Hook, listening to Tom Dewey, he remarked, "No one could vote for

that man unless he disliked Roosevelt as much as I do."
Another night and another Dewey speech, and my father
exclaimed, "God damn it, I can't vote for that man." He
didn't detest Roosevelt as the Best People did, but more on
personality grounds—the automatic smile, the Rooseveltian
humor, the Harvard accent and manner.

One late fall, when my father and mother were about to
embark on their winter cruising, she complained of a difficulty
in breathing through one nostril. She had no intention of
consulting a doctor, though, and her difficulty continued when
they sailed; it continued still when they were back at Fish
Hook in the spring and early summer. Now she was persuaded
to see a specialist, and by degrees, as so often happens, a
grave diagnosis was made and confirmed—cancer of the eth-
noids and antrum.

All of us should have known, as the surgeon surely knew,
that the case was hopeless after so many months. But the
profession of surgery demands operations, and my mother
underwent one of the cruelest that could be imagined. In the
period of after-care, even the relief of aspirin was rationed,
and she was to be fooled part of the time by substitution of
bicarbonate of soda pills. When, finally, she lay in her own
bed at Campbell Street, the room above the one where I was
born, Dr. Daniel P. O'Brien, long-time friend and family
physician, prescribed morphine. She had no more conscious
pain, but only a few lucid intervals, during which she talked
of her childhood in Holmes Hole. From July to November
her ordeal lasted, and what had been the gain of that
desperate operation?

This was a time of my rediscovery of New Bedford, which
I had not explored for many years. I walked with my father,
as George walked with him at other times, and we visited the
North End. I tried to find where the Athletic Field had
been, with the Bull Durham sign in the outfield, and the short
field where I had watched Rabbit Maranville, his speed and
famous basket catch, when I was a boy. Brooklawn Park,

Daniel Ricketson's old estate, was no longer beyond the city but had been surrounded and engulfed.

Some years later the New Bedford fire department wanted to burn Ricketson's house for practice. I subscribed $25 to a fund to save the house, doing this for Thoreau rather than for Ricketson, and at the time it was rescued. Whether it still stands I hesitate to inquire.

With my father on these walks I also tried to find where the first circus lot of my memory had been, but I failed. We walked across the Jean Bridge near the head of the Acushnet River, and across the Coggeshall Street Bridge, past the ruin of one demolished cotton mill, through Fairhaven on the other side of the river and back by the central bridge, construction of which had been a marvel of my childhood. It had become a constant roar of automobile traffic, a channel of speed and hazard in what had been a peaceful crossing of a peaceful river.

In the center of New Bedford old stores had disappeared, some that remained were dressed with modern, shiny fronts, and chain stores and discount stores were strung along in the shopping district. I missed the lettering high on the yellow brick side of the Household Furnishings store which had puzzled me in my boyhood: "A Dollar Down, a Dollar a Week."

I had become an outsider of all outsiders, a native son returning in jealous retrospect and a certain unrewarded longing. I had become, moreover, a prejudiced historian. All the same, this was the depressing ruin of a city that had once been fair.

Another time, many years later, I returned to New Bedford when I was writing the centennial history of Wamsutta. That was when I drove through our old block on Campbell Street as if, in two or three minutes, to review again the first eighteen years of my life. No more vacant lot across the street. No more Jamie Blossom or Frank DeTerra or Brick McDermott or Killigrew boys. It would have been a mistake for me to stop, for time had not stopped, and what was gone was gone forever. I did not even pause to see whether the sweetbriar rose of my mother still grew in the side yard.

We took my mother to Vineyard Haven, and when all was ready at the grave in Oak Grove cemetery in the morning, we saw the North Tisbury neighbors approaching through the bare November trees where they had been waiting. They were all there, standing a little way off, beside the grave. So my mother was buried in the same ground and not far from Captain Henry W. Beetle, Eliza Ann, the nameless infant boy, and dark-eyed Aunt Ettie; not far, either, from Uncle Press and Aunt Addie, and Uncle Ben, and Uncle Garry.

Gone now was the past that lived in my mother; and the usages of her past; familiarity with ships that sailed close-hauled, or lay off and on; with winds that backed in or came around, and with the right time of day for clearing weather; memories of Uncle Press and Uncle Ben; sayings offered wryly or otherwise, such as "A lie well stuck to is better than the truth wavering."

My mother had been born in the presidency of James Buchanan, and in the month of her death we reported in the *Gazette* the election of Franklin D. Roosevelt. The span was long and I thought of it as awesome, but I myself have lived from Grover Cleveland to Gerald Ford.

9

In the late fall and early winter of 1933 I wrote a history of Martha's Vineyard as a summer resort for publication serially in the *Gazette*. I began with Bartholomew Gosnold's visit of discovery in May, 1602, regarding him and his gentlemen voyagers as our first summer visitors, and went from there to Nathaniel Hawthorne's sojourn in 1830, when he talked with a philosophic stonecutter about the propriety of graving an epitaph for an infidel. I paid closest attention to the camp meeting in the oak woods that became Wesleyan Grove and eventually the foundation of Cottage City and Oak Bluffs. I found a good many first-hand sources, including Theodore Wimpenney and James E. Chadwick.

After the history had run in the *Gazette* I submitted it to a publisher, who rightly judged it too detailed and local for book publication for a general audience. Accepting this, I arranged to have it privately published nevertheless, borrowing the money. It seemed an appalling amount—an edition of 2,000 copies, 1,000 bound in cloth, 280 pages, including twenty-four pages of illustrations, for $1,500.

I neither gained nor lost financially, but in recognition I

found unexpected reward. I sent out review copies, expecting little or nothing, but Ralph Thompson devoted one of his daily columns to it in the New York *Times:*

Every once in a while an important local history puts in an appearance. We have such a one today in Henry Beetle Hough's "Martha's Vineyard". Though it concerns but an area of 100 square miles, and an Island at that, it is in a real sense of wider scope, and deserves the attention of those who would understand nineteenth century America.

Nothing came immediately of this review, but in late 1937 I sailed with my father on a cruise to South Africa aboard the rusty World War I freighter *West Isleta.* James A. Farrell, Jr.—"Jim," to his many Vineyard friends—told me that she was the first vessel he ever bought. Since my mother's death, my father had taken his two grandsons on winter voyages, and had made some alone. He and Betty urged me to be his next companion and, mistakenly, I went. If anyone was born not to travel, it is I. I understand that the home of man is in the cosmos, but I belong on Martha's Vineyard.

We were to have sailed from New York, but departure was shifted to New Orleans, whither we went by train. From New Orleans to Capetown required of us the slow tribute of thirty-one days, including a stop at Trinidad, where we took on asphalt in drums, loaded by conveyor almost directly from the asphalt lake. It happened that Trinidad had significance for me precisely because of that lake.

At Parker Street School, circa 1910, I had been introduced to something new—a book on commercial geography. Several of the illustrations remain as clear to me now as then: the Trinidad lake, the stockyards of Chicago, the above-ground cemetery at New Orleans, and the big hole at Kimberley. By the time I had reached home from this voyage, I had seen them all and had no reason for any further travels whatsoever. I had fulfilled so much—really all, if I have my way—of my appointed itinerary here below. Incidentally, when you walk on the asphalt lake it does not stick to your feet; and it fills up again as fast as asphalt is dug out.

The cruise of the *West Isleta* was advertised as the world's longest fair-weather voyage, and this proved an honest prophecy. Only for one rough last day did I stay in my bunk, and even then emerged to see a great albatross keeping us company overhead, and the Southern Cross so bright in the sky.

When the engines stopped at last, I wakened and went on deck to behold Capetown revealed in the blue of coming dawn, the stars still shining overhead, the lights of the city glimmering under the straight line and mass of Table Mountain. I had not then read my grandfather's letters or I would have marveled at what he must have seen and did not write about.

We were met by an agreeable young Englishman representing a tourist company with which my father had had previous dealings. He took us in hand, and I soon added to the unfortunate reputation of Americans traveling abroad. Most certainly, I should have been left at home. I remarked on the fact that at the huge, busy railroad station in Capetown one could not get lunch until the stroke of noon.

"Would you expect to get lunch at any hour you happened to feel like it?" asked Mr. Piper.

I was in too far to back out. I said, "Yes."

Worse still, two attractive young South Africans of English descent were speaking of the excellent reputation of an express train scheduled between Capetown and Johannesburg. They said proudly that it always ran on time. I heard myself saying, without the least harmful intent, "Why wouldn't it run on time? It only runs once a week."

Then there was the time on a scorching-hot day in Kimberley when we were lunching at the Queens Hotel and I asked for a glass of water. The waiter had to make a special trip to the bar to get it while all the Englishmen, sipping their hot tea, looked at me with cool surprise and disapproval.

From Capetown we journeyed northward across the Great Karroo to Bloemfontein, tree-shaded and lovely, lying close to a native "location" of blazing ocher sand and low galvanized iron huts. In Bloemfontein we saw Margaret Wycherly in the movie version of *The Thirteenth Chair*, and the next time I saw her was in the flesh when she uncannily opened the front door of the house on the Vineyard where Ida Wylie and Dr. Louise Pearce were staying.

We peered into the big hole at Kimberley, bigger and deeper than I could have imagined. We stopped at Bulawayo, with its wide streets, and drove to the Matopo to see the grave of Cecil Rhodes, who had called this place "World's View." A barren view, I thought, and not enough distance to justify the name. Our driver, even then, expressed the opinion, fatalistically for him, that the blacks would one day repossess their land.

We reached Victoria Falls in the afternoon, registered at the hotel, and walked a short distance to view the falls, passing by the way a few baboons walking in the opposite direction; that deep, twisting gorge runs more than a mile in length and 355 feet in depth, sending up in mist and rain "the smoke that thunders." As we walked back to the hotel my father said, "Now we've got that behind us." On the hotel porch we watched the Englishmen, with their sundowners, flipping ice cubes out of their glasses.

Of course we did view the falls again, and more of them, and went across the bridge into Livingston and acquired dark wood animals carved by the Borotsis. Our waiter at the hotel was a handsome young Borotsi who asked where we were from. We said, "New York," and he smiled and said, "That's a long way."

We were in Pretoria on a Sunday, and a Sunday-quiet city it was. We visited the grave of Oom Paul, which my father had seen before but did not tire of looking upon. He was delighted that the tall hat of Oom Paul's statue in front of the railroad station served as a birdbath, the hat having no lid or top. The jacaranda trees were in blue flower, and the Parliament buildings stood aside in stately serenity.

Then to Johannesburg, modern city of Witwatersrand gold, where we stayed at the Carlton, which served no breakfasts before 8:00 A.M. but sent up breakfast things to our room when we had to catch a seven o'clock train. Then to Durban, on the Indian Ocean, a favorite city of my father's, its deeply indented bay filled with shipping, where we also saw the rickshaws and the ocean resort beach, and went by sightseeing bus to the Zulu reserve in the hills. A chief, after having been viewed by the tourists, stepped behind one of the huts and put on his pants.

By car we rode to Umtata, native capital of Pondoland, and stayed at a curious-looking hotel where we met a Conrad-like English character before taking a bus to Port St. Johns. We forded a river and rested for a day or two in that scene of river, mountains, and sea; but I did not swim in the Indian Ocean until we got to Port Elizabeth. There was nothing different about it from our own ocean at home.

We reached Capetown again by the Garden Route, which goes through a town named George and a resort called the Wilderness where stinkwood trees grow. Then it was embarkation again. By wireless we were instructed at sea to proceed to Halifax instead of to New York, which meant that we went directly through the Sargasso Sea and could watch the Sargasso weed idly floating.

We went to a movie in Halifax but it turned out to be an animated cartoon and we were so bored in a few minutes that we went back to the hotel and to bed. The picture was Walt Disney's *Snow White*, which we hadn't heard about because of our travels.

That was the spring of 1938. In the fall came the great hurricane, refuting the experience of living men and women, bringing a kind of consternation unknown to twentieth-century

Martha's Vineyard. Violence flailing inward from the south on a warm wind? Nothing seemed more unlikely.

I had gone that afternoon to a council meeting of the Dukes County Historical Society in the Squire Cooke house. Marshall Shepard was there, and Ulysses E. Mayhew, who, as a boy, had shipped on one of the whaleships burned and sunk by the Confederate raider *Alabama*, and put ashore on the island of Fernando de Noronha off the coast of Brazil, past which the *West Isleta* had closely steamed; and Emma Mayhew Whiting, as remarkable a woman as Betty and I ever knew, a farm wife proud of being one, and a historian of energy and infectious interest. She began a history of the Vineyard wives who sailed on whaling voyages with their captain husbands, and when she died before its completion I went on from where she had stopped. Present also at the council meeting was Francis A. Foster, at the time secretary general of the Society of the Cincinnati, a retired country gentleman of historical predilections.

During our meeting the front door of the house came open. It didn't seem to have been blown open—it just opened. I shut it again, and we went on with our history. A bit later, when I got back to the *Gazette* office, Betty told me that Columbus Iselin had telephoned from Woods Hole and that an entirely novel and tremendous storm was heading up the coast toward us. The ancient Squire Cooke house had known about the storm before this scientific word. In fact, the wind had already freshened by this time.

Betty and I went down to the sloping lawn of the Mayhew house above the harbor and watched the might of the Atlantic come streaming through Katama Bay and the harbor like a river of unimaginable proportions. The main force of the winds passed us by, but the tide overwhelmed the fishing village of Menemsha and left wreckage of piers, boats, and houses wherever land met sea.

The hurricane of 1938 was to stand as one of the two or three biggest stories of our *Gazette* experience, but that of 1944 proved bigger because in that year the Island was spared neither violence of wind nor violence of sea. The storm came late on Thursday, and as we quit work on the next day's paper we said to one another, "Either it will be all right, or it won't be." There was no use in trying to work through the night—and even if we should try, we would not be able to report the storm expected to break around us.

At eight o'clock there were flashes of blue lightning like a stage effect on a grand scale. Tree limbs began to shudder, and we heard far-off blustering in the sky. I went outdoors and picked our yellow apples from the tree. Night blackness came on more quickly than usual, the wind roared, and I took our collie Matrix out for a walk in Pierce Lane. Suddenly the pale trunk of a dead tree decided to lean over and collapse on the ground. Flickers had nested in that tree, and I was sorry to see it go.

Two fields away a mother and her three-year-old baby were still in a summer cottage, and at about ten o'clock I went with a flashlight to escort them to our house. The storm was rolling and tossing, shrieking and thundering in the sky—and the baby went to sleep.

This was our great adventure with disaster. When I started downtown in the morning, climbing over fallen trees, someone said, "Have you seen the water front? There's nothing left." But there was a good deal left in spite of all the havoc.

Electric current, of course, had failed—it wasn't to be restored for a week or ten days—and Bill, Everett, and I took the *Gazette* forms to New Bedford and finished setting type at the Reynolds printing plant there; then we were off to Plymouth to print the paper on the press of the *Old Colony Memorial*, which was identical with our own. We lost track of the war news and of all else until at last we were back with the completed edition.

Our next most serious hurricane occurred on a Saturday. Betty and I, home from the office, sat in our kitchen listening to the radio. At last an announcer said, "I have goods news for you—the hurricane will pass out to sea over Nantucket and

Martha's Vineyard." A few minutes later the radio failed and the hurricane had arrived. At noon the wind subsided, the sun came out, and we walked down to the harbor, now unnaturally, cloyingly calm and serene. "Torpid" was perhaps the word for it, and the air seemed tropical in its sudden warmth. Adults as well as children were wading, poking into this yard or that, remarking on damage here and damage there. We were in the eye of the hurricane.

Then the wind rose again, this time from the northwest, and blew harder than before. Our two greatest elms were canted over, and our yard again filled with storm wreckage. But the elms could be pulled almost straight again by Grant Brothers' truck, and by this time the aftermath of a hurricane had become a sort of rehearsed experience.

The later years of the 1930's somehow came to be a time of steadier awareness and of getting ahead for the *Gazette*, though the depression continued and nothing seemed to have changed for the better. We were inured, I think.

We employed summer reporters, not because of increased prosperity, but because they wanted to be summer reporters and wanted to write, and would work enthusiastically for about five dollars a week. Who they were: Joan, Barbara, and Polly Woollcott, daughters of William and Marie Woollcott and nieces of Alexander; Caroline Rabell, who would have become a woman lawyer but got married first; Bill Attwood, later successful journalist and writer, traveling companion of Adlai Stevenson, editor of *Look*, ambassador to Kenya, publisher of *Newsday;* Howard Young, scion of a summer family who took to newspaper work quickly. These in the 1930's and others after World War II. How could we have been gifted with such youth and ability and the later reward of lifelong friendship?

World War II, of course, would be interrupting. But before that I had written *Country Editor* and also a novel.

I had been fooling around for several years with the idea of some sort of country newspaper book, and on the strength of *Martha's Vineyard, Summer Resort* had gained an agent and friend, Harold Matson, who said what I ought to write was a book of the genre of *The Story of San Michele*, relating my own experiences. *San Michele*, though, so overawed me that I did not know where to begin. Presently Bellamy Partridge's *Country Lawyer* came out, gained sales of 40,000 in a short time, and the open season for "country" books was on.

Hal wrote to me, "You're an author though you don't know it." He had agreed with Doubleday, Doran, as the firm then was, for the book that was to become *Country Editor*, though everyone tried to think of a better title; and what I must do was to go to New York, lunch with Hal and the Doubleday editor, Jim Poling, sign the contract, and get on with the book.

This was the autumn of the "phony war," when, after the fall of Poland and the declarations of war, nothing seemed to be happening. Maybe the Maginot Line really was impregnable, maybe General Gamelin really was a military genius, maybe hostilities would somehow stop where they were. Meantime the fall weather on the Vineyard was as golden and relaxed as always, a breathing space in the progression of the year. And the *Gazette* experienced weeks of good feeling, without emergencies or anxieties.

I wrote at home each morning until ten, Betty managing without me at the office. I finished 150 pages of the book in ten days, which was not remarkable since I had so much collected material, sketches, notes, abortive essays, and so on. Doubleday liked the finished manuscript and planned to delay publication until August to allow for elaborate promotion. Before August, though, Hitler's armies had swept through Holland and Belgium, and on to Paris. There had been the historic withdrawal of the English from Dunkirk, and Churchill had uttered his "blood, toil, tears and sweat" speech to his own people, to Hitler, and to the world. The time held little promise for a quiet book about life on an island with a weekly newspaper, priced venturesomely at the high figure of $3.50.

Nevertheless *Country Editor* brought front-page reviews in the New York Sunday *Times* and *Herald Tribune*, window displays in New York stores, and more favorable attention than I could have anticipated. It also brought an appearance for me on the radio program "Information Please," on which, to say the least, I did not excel. After the program Hal Matson and I sat at a table in the sunken terrace of Radio City, had a drink or two, and felt the ease of the city on a warm Manhattan night.

The novel I wrote a little later. I had sold a short story to *Esquire*—"Jacob Smiles on Fortune"—based on my impressions of a black youth at Port St. Johns, and of the odd little hotel there. An editor of *Dial* wrote to ask if I would care to submit an idea for a novel in the same vein, and I did; but he didn't like my outline well enough. Eventually I went ahead anyway, and Doubleday published the novel under the title *That Lofty Sky*.

Lewis Gannett liked it. He wrote in the *Herald Tribune* that it might be read "as a semi-philosophic story of the slow, unconscious de-Nazification of a young Nazi . . . or as a sunny, somewhat sentimental love story set against a gorgeous South African background; and young love has an infectious quality, in and out of novels. But if you start reading, you will find yourself carried, eager and chuckling, from chapter to chapter, primarily because Mr. Hough seems to combine the inventive qualities of P. G. Wodehouse and Robert Nathan, both of whom are masters of plot, fantasy and style."

He went on: "This is a lot to say for a book. Perhaps it is too much. . . ." Well, of course it was too much, but Betty and I loved having him say it, and it would be heartening in harsher interludes ahead.

I had taken the young Nazi from a group of young Germans at Capetown, on leave from the cruiser *Schleswig-Holstein*, which was there on a training cruise. This was the ship that later fired the first shells of World War II into the fortifications of Danzig.

"In the parliament of man," James Russell Lowell wrote, "every man represents a constituency of the past."

My constituency, as anyone may see, is one of the rottenest of rotten boroughs. Three decades of my active life, generally taken as the span of a generation, are accounted for by a few stillborn years in the 1920's, the Great Depression, and World War II, followed by an anticlimax of inflated expectations and inordinate desire. Few votes can be counted on from such a past, an era mostly of aberrations, part of the American experience, not mere patches on the American myth. No wonder I am on the losing side.

Yet by contrast with today the depression proved a good time, good to be remembered. Its virtues might be compared to those of sleeping in a heatless bedroom during a bitter winter, but they were virtues and not without satisfactions. We of the Island were more than reasonably self-sufficient. City people envied us, and a good many came to the *Gazette* office and asked if we had any jobs for them.

Betty and I ate lunches day after day at the restaurant on lower Main Street run by white-haired, ruddy-faced Mr. Hallowell and his competent, heartily old-fashioned wife, who, together, had been the crew of a coal barge in coastwise transport. They had answered a Help Wanted advertisement for a postmaster in Chilmark, the office going along with a clerkship in a general store.

One day we had beef stew, a steaming bowl of it, rich with cubes of beef, for twenty-five cents; then followed in daily sequence haddock or cod chowder, clam chowder, quahaug chowder, all at the same price, and back to beef stew again. For a nickel we could have a wedge of Mrs. Hallowell's cream of banana pie surmounted with lofty meringue. The only thing was that the pie had to be fresh; left over for a day or two it would lose heart. We had to find out its age by guile, not wanting to ask Mrs. Hallowell direct.

"Simplicity" Thoreau had said, and for a while many people

who had never known of him followed his injunction in important, necessitous ways.

I wrote to Betty, on a visit to Baltimore in 1933, reporting on the finances of the *Gazette:* gross receipts 1932, $15,792.58, 1933 $15,981.62; salaries and wages, 1932 $12,855.13, 1933 $11,733.56; net loss, 1932 $2,612.56, 1933 $633.10.

"Of course," I wrote, "not all the $15,981.62 of the gross income has been collected, and not all of it ever will be. The outstanding accounts are a little higher than last year—something more than $8,000." Our happiness may have been of a Micawber type, but it was genuine. Since we were at the office all day, I kept the house locked against the meter reader for more than six months and thus deferred payment of the electric bill. This stopped being a good idea on the day the bill finally had to be paid.

The *Gazette* finances did not encourage enterprise, but we had a certain amount of enterprise within ourselves, and Bill and I went up to Boston to see about trading in our old Model L Linotype for something better. The down payment would be relatively small, and we could trust to luck for the installment notes.

There were two possibilities then, the Linotype or the competing Intertype, which followed the same principles and appearance but had been designed as a simpler machine. I liked the Intertype and I think Bill liked it well enough, but he was reluctant to go back on the Linotype Company and its New England sales manager, Mark Boynton. This matter was settled when we saw on Mr. Boynton's office wall a framed certificate attesting that he had made a hole in one. Bill decided that he belonged to an advantaged class, freeing us to choose as we liked.

We contracted for the Intertype, a matter of such importance that Ray Daigle, Intertype sales manager for New England, boarded a train for Philadelphia and delivered the order in person. The N.R.A. codes had just gone into effect, and I think we were set back about a thousand dollars on the allowance we might have received for our old machine. We charged this up as a contribution toward the reconstruction of the national economy, a sample of the American tradition of levying on little people to keep big people going.

Our complaint against the N.R.A.—which was intramural in any case—amounted to nothing compared to the conservative resentment against Roosevelt, and oddly enough we who were generally for Roosevelt, although I voted once for Norman Thomas, benefited from this resentment. A retired engineer ran a series of front-page advertisements in the *Gazette* pursuing a theme set forth in the first one, "Arming the Magistrate." The phrase was Thomas Jefferson's and F.D.R. was the magistrate who was certainly being armed.

Sprigg D. Camden, of West Virginia, calling at the *Gazette* office, remarked that Connie Lee was going overboard on the anti-Roosevelt line. But when we tended to agree with him he said, "Of course I look upon Roosevelt as a very dangerous man."

The wife of the "Arming the Magistrate" man said to Betty, "Don't you think it's terrible, our selling all that silver to Japan, or buying it, whichever we do?"

Our house wasn't paid for, but we owed on that to one bank and could borrow $8,000 from another bank in 1939 toward acquiring a new and adequate office. The occasion came about because at last there was an opportunity to buy a pre-Revolutionary house at the corner, only one door removed, bordered at the side by Davis Lane, known to generations past as Davis Strait because of the noble stream into which it was turned by every heavy rain. We had desired the property, and at last it became available because of the settlement of an old estate.

In recent years eight families had lived in the house and had given it the popular name of "Beehive." But during the Revolution it had been the home of a militia captain, Benjamin Smith, and later of Isaiah Mills, a Noank fisherman. We removed a big modern addition at the rear, which our architect referred to as a rabbit warren, constructing in its place a roomy shop under a trussed roof which eliminated any need for interfering posts. We respected the integrity of the old house itself, subjecting it to no more indignity than the removal of one first-floor partition to provide a spacious editorial and business office. After relative harmony for a few years the two were separated.

Betty used a big shovel to break ground for the shop that fall, lifting a generous hunk of black earth, and we moved into our new quarters in March with a glorious housewarming attended by more than 500 Vineyarders who, we were sure, came in friendship.

Now we had not only an efficient office but also one that Roger Baldwin and others could term the most beautiful newspaper office in America. It must be toward the top, anyway, with its symmetry of age, weathered shingles, eight fireplaces, and a lot of contributing eloquences.

We lived then in conflict, as everyone did, walled in by the depression and threatened by rumblings and events abroad. Hitler and Mussolini held our future in suspense. The march into Austria occurred in March, 1938, while my father and I were at sea, and in September Chamberlain had returned from Munich waving his umbrella and proclaiming "Peace in our time!" How much time would that be?

Donald Tarr, minister of the Edgartown Methodist church, arranged a series of forums, with which we helped him all we could. Rabbi Israel Harburg, of Lynn, spoke on "Racial Animosity, Its Cause and Cure." He said Germany was more truly represented by Thomas Mann than by Hitler. It was reported that this was the first appearance of a rabbi in an Island church pulpit; if so, it wasn't the last.

Donald launched another forum series in March, 1939, on the theme "Toward a Christian Democracy." When another minister, Opie Eskridge, of the Federated Church, stopped at the *Gazette* with his church notes, he and Betty, and I if I happened to be on hand, seldom missed talking of war and peace, and the threatened tragedy of World War II.

Yet we were at peace. In May Mrs. Mona Worden poked her head inside an open window on Davis Lane and reported that there were seven different kinds of warblers in the newly green maple tree across the way. Summer came with little difference in our outer lives except scattering events such as an address in Donald Tarr's church by the Reverend E. A. Turner, who had been for four years pastor of the American church in Berlin. He spoke on "This Bewildering Germany." And summer passed.

Ezra Bowen, leaning against the fence at the corner of Main and Summer, asked me if I thought war was inevitable. I said yes, I did, and so did he. He talked of the nature of sovereignty and the jealousies of power. The attack on Poland may have begun already, events had moved so fast. The next day, Friday, everyone knew, but just the same we put a paragraph on the first page of the *Gazette* for the sake of history.

On Sunday evening Chester Lane, general counsel of the Securities Exchange Commission, spoke in Donald Tarr's church on the topic "Democracy in Crisis." He said, "Even though the machine may run us down before it gets through, our lives are still our own for a little while at least."

After we left the church I sat with Eddie Greenbaum, later General Edward S. Greenbaum, to listen to the President's address over a car radio. I wanted to hear something like Roosevelt's "again and again and again" campaign speech—none of our men to fight overseas; but of course there was no chance of that. I asked Eddie what he thought.

"That's all he could have said," Eddie replied.

Betty and I went to the dog show out near the Oyster Pond, run for the benefit of Miss Katharine M. Foote's Animal Rescue League, and our copper-colored collie Matrix went best of show, judged by John G. Bates, former president of the Westminster Kennel Club. Life as usual. Presently we were asking editorially for balance in thought and speech: balance, not indifference. I wrote earnestly to Congressman Charlie Gifford, and he replied that he intended to remain neutral in his own thoughts until all possible evidence was in. I wrote to Senator David I. Walsh, who praised the "impartial and patriotic tone" of my letter and promised to read an article by Charles A. Beard I had recommended. I knew, of course, he wouldn't.

A circular letter came from Pitkin, a call to peace in his pungent style in the name of some organization or other, offering antiwar stickers for a price. I sent a check, but Pitkin had already gone on to the "American Majority" movement, which had as its slogan "We Who Pay Demand a Say."

Opie Eskridge, as president of the Island Pastors' Council, planned a mass meeting for neutrality and peace. He asked our help in finding an appropriate speaker, and we turned to McAlister Coleman, that outgiving friend of ours and the common man. He tried but didn't hit upon an answer. We wrote Pitkin, who said it "was hard to pin the good guys down" and added: "I may sail up this fall to see you before I go south in my schooner. Got 8 feet of water at low tide near your Linotypes? If so, set out a mooring buoy for me early in December."

His "W.B.P." signature filled almost half a page. His active spirit must have shot ahead again, for he couldn't have been planning to take the American Majority on his schooner with him. For a speaker we finally got Dr. J. Max Weis, director of World Peaceways, which had been running full-page ads in the *New Yorker.*

The mass meeting took place in the Tisbury school auditorium on the Sunday afternoon following Armistice Day, the Island clergy almost in unanimity seated along the front of the platform. A sunny afternoon on the Vineyard, our lives, our awareness of the distant thunder, a crowded hall, a talk—a gesture of hope rather than of faith.

Yet had not Roosevelt in Boston, near the end of his election campaign, uttered his "again and again and again" declaration to which I have referred, declaring that "your boys are not going to be sent into any foreign wars." Mrs. Roosevelt the next day showed greater candor: "No one can honestly promise you peace at home or abroad. All any human being can do is to promise that he will do his utmost to prevent this country being involved in war."

The Willkie campaign had been vigorously pressed on the Island, with big advertisements in the *Gazette:* "Do You Want a Dictator in This Country?" Willkie would carry the Island, of course, but the Democratic strength was growing. We worked all night and got out our third and last election extra with three banner lines at the top of the first page and a huge "Roosevelt Wins Third Term" at the bottom in what Bill called "horse type."

Russia invaded Finland, inflaming anti-Russian feeling again, but, for all the outrage, this was a side show of a war. The great confrontation remained in suspense through the winter, and the late fall had been warm and sweet. I wrote an editorial, "Our Own Reality," and our own reality was what we hoped to attend to.

We joined Donald Tarr in a forum series, "How Can We Improve Our World?" and in February Frank Aaltonen, a ruggedly typical and persuasive Finn, talked of the co-operative movement in which he had worked for many years. The co-operative idea made progress on the Island, the Rochdale principles were examined and approved. Dr. James P. Warbasse, elder statesman of co-operatives, came from Woods Hole bringing a mixture of practicality and missionary zeal. Ironically, the result proved to be a retail co-operative store rather than the fisherman's marketing co-operative we had hoped for. As Carey Luce put it, "They went into the grocery business."

That period—so much hoped and worked for, nothing apparently foreclosed, Islanders coming together to talk and plan— might have been the most fruitful of our *Gazette* experience. It is too bad that in the long accounting it came to nothing. The threshold could never quite be crossed; then the war and postwar prosperity launched us all into modern times.

10

Everyone knew that Katharine Cornell, quietly and characteristically, was giving of herself for the human needs of wartime—especially those who had seen her in predawn bleakness, breakfastless, bound for New Bedford to give blood to the mobile unit which at that time could not come to the Vineyard.

Then, for her friend Laura Johnson, who ran the express office in Vineyard Haven and now headed the U.S.O., Miss Cornell, her husband, Guthrie McClintic, and her friends Nancy Hamilton and Brenda Forbes, put on a U.S.O. jamboree in the Tisbury school gym. What a willing, bursting, happy show that jamboree turned out to be—also a bit of stage history spun out of Martha's Vineyard's friendship and good will.

Miss Cornell sang for the first time in her professional career —"and the last time," she said then. She sang "Lazy Days," the words by the abundantly gifted and spirited Nancy Hamilton, the music by Morgan Lewis. The *Gazette* spoke of her shy, friendly smile, her wistfulness, and the little gesture with which she finished. No one was likely to forget the three on the stage together—Miss Cornell, Guthrie, and a young actor not yet much known, Gregory Peck.

Nancy Hamilton sang "My Day," a parody of Eleanor Roosevelt's column, and Brenda Forbes, fresh from *Mrs. Miniver* in the movies, sang, cockney fashion, "Oh He Shouldn't Come to Bed with His Boots On. It's the Little Things of Life that Bother Me." And Freda Cohen did something called "Birds Which May Not Be Shot in Massachusetts."

A master of ceremonies named Bob Hawk provided the linking moments that bound all together, and the show bubbled its own gifted way from first to last, with Katharine Cornell shyly and effortlessly lovely.

All that was long ago. So I write now on a foggy morning in 1974. Graham and I have walked to the white lighthouse tower at the end of the causeway from which the lights of the town showed indistinctly, apparitionlike, reminding me of the gaslights of New Bedford in my boyhood. Long ago and a mythic time.

Strange to think of a traveler bound for Martha's Vineyard and, having asked in Grand Central Station about the boat schedule, being told, "Madam, we can't give out that information. Don't you know there's a war on?" Cuffs were ordered off men's pants in order to save cloth, and fertilizer was late in reaching farmers because the bags had to show pictures of vegetables instead of flowers.

The newness and strangeness of wartime overtook us as we tried to live our ordinary lives still. Joe Allen joined the State Guard, Bill Roberts was appointed to the Ration Board, Betty took the Red Cross course, and both of us became airplane spotters at the post up beside the standpipe on Mill Hill. So often there at night, winter and summer, we were to listen to the landing craft at practice in the harbor against the time of the invasion overseas. And we saw bluebirds in the snow, flying from thicket to thicket; and the town basking in sunlight or starlight, blue harbor aglitter.

I kept a journal and wrote in it that the first rosa hugonis was in blossom, and Everett labored mightily with an item which turned out this way: "Clifford Fisher has returned from his trip to the mainland. He attended funeral services for his brother in Edgewood, R.I. He also enjoyed a day at the horse races." That was the week the government commandeered the largest Island steamer, *Naushon*.

And again: "A misting morning but still a fair one because the dark purple iris are out and the flowering crabs are covered with blossoms. . . . Jared Vincent's boat has been taken by the government. A hard case. The boat was just what Jared wanted, and the fruit of long years of work."

"Clarifying questions and answers" came from C. D. headquarters:

Q. If a community in the past has sounded an audible signal on the "yellow" signal, may it continue to do so?
A. No, the "yellow" signal is a non-audible confidential signal. (see par. 18)
Q. Do the regulations prescribe a public, audible All Clear signal?
A. No, a public audible All Clear (white) signal is not prescribed nor can one be used unless it is sufficiently differentiated from the prescribed "Blue" and "Red" signals so as not to be confused with either.

At a Civil Defense meeting it was decided to have wardens blow whistles for the All Clear signal, but Abner Draley, C. D. chairman, said they would have to be ten-cent whistles. He wouldn't approve fifty-cent whistles for the purpose.

I wrote in my journal:

The temperature was 25 at 7 o'clock but now it is 35 and warming up steadily. Heavy white frost and a chill haze in the air at breakfast time. . . . Saturday night I took Grace Morris to Mrs. Orr's, where there was a preliminary meeting looking toward a series of classes on the identification of planes. When we arrived Dr. Wilson was explaining why such a course was not only unnecessary but likely to be harmful. This was the way the meeting went—it was a cold water session. Dr. Wilson is bearish on the intelligence of some observers. He cites with wrath the query Christine Pease made at a meeting at which Dave McBride, chief observer, was explaining how to report a plane you have seen, and one you have only heard. "What do you do if you have neither seen nor heard it?" Christine asked.

On Friday morning Dr. Cosgrove came into the office. He wanted to know if we would have room in the "Gazette" for some articles preparing people for the great tasks to come. What he had in mind was nothing political but a treatment of fundamental things, going back to the nebular hypothesis—"the world in its gaseous state"—and coming on right down through, so simple that anyone would grasp it. . . .

A grave and saddening time, too. The *Gazette*'s own Douglas Brown had gone into the Navy. He had started working for us part time when he was in high school, playing basketball and getting high marks, too. He had a chance for a scholarship but no money, so he began learning the trade of printer. We liked him. He was good looking, with crisply curling light hair and blue eyes. He sang in the Federated Church choir. Then he joined up as a naval aviation cadet, and it turned out that he was going to college after all, though for special training. He sailed along close to the head of his class and was chosen as one of several exceptionally promising boys to be finished off in a hurry as navigators.

He came back to Edgartown a few times, and finally we saw him in his ensign's uniform, gentleman navigator, and still the same friendly Doug with the shy smile. He said good-by to us, to his mother, to his girl, and went away. The next we knew, he was in the Pacific.

He flew as navigator on one of the giant planes on a long photographic mission, and when it was necessary to make an emergency landing he figured the position so accurately that rescuers were ready as the great plane went down. The others thought Doug had got out with them after they struck the water, but he was never seen again.

Out of the scrub oak of the Island's central plain a Navy flying field was cut for the training of carrier pilots. We didn't always get along with the imported personnel.

Low-flying planes over the Island had become a nuisance, and one morning I noticed that the wind vane atop the Federated Church steeple had been bent. I wondered aloud to Ed Vincent, who happened to be going by, whether a Navy plane had struck it. Ed grinned and said he didn't see what else could have happened. We printed an item suggesting the possibility, even the likelihood, after which a public-relations officer came hurrying down from the field with an indignant protest.

Following a change in commanding officers, the *Gazette* came out with a wrong subhead in the story of Commander Webster's departure, something about a New Year robin redbreast. It sounded derisive. Someone had put four lines of corrections in one galley instead of three in one and one in another.

The hottest free-for-all of words in our *Gazette* experience came when a Navy wife about to depart from the Island sent in a communication berating Islanders for exploiting their wartime guests. The communication was signed with a pseudonym, but we didn't know that at the time. A resident newly established with us replied to the Navy wife with counteraccusations and slurs almost abusive. The storm was up. From all sides the letters came. For a week or two we published them all, some written in fishwife anger, some haughty and above the battle, and many chastising the *Gazette* for airing the controversy. An indirect result was that Betty and I made some friends among the Navy men and their wives.

Then there was the war of the Armed Forces against Ed Vincent. The Army had leased a tract of lonely plain land near the ocean and began landing great quantities of pipe on the town wharf and trucking them to the plain, where, as it would happen, Ed Vincent pastured his cows. The Army told Ed it would be all right; he could put his cows out and take them in whenever he liked.

That was in the afternoon, but by evening the sentry lines had been advanced and Ed was ordered to halt until he got a pass from a lieutenant. Ed said he had no intention of asking for a pass to go on his own land. The sentry threatened to shoot. Ed told him to shoot, he was going for his cows anyway, and he did. Meantime the Army had taken down a good deal of fence.

"It wasn't the best fence in the world," Ed said, "but it kept the cows in. It would cost $500 to put up another. I went down to look around. I figured it would be the last look I'd have at my land. We saved a few posts and a little barbed wire and let the rest go. I decided to try to forget about it. I'm too old to begin building up new land."

All that mysterious pipe, we learned afterward, was for training purposes, to be laid again and again through the South Beach surf in preparation for similar pipe-laying across the English Channel to provide gasoline for our invading forces. But the British had developed a system of their own, Operation Pluto, which was the one employed.

Then it came the Navy's turn to confront Ed Vincent, for the Navy built an immense plant near the South Beach, intended for quarters and for a firing range, including tracks that would run with a target among bunkers and sand piles. This was never used, because the hurricane of 1944 moved in ahead of the naval aviators and their support. Just the same, the war with Ed Vincent continued until, after the end of hostilities overseas, the Annapolis football squad arrived by submarine for early fall practice on the Vineyard. In the name of sport a harmonious agreement with Ed was at last concluded.

Changing times as recorded in my journal:

Betty went to the Legion show Wednesday night and heard, among other things, Buddy Minstrel sing "God Bless Ameriker." Someone in the audience yelled, "Where's your teeth?"

Fair but rather gray after the rain and still only a little above freezing. Went to see Miss Annie Mayhew for facts as to Will Mayhew's obituary. . . . When the low-flying plane came over on Friday, Eldon Willoughby, the wounded parachutist who had jumped in Sicily, leaped out of bed and yelled, "Jesus Christ! Son of a bitch!"

This p.m. went to see Mattie Modley with Marshall Shepard to view a drawing dated 1847 of the Mayhew family tree done by Frederick Mayhew which Mattie wants to sell to the Historical Society. "You ask her what she wants for it," M. S. said. I asked her. She said that whatever the price was she would throw in a piano that had belonged to David Davis. After more talk I asked her again. She said that whatever the price was she would throw in a set of antlers her father had brought around Cape Horn—etc., etc. At long last she thought valiantly and brought out her price— $1100. We excused ourselves and departed.

Mrs. T. A. Dexter improving at the M. V. Hospital after having been at the point of death with pneumonia. She has asked for some special crackers and a lively detective story. She told Alice that the turkey dinner was good at the hospital but she missed the turnip and squash she would have had at home. Meantime Tom, the sheriff, has had eel stifle for dinner, breakfast, supper, breakfast, and again dinner—and at last he said to Alice, "My eel stifle seems to be all gone."

At Fish Hook that remarkable man, my father, did his own chronicling of the war in the log. He had now reached his mid-seventies with undiminished spirit. Sometime before this he had acquired the Ephraim Allen house as an extension of the Fish Hook domain, and he was now prompt to offer it for the use of the Army on maneuvers.

This was how it went:

The war is on. Awakened at 5 a.m. by the roaring of motors of boats and planes, and shots in the direction of Seven Gates sounding like the Fourth of July. Out of bed before 6 and put on my hip rubber boots and went up on the hill. Nothing to be seen but hundreds of boats in the Sound and planes overhead. . . . Detachment of soldiers—the invaders—came to the house and I guided them over to Indian Hill. Later a jeep arrived with two lieutenants seeking the way to Gray's Beach. Rode over to my boundary line with them. . . . Virginia Berresford came down for supper bringing a big casserole of jambalaya of her own composition. Superb! Three soldiers turned up as we were eating supper and asked for water. "Had you rather have beer?" I asked. They preferred beer and consumed two quarts. Open house for the Army at Fish Hook. Had a jolly hour with them until Virginia had to leave before darkness in blacked-out Chilmark. The boys lingered and started for camp in the dark. . . .

Awakened at 7 a.m. by the arrival of a big military truck. "We're lost," the driver said. Pointed him on his way. Went to the Allen house to express my sorrow to General Keating whom I poisoned. He was taken violently ill Tuesday night and attributed his illness to the water and asked to have it boiled. It smelled like sulphurated hydrogen. Investigation revealed a dead rabbit and two dead rats in the Allen house reservoir. Mary DesChenes and her family had been using the water for nearly a month so I did not feel culpable. . . . The war ended tactically at 10 a.m.

So different and long ago now were those innocent summer days when my father took us all to the Chilmark hills to watch a squadron of the Great White Fleet firing over the sea. History unobserved takes long hurdles.

The Army came back in October, and it was then that Lieutenant General Lesley J. McNair watched a practice invasion of Martha's Vineyard by landing craft crossing Vineyard Sound. General McNair, commander of all United States forces, was soon to die in Normandy. The room where he slept in the Allen house was marked with his name.

Meantime the Army fixed my father's ailing radio, removed boulders from his road, placed itself as much as possible, from generals to privates, at his service. Drinking Scotch with the Army on the front porch was his pleasure.

When he had no guests, preferably young guests, and when no unusual events impended at Fish Hook, he sank into gloom, loneliness, and even despond. At each departure in late fall he expressed a conviction that he would not live to return the following spring. But he did return, and fresh interests revived him. I come upon entries in the log about Betty and myself:

Read H.B.H.'s latest story in the Sat Eve Post, "Nearer to the Heart's Desire" and didn't enthuse. I am very, very proud of my son and like to see him in the money, but the Sat Eve Post technique of which he is a master doesn't appeal to me. To bed at 10.

Not so much money and not so much technical facility as all that, but the money did help. Later:

Thrilled and proud to hear a radio broadcast of a dramatization of H.B.H.'s story, "Nearer to the Heart's Desire" over the Blue Network. Perfect reception over W.B.Z. A laugh for his father and his wife when he was described as the great American favorite writer of love stories.

This was a weekly promotional device to boost the sales of the *Saturday Evening Post*. I didn't write many love stories, but the stories the *Post* bought of mine were love stories.

Benedict Thielen—"Bob" to his friends, emphatically including my father—wrote of him as an "Unforgettable Character" in *Reader's Digest*, and this is his description of Fish Hook in my father's later retirement years:

Like one's first glimpse of a crowded museum, it is slightly overwhelming. On the living room walls there are, among other things, a dried snakeskin, a Maori dancer's charm from New Zealand, a swordfish sword, ship's papers signed "A. Lincoln", a strip of Batik from Sumatra, a painting of the famous New Bedford barque "Catalpa", and an outsize Christmas card from Denys Wortman showing Mopey Dick and the Duke under a crate labeled "Greetings to George A. Hough." Between a boomerang from Australia and a dried wasp's nest hangs a signed picture of a bishop, and farther on there is a picture of a clown—memento of a vacation once spent traveling with a circus.

Bob Thielen wrote his "Unforgettable Character" in September, 1951, and my father lived a little more than four years after that, afflicted with Parkinson's disease but spending all the time he could at Fish Hook. He suffered a stroke there on Columbus Day, 1955, and died the next day at the Martha's Vineyard Hospital, having lived only a few weeks short of eighty-seven years.

The war years were set aside in friendship which filled the war-decreed gaps in what would have been the activities of normal life. Lacking the war, it is unlikely that W. Somerset Maugham would have come to Edgartown, and completely unlikely that Edgartown would have had claim to the world premiere showing of the motion picture made from Maugham's novel *The Moon and Sixpence*. It was a benign conjunction, too, that brought Curtis Moffat, who had known Maugham well in London and addressed him easily as "Willie." And not a bit less, Francis and Signe Hackett, who had also known Maugham in England.

Maugham, of course, was easily recognizable. I thought something about his mouth and at times the expression of his eyes signaled the sensuous, darker side of his character. He was affable to us, and Betty thought, accurately, I'm sure, that he considered himself a wartime ambassador of good will to America. The winters he spent as a guest of Nelson Doubleday in South Carolina, and a bridge-playing acquaintance, a woman who knew Edgartown well, recommended it as a place where one could manage nicely without an automobile.

Maugham liked his bridge. He didn't see what you could do when you became old if you didn't play bridge. He was sixty-nine then and liked to describe himself as getting to be "quite an old party." I asked for an interview, and he invited Betty and me to dinner at the Yacht Club. My interview was on the adulatory side, for I admired Maugham as a writer and story-teller, and still do, and naturally he liked it.

But we wouldn't have seen so much of him if it hadn't been for Curtis and Kathleen Moffat. Curtis, really an American, had come to America to see his mother and had been prevented by the war from going back to London. As to what he had been there, I learned later when Kathleen sent us a copy of *Museum Piece* by James Laver. Laver wrote of fine arts and also of London's "literary and gastronomic activities," including the Wine and Food Society and the Saintsbury Club. He wrote:

> Involved, in his casual way, in all these affairs was Curtis Moffat, the well known decorator. . . . He lived in Fitzroy Square in a flat with what seemed in those days a startlingly modern decor. But his real interest was food and drink. He was softvoiced and modest; and I suppose the most complete Sybarite I have ever known. His taste in claret and the fineness of his taste buds were remarkable.

Laver wrote of a dinner given by Richard Wyndham at which five splendid clarets were provided, "of which the two most outstanding were both pre-phyloxera vintages. And as we were sipping the first, Curtis Moffat said, 'Oh, but Dick, you've got them out of order. This is not the Lafitte 1874; it is the Margaux 1870.' It was even so; and I had to ask myself how many times one would have to taste these wines—and how seldom ordinary people would have had a chance to do so—in order to identify them with such certainty and precision."

Transport, now, this Sybarite, as Laver termed him, to a stool at the counter of Captain St. Clair Brown's dog wagon, so-called, at the wharf at the foot of Main Street in Edgartown late on a June evening in 1942. We all had lobster—Curtis, Kathleen, and I—except Betty, who never ate it. The lobster was excellent, and Curtis slipped up to the Harborside Liquor Store and returned with two bottles of a white California wine. No corkscrew was available at Captain Brown's. Not at all disturbed, Curtis announced that he would open the bottles with a cleaver. A formidable cleaver was brought by Eleanor, the pretty waitress. The method, Curtis said, was to strike the lip of the bottle sharply with the cleaver so that the head of the bottle would come cleanly off.

In the next few minutes he paused several times to address a bottle with the cleaver in the manner he had described, making a few tentative passes that caused Betty and me, and I think Kathleen, to shrink back in apprehension. At last, without hesitation and so quickly that we hardly saw his motion, he delivered one precise stroke, severing the bottle top cleanly and perfectly.

Curtis and Kathleen not only accepted Edgartown; they opened themselves to it. Kathleen taught classes for air wardens and Curtis planted a garden, cultivating one summer all possible types of lettuce and tomatoes. This wasn't easy in a dry season, and he carried water in jugs to keep his plants growing in a plot set aside for wartime gardens.

Betty and I were guests of the Moffats one night when they

were staying in the big square house at the head of Pierce
Avenue. But first we went to Mrs. Alfred Edey's, overlooking
the Eel Pond, for cocktails and to meet Mr. and Mrs. Harry
Scherman. Later, when we arrived at the Moffats', the other
guests, Mr. and Mrs. I. Richmond Hoxie—Pat and Eleanor—
and Maugham were already there. Presently Curtis remarked
that the Schermans had so insisted on having their regards sent
to Mr. Maugham that "I'm afraid I asked them to come in later
for "coffee."

"The only Sherman I know is General Sherman, and he's
dead," said Maugham.

Betty remarked that Mr. Scherman was president of the
Book-of-the-Month Club.

"Oh, those Schermans," said Maugham, and went on to tell
how Harry had been a clerk in a Doubleday bookshop and
had got this book-club idea and put it over. "Of course, it's a
racket," he added.

The dinner was superb, as always with Curtis and Kathleen.
Betty asked Maugham what he thought about Edmund Wilson
as book reviewer for the *New Yorker*. Maugham said they had
given Wilson a contract and were now debating whether to
pay him $10,000 and get rid of him at once. "Of course he is
one of America's most distinguished critics, but Harold Ross
didn't dream he could be so boring."

We knew but did not mention Wilson's opinion of
Maugham: ". . . a half trashy novelist who writes badly but is
patronized by half-serious readers." As to the Book-of-the-
Month Club, Maugham said he was told by his publishers—and
he advised taking it with a grain of salt, since one is never to
believe everything his publisher tells him—that most customers
of the club would not buy a book in any other way, and therefore represented a new public.

We were still at table when the Schermans arrived. Curtis
liked to linger, even so long that the lingering became a trial
to Kathleen. Curtis rose as they knocked, but Maugham was
on his feet first, saying that he would look after the Schermans,

and beating Curtis to the front hall. Kathleen followed, returning shortly to report that there had been a three-way contest. Curtis had wanted to bring the Schermans to the dining room, she to take them to the living room, and Maugham to have them to himself.

Curtis came back to the dining room alone. Pat Hoxie said, "Why don't we go out on the porch?" And a little later, "We might play cops and robbers and run all through the house."

Curtis continued to be droll in describing how Maugham had taken charge of the Schermans, but presently his resolution hardened. "After all," he said, "this is my house," and he would bring them to the dining room if he wanted to. He did. When Kathleen came down from upstairs, where she had gone to see their daughter Penelope, she found the full assemblage around the dining table; and there we all remained until about ten o'clock, when Maugham suddenly took off, with a few whispered words to Kathleen.

Maugham was working on an anthology, his fifty-third or fifty-fourth book, whereas my second novel, and fourth book, was just appearing under the same imprint. This novel of mine was based on the career of Lillian Norton, of the Vineyard Nortons (though she was born near Farmington), who became the great opera singer "Gigli" Nordica, Lily of the North. It concerned also Joseph Raphael DeLamar, deep-sea diver, remembered by Uncle Ben and my mother, who had gone west without paying his crew for a salvage job off Bermuda, and had come back as the Idaho Monte Cristo. He never won Nordica, but he did marry the beautiful Nellie Sands, daughter of a Madison Square drugstore proprietor, who was known at Cottage City as the Woman in Red. She was pictured in the sensational press as one of the four most beautiful women in the world, the others being the Czarina of Russia, Vera Boardman, and Princess Henry of Pless.

There was much more—too much for me to handle in a novel, but I could have done a lot worse. Maugham wrote to me from South Carolina that fall: "You did not send me a copy of 'All Things Are Yours' as you said you were going to, so I got one from the office. I finished it last night and I want to tell you how much I enjoyed it. I think you have recaptured very cleverly the spirit of a time that has passed away forever. It is very readable, which is what a book should be & I think you have run the parallel stories of Lottie & Van Deveren with great ingenuity. The end is logical and right. My respects to your wife. Yours always, W. S. Maugham."

Of course I treasured this note in Maugham's own hand, and not less later on when I happened to see a piece of his in a magazine in which he spoke of a young writer who had chosen to write a novel about an opera singer, little realizing that opera singers were among the most hackneyed of literary subjects.

One fine August day Betty and I drove Maugham, Francis and Signe Hackett, the Moffats, and Mrs. Nelson Doubleday to Fish Hook, where my father made them welcome in his casual, cordial way. Maugham seemed concerned about the impending arrival from Hollywood of film emissaries bringing the film of his *Moon and Sixpence*.

He needn't have worried. The world's first showing of *Moon and Sixpence* came off as a triumph for him and for Alfred Hall of the Vineyard movie theaters, who showed characteristic resourcefulness. A congenial consortium of newspaper people came for the event, including Marjory Adams, of the Boston *Globe*, whom we had not seen since the S. of J. days in 1918; dark-haired, pretty Elinor Hughes of the Boston *Herald*, and an agreeable cynic from *PM*, then still extant in New York. All celebrities on the Island were invited and practically all came. Katharine Cornell couldn't, but with her unfailing kindness was photographed in front of the movie theater, which did just as well.

Maugham sat on the aisle, far back. One of the film emissaries, a personable and instantly likable young man, asked me to introduce Maugham to the audience. I didn't know whether he would want to be introduced—whether he would be bothered by his famous stutter, though it seemed to give him little trouble—so I asked him. Of course he nodded assent. All I had to do then was to think of something to say. Happily the *PM* man recorded my brief introduction for posterity. I claimed the odd duty of introducing a man "already known to every literate person on the face of the globe."

The evening, Elinor Hughes wrote, was "unbelievably beautiful, for the stars, apparently encouraged by the lack of competition on the ground, were unusually brilliant and so close that it seemed as though a few of them were coming down to see what was going on."

Ida Wylie—more formally, I. A. R. Wylie, as she signed her stories and books—had written that she would like sometime to meet Maugham. Here in Edgartown of all places she did. And at the Yacht Club that night, Francis Bowes Sayre told me he had read *Country Editor* on Corregidor during the black time before he and MacArthur were evacuated to Australia by submarine.

In the matter of friendships through the years, Cedar Tree Neck exerted a benign influence. This promontory—undecided as between boldness and mildness, and achieving a magical, changing blend of the two—gave the Vineyard a point for its triangular shape and its farthest extension into Vineyard Sound. From the high point of the Neck you could look both ways. The Neck was also almost islanded itself by a large pond just to the west, a smaller pond and marsh in front, and the deep bend of the Sound on both sides. From its height, atop an impressive bluff, one commanded a real choice of views.

The sky over Cedar Tree Neck seemed always purposely vast, the air, whether on a sunny day or in dark winter chill, invariably and stimulatingly fresh for breathing. The elements mixed themselves in bracing proportion. Gales from northeast or northwest brought rollers crashing in with slantwise shifting; but the true nature of the Sound at this place of division seemed to be the blue glimmering serenity to which it always returned.

From the shore old dirt roads ran up through the woods, past broken ridges, a tumble of glacial basins and ravines, and at last, after a mile or a bit more, to the smooth open fields and summits above. The native growth included oak, beech, red maple, tupelo, and sassafras, and among the thickets the most fragrant of all wild summer shrubs, swamp honeysuckle and sweet pepper bush.

Always in my day the Obed Daggetts had taken boarders, but this did not mean that they kept a boardinghouse. Their Cedar Tree Neck homestead was an establishment apart. The population at Obed's wasn't numerically great but it always evolved toward distinction. To Cedar Tree Neck came, among others, Pen and Hermine Dudley and their two daughters; and eventually Pen alone until a summer or two before his death. To the Neck came Hiram and Mary Haydn on their honeymoon long ago, fortunately for me making an expedition to Edgartown and to the *Gazette*.

Hiram and Mary returned to the Island often, though not in every year, and when Hiram was editor in chief of Random House he accepted my novel *The New England Story*, with an enthusiasm that rallied my spirit and intention. Hiram was then and continued to be always a towering help and influence for me as friend and editor—teacher, too, for that had been not only his profession but also a deeply living skill and earnestness within his nature. He loomed physically, tall and rangy, looking with humor or almost any kind of eloquence from his large expressive eyes. He remains for me a complete scholar and human being, bringing all worlds together with patience and understanding.

I followed him from Random House to Atheneum for publication of two more novels, *Lament for a City* and *The Port*, which latter I liked best because it was the only one in which I took pleasure during the writing. Then I went with him to the fortunate fulfillment of the publishers of this present work.

He and Mary became tenants of Fish Hook for some years, loving the place well, as they had loved the neighboring Cedar

Tree Neck, and understanding it, too, in a continuing exchange or realization.

With *The New England Story*, Hiram—and Bob Thielen, too—recommended Henry Volkening to be my agent. Henry very soon became my friend, at once one of the most unfailingly helpful and delightful relationships of my life, though his death came after a dozen years. To me these years meant as much as many times a dozen because of Henry's clarifying intelligence in all writing matters past and present, and his gift of laughter, dedication, and phrase. He and Natalie came several summers to Edgartown, where constraint was almost nil among us and understanding flourished. I drove them once to Cedar Tree Neck, and Miss Emma Daggett, who had succeeded to the management and tradition of the place, enlarging and enriching it as well, showed them through the Daggett homestead. I have always been glad the day was sunny; and I have the colored photographs that Natalie took.

The David E. Lilienthals didn't come to Cedar Tree Neck at first, though they were not long in being welcomed as familiars there. Miss Emma, after she knew them well, even put aside her ancestral Republicanism. Events began and fell about this way:

Mrs. Theodore H. Dillon, wife of General Dillon, who was Deputy Chief of the Transportation Corps of the Army in World War II, was a cousin of Betty's. When General Dillon retired for reasons of health, they lived in Edgartown and he filled in as principal of the Edgartown High School, later going to Los Alamos. And there he suggested the Vineyard as a vacation place and refuge for Mr. Lilienthal, then Chairman of the Atomic Energy Commission.

This seemed to point to the Ephraim Allen house, not long ago loaned to the Army on maneuvers. Betty wasn't quite sure, for the house stood in a fairly remote landscape and lacked a good deal in basic facilities. But the experiment was to be tried, and she met the ferry at Vineyard Haven late on a darkening afternoon and guided the Lilienthals to their destination. When she discovered that they had not had supper, she took them to Fish Hook, where my father had prepared one of his split pea soups. The friendship begun then was to last through, and in memory even beyond, my father's life.

Dave's own account of his arrival may be found in Volume Two of his *Journals,* published in 1964: ". . . it was a misty-moisty day, cool, and half rainy and dark. We were met at the ferry by Mrs. Henry Hough, who kept wailing that she was sure it wouldn't do, the house, but the Dillons said we loved roughing it. . . ."

Later, on the night of September 19, 1949, he and Helen dined at our house in Edgartown with the Robert L. Duffuses, those rarely sensitive and wisely articulate friends. Returning to the Allen house, they reached the end of the town road, Norton Circle, and the headlights showed a man waiting, peering against the glare. He was Brigadier General James McCormick, AUS, Director of the Division of Military Applications of the Atomic Energy Commission, and his errand was to report that our detection system had evidence of an atomic explosion by the Russians. Headlines would shortly erupt: RUSSIA HAS THE BOMB. Dave spoke in his *Journals* and afterward of the "Wuthering Heights atmosphere" of that night at the end of the Indian Hill Road.

He and Helen, one summer, were tenants of Fish Hook for a while. But their own Island roots were put down on a shoulder of Indian Hill, where they built a small but adequate house, Topside.

Cedar Tree Neck again: it was there I last saw J. Donald Adams, book editor of the New York *Times Book Review,* onetime reporter on the New Bedford *Standard,* and loyal friend of my father's. We had reunions several times at Miss Emma's, and on the hill leading into Vineyard Haven he had what must have been a unique experience. The brakes of his car failed and he caromed into Main Street in a helpless zigzag, striking five different automobiles before coming to a halt, and without injuring anyone, even himself.

The west beach of Cedar Tree Neck adjoined the Fish Hook beach, and when George and I discovered that, with the new and formidably rising land values we could not hope to keep the Fish Hook property in the family past the first Internal Revenue Service levy of inheritance taxes, Emma, Bob, and Jack Daggett, now the three owners of the Neck, found themselves in the same situation. George and I made provision that, after us, the Fish Hook beach and some sixty acres of woodland ridge, ravine, and marsh should go to the Sheriff's Meadow Foundation; and the Daggetts, reserving the homestead and some ten acres, agreed to sell the remaining 200 acres at a favorable price to be preserved in the natural state by the Foundation.

This venture in environmental rescue could never have been accomplished if it had not been for the counsel and encouragement of Allen Morgan, of the Massachusetts Audubon Society. He said the money could be raised to buy the Neck, and because he said it could be done we had the courage to campaign for funds in the *Vineyard Gazette*, the response was generous, and it was done. But one other help that seemed heaven-sent stands out as clearly indispensable. Fairleigh Dickinson, Jr., who loves the Island well, offered to guarantee thirty per cent of what was needed, for he said that experience showed if you began with a third, you would really be able to make it. We might have fared quite differently without this practical wisdom and this all-important stake at the outset.

So Cedar Tree Neck is, as far as human provision can now go, a sanctuary, a natural heritage, as the eons—and also the generations—have left it. Happily, the generations have left it well. But I know there are many who say, "What good is it? All you can do is take a walk."

Another prized friendship with Cedar Tree Neck associations was that with Whit Griswold, always deeply attached to the Island and latterly president of Yale, and with his wife, Mary. He came first to Edgartown, she to Oak Bluffs, and later, together, they acquired a place at Lambert's Cove, on the

North Shore, not far from the Neck. Whit's uncle was a Daggett boarder.

Among our later reporters was John Molleson, a Columbia S. of J. graduate, who went from the *Gazette* to the New York *Herald Tribune*. Peter Bunzel followed him, first as summer reporter while he was still at Princeton, and then, as was planned, for all year. But his car ran off the road one wintry night and he suffered a serious leg injury, which almost miraculous surgery overcame. Peter, like so many others, was the subject of an F.B.I. inquiry—I have forgotten why. Betty assured the F.B.I. that Peter was O.K., in fact, she said, he had been flown off the Island after his injury with an American flag draped over him.

Peter wooed the lovely Jane Cole at Edgartown. They were married, and quite a while afterward Betty and I stood at the font in St. Andrew's Church to be godparents for Bob and for Jeff Bunzel. The other day Peter and Jane came to Edgartown after a long lapse of years, Bob, now of Harvard, and Jeff, freshly graduated from Exeter, with them. Peter had left the *Gazette* after his accident and joined, first, the *New Yorker*, then *Life*, then the new *Seattle* magazine, across the continent, as editor. Most recently he has been a staff member of the Los Angeles *Times*.

Sometimes one travels far, like Peter, but no *Gazette* graduate has traveled more widely than Phyllis Meras, who, at Wellesley, had seemed destined for a teaching career. She came to us in summer—for she had known the Island from early childhood—and wrote well and discerningly, turning out an incredible volume of good copy, copy that would have been good anywhere; and the *Gazette*, by a sort of mutual adoption, deflected her to the Columbia School of Journalism and a graduate degree. Then it was the Providence *Journal*, a hitch with *Ladies' Home Journal*, editing a Swiss weekly in Geneva for a year, and by progression to the travel department of the

New York *Times*, until she came back to the *Gazette* as managing editor.

Bill Jorden, who did his first newspaper work on the *Gazette*, also went on to Columbia, and to both Tokyo and Moscow—at different periods—for the New York *Times*. He was then in Washington for the *Times*, and now, after an interlude with the papers of Lyndon Johnson in Texas, has lately become ambassador to Panama.

The *Gazette* had Island affairs to look after, but always with a sense of the world outside and what the world was doing. When the McCarthy era came we sat in the manner of Walt Whitman and looked out, and saw ". . . all the meanness and agony without end"—saw, heard, and didn't want to remain silent.

That successor of a free and enterprising newspaper in New Bedford, the *Standard-Times*, supported McCarthy with implacable enthusiasm. Comment in Boston newspapers was muted because of the strength of McCarthyism there. The very atmosphere brooded uncannily. When President Eisenhower finally declared himself, the New York *Times* observed the next day that not a single Republican senator unequivocally supported his position. I wrote to Senator Saltonstall to inquire why, and he didn't answer my letter.

We could feel the McCarthy intolerance on the Vineyard, a division among us. Betty said the *Gazette* couldn't go on in silence; I agreed. No, it couldn't. It must speak out clearly. Oddly, though, we would be speaking out on a national issue for the first time in all our independent years, an issue on which we had no special source of information, nothing to grasp except what came to us directly or indirectly in the press and on the radio, and our own principles and sense of history.

Just about then, Gerald Chittenden, retired from teaching at St. Paul's in Concord, New Hampshire, who had opened a bookshop in Edgartown, arranged an anti-McCarthy table, displaying such books as the works of Tom Paine, *It Can't Happen Here, Nineteen Eighty-Four,* Elmer Davis's *But We Were Born Free,* and, along with many others, Whit Griswold's *Essays on Education.* So we endorsed Gerald Chittenden and his project, denouncing McCarthy and McCarthyism.

We wondered what the response would be. "To me a light seems to have gone out, an old and valued friend has let us down," wrote one subscriber. "Sorry you are so violently anti-McCarthy," wrote another. "I do not like the *Gazette* so violent. I want to argue with you." But another considered our editorial "mild but firm," and a good friend warned that we would face ruthless opposition if we advocated "emancipation from fear."

Then a balance began to appear. "It may come as a surprise to our summer friends that their lotus-eating Island should become aroused by such a non-local issue as McCarthyism," wrote a West Tisbury correspondent. "To some it may have been a distinct disappointment and seeming breach of faith. It seems to me, however, that such expressions as have appeared publicly probably indicate a widespread interest on the Island, and that such interest is a helpful sign of liveliness and intellectual curiosity on the part of Vineyarders."

"More power to McCarthy," said another. "May I be permitted a place beside you to receive a portion of the bricks that are being hurled at you for your failure to approve of a certain man whose name I will not mention," said still another.

So we rode the storm out, more at length supporting us than denouncing us, and it all came right in the end. Why, then, did it seem such a near thing? Perhaps because it really was a near thing for us and for the country, and I wonder about another time and, in different form, of course, another McCarthy.

A week or so after our editorial challenge we reprinted from the New Bedford paper this item: "Senator Joseph R. McCarthy was voted 'Man of the Year' in a senior popularity poll taken in the New Bedford High School publication, 'Student

Highlights'." Over it we put the caption: "News from the Cultural Center of Southeastern Massachusetts."

The Reverend William M. Thompson—Bill Thompson—who had gone from the Federated Church in Edgartown to the United Church in New Bedford, referred to the *Gazette* in his Sunday leaflet, devoting a page to anti-McCarthy views. He added, "Perhaps the above may offend some, but I felt it was about time someone in New Bedford opened a window and let in some fresh air."

Pitkin, in one of his generalizations suited to the age and condition of those he was instructing in 1916, defined three levels of conflict: between man and nature, man and man, and different forces in the same man. There was quite a lot to this.

Betty and I were spiritedly aware that the Vineyard when we came to the *Gazette* was largely involved in equations of man and nature. We liked it that way. Winter storms, seasons for scalloping and swordfishing, harvest time for picking cranberries, a time to pot eels, a time to cut ice, a time for opening Katama Bay to the ocean.

The tone or temper of the Island was fixed by the relationship of the Island and nature entire and in the wild, not always an adversary relationship, sometimes a friendly competition, sometimes in genuine co operation. Forty years were to pass before nature became nothing more or less than a merchantable commodity, usually expendable, and less significant to man than the bulldozer with which he could advance his money-making plans.

Other conflicts, whether new or hitherto variations of the old, emerged full blown: the conflict of customs and manners involving man as a consenting member of a social conformity without real will of his own; the subtler opposition of new times and old times, complicated by differing vistas or surveys and by the fact that it became easier to look at television than in either direction outdoors; the outdistancing of evolution in its slow pace by the quickening of technology and economics, with evolution slowly, surely, and surprisingly fighting back.

Martha's Vineyard underwent a loss of identity in these happy, hapless postwar years, or, if one prefers, gained a new identity as a colonial outpost of the exploited and brazenly prosperous mainland. "There are no islands any more," television pundits said, and they were right.

From that most wonderful of times, time immemorial, the Island character, its people, its ways, its shores and landscapes, had been influenced but never controlled by a succession of individualists in a culture and society oriented toward nature and away from the evolving megalopolis. When one spoke pridefully of the past, one reeled off family names that had been current on the Vineyard for three centuries or almost that: Allen, Cottle, Daggett, Hillman, Luce, Look, Norton, Pease, Mayhew. These names and others that served our pride well enough.

But there was much more to be filled in. Ben Lumsden, the deep-sea fisherman who was elected selectman of Edgartown and ran Bill Cottle's old store at the corner of Summer and Main, came from Canso, Nova Scotia; Captain St. Clair Brown, fisherman and sailing master who went into the restaurant business, was from Freeport, not far from Digby; Captain Claude Wagner, of the schooner *Liberty*, hailed from West Berlin, also in Nova Scotia.

Sam Cronig and his brothers, successful in business in Vineyard Haven for more than a generation, were from the region of Vilna, in Lithuania; Judal Brickman, who built up a remarkable business enterprise from nothing, came from Lithuania also. The Reverend Oscar E. Denniston was from Jamaica and reported the Jamaican earthquake of 1907 for the *Gazette*. In our time he served as pastor of Bradley Memorial Church. "Tailor" Bradley, for whom the church was named, came from Connecticut, directed by visions, as recorded in *Varieties of Religious Experience* by William James.

Jimmy Green, who lived on the West Tisbury road, came from St. Helena. Olaf Carlson, of Middletown, came from

Sweden, and Captain Dan Larsen, of Chilmark, from Aalesund, Norway. Ole Borgen came from Norway also. Then there was German Charlie, whose farm was on the central plain, and Robert Schwemmler, also from Germany, who kept the bakery on Circuit Avenue. Lady Katherine Graham, Mike Keegan, John Bent, Manuel Silva, Jr., Antone King Silva I have spoken of already, and the list of all those others who came from the Western Islands runs on and on.

Ilse Marie Crawley came from Vienna and was once dug out of a snowbank by a nephew of Freud, who married her. The family of William Channing Nevin came from Philadelphia, and the Gay Head Indians, for all practical purposes, have always been here. So, too, with the Indians of Chappaquiddick. Think also of the schoolteacher wives who have come through all the years, from the undefined terra incognita from which schoolteachers come to teach and to wed.

So many of these I have named hailed from islands or sea-coast places. They were drawn to Martha's Vineyard by an ancient kinship, or found the kinship when they settled here. They fitted into the historic homogeneity of Island life and culture and did not mind having the culture designated by the names of Mayhews, Nortons, Luces, and so on.

Three centuries—and the Vineyard was still the Vineyard; and then came the overpowering surge of mainstream America, and the Vineyard would never be the Vineyard again. The conformity of prosperous, forward-looking America allowed few and transitory exceptions to its spread through communications and education, the beacon lights that allowed only a single glare. Phrases such as "tourism," "second homes," "day trippers" were adopted to suggest the terms we were to come to with economics and the mass world.

So much change had taken place already that the old ways were weakened against greater change. During World War II the government decreed that milkmen should deliver milk only every other day. This plan worked all right in an era of pasteurization and electric refrigeration, and the old way was never resumed. The Island milk producers formed a co-operative at last, one delivery system serving them all. But, as standards changed, who really wanted to keep cows any more? So many easier ways of making a living! The co-operative lapsed, and almost everyone buys milk in waxed cartons at the store.

The last deep-legged fishing vessel at Edgartown was sold in 1952, the old fleet of handsome schooners replaced by heavy, factory-type draggers operating out of New Bedford and other mainland ports, making passages easily under power, staying at sea for trips of almost any length. Vineyard farms gradually diminished in size and number, the survivors usually becoming market gardens with roadside stands. Children didn't grow up into farmers any more, and what if they did? There could be no competing with the lush volumes of produce arriving by mammoth truck from the mainland. No more drays, no more local trucking to and from the wharves—mammoth trucks on and off the ferry in unbroken trips from point of origin to destination.

Electric power was no longer generated on the Island but came by cable from a distant plant or network. The Island telephone manager now lived on the mainland. If you paid your electric and telephone bills by check, your check would be mailed to Hyannis or Boston. Centralization, so briefly out of favor during the Great Depression, as one could see now, had more than regained its old ground. Sometimes we had to look at the financial pages of the Boston or New York papers to learn whom we belonged to.

Lighthouses were automated, dispensing with the keepers who had been characteristic of the old times, mediators between land and sea; but the number of state or federal or state-county-federal employees increased steadily with the multiplication of agencies and projects made possible by federal funding.

Vandalism increased from the rare or occasional to the usual and expected. One could no longer with safety leave doors and windows unlocked as always in the past; and vandals were seldom if ever caught. All this in an age of communications that didn't communicate and of education that didn't educate —but watching television catered to a mass appetite, and the conscience of the community could always be satisfied by adding a few more thousands to the annual school budget.

I heard on the radio this morning that Utopia Boulevard was blocked beyond the Long Island Expressway. Of course it was blocked in one place or another; you have to turn off Utopia Boulevard somewhere and it might as well be on the Long Island Expressway. But I did not feel communicated with.

I remember that bright, starry night in August, so warm but also a little cool as you walked through an occasional hollow, the path going down and then up. "Radiological cooling," the meteorologists would say in the morning. The strumming of the cicada and the cry of the black-crowned night heron over-head were lonely but also in an old companionship; the night air was softly fragrant with the scent of sweet pepper bush, bayberry, and sweet fern.

Graham and I completed our walk and arrived home much later than usual. The telephone rang, and it was Rose Styron calling. She said Ted Kennedy was with them—I could imagine his young voyagers from the Cape bivouacking on the wide green lawn near the shore of Vineyard Haven harbor—and would I talk with him.

I had met him once long ago when Bob Carroll introduced us in front of the Coffee Shop in Edgartown when Bob had brought him to the Island to help his brother's campaign for the Senate against Henry Cabot Lodge. Now he came to the telephone and talked of the Vineyard and of his concern to protect its character and quality and resources lest all be changed in the onrush of development. He wondered about some concept that might be found for the purpose, something innovative, perhaps something drawn from the experience of the Old World. Then he added: "I'd be willing to stand considerable heat to do it."

I recognized, as one can at times, that he felt as I did; the Vineyard and the other islands were strongly in his youth, too, from the beginning, though his home port had been across the Sound on Cape Cod.

Preservation had been talked about more and more often on the Vineyard. There had been discussions and even studies. In 1964 a study by the National Park Service brought about by John B. Oakes resulted in a memorandum: "The blight of unbridled subdivision and the inroads of tasteless commercial exploitation are only just beginning on Martha's Vineyard." Maybe this was too complacent, but there was still time.

In October, 1969, the Dukes County Planning and Development Commission, just formed with federal funding, along with the Massachusetts Department of Community Affairs, contracted with the Boston engineering firm of Metcalf & Eddy for a comprehensive study and plan. Meantime the Interior Department took another look: "All preservation is obviously wrong, and all expansion is worse. The question is, how can we preserve an area in its natural state and then see how many people can use it without overusing it. . . ."

That wasn't helpful; when you go at something on the principle of maximum numbers you are under heavy pressure to let in more and more. But it was soon evident that the Interior Department wouldn't do anything at all.

We were in for some noisy, crowding, polluting, uneasy summers. Anthony Lewis, able votary of the Great Pond region of West Tisbury, wrote in the New York *Times*: "Privacy may be the most deeply felt interest. . . . Our parents and grandparents had a sense of space that will be quite beyond our children. . . . But need that mean that everyone has to live alike in an Aldous Huxley world, see alike, play alike? Will there be no isolated places, resistant, hard to reach? Are there no new forms of privacy to be developed? Must we lose variety, that beneficent result of private property?"

But the restlessness of growth and enterprise was on, and the ingrained faith that land was intended to be built on—for profit —found expression in direct and indirect ways. Open space, land, attracted a rising value in the market, no upper limit in sight. Cape Cod was built up, gone the way of "development" except for the National Seashore and an enclave here and there. Where could land speculation profitably feed now except on Martha's Vineyard?

After two years Metcalf & Eddy submitted a report that was, unexpectedly, a confrontation. Dukes County, "one of the few bastions of rural environmental splendor along the eastern coastline of the United States," was faced with clear and present danger from despoilers. The perils were defined: "contamination and loss by overpopulation and misuse; vehicular congestion and noise and air pollution; indiscriminate misuse and overuse of land and buildings; and loss and destruction of its animal and bird life, and danger to human life by people, vehicles, water pollution, and salt water intrusion."

The Commission hadn't asked for this. Federally funded reports are supposed to be bland or, better still, turgid. Had Metcalf & Eddy overlooked the phrase "Economic Development" in the Commission's title? The report struck squarely across the gospel of enterprise and growth and the preference for slick talk; across the shady side of the gospel, too, and the settled folk belief that Martha's Vineyard would always be Martha's Vineyard. Why should outsiders come here and tell us it won't?

So the Commission found "philosophic differences" with the report as well as "differences of opinion related to interpretation and emphasis." This could be translated as "We don't like what you said." A different set of planners was hired, with another infusion of federal money, and the way of enterprise was kept open.

This was how things stood in April, 1972, when Senator Kennedy introduced a bill to establish the Nantucket Sound Islands Trust to preserve and conserve Nantucket, Tuckernuck, Muskeget, Martha's Vineyard, No Mans Land, and the Elizabeth Islands because of their "unique scenic, ecological, scientific, historical, recreational and other values. . . ." The bill was offered as a working paper and it looked toward "maximum coordinate action by state and local governments and private groups."

It wasn't to be expected that those who had found "philosophic differences" with the Metcalf & Eddy report would welcome the Trust bill, but the violence of opposition outran any reasonable prediction. The "elected officials"—a phrase that was to be used over and over as describing a degree of final authority—reacted with stinging resentment because they had not been consulted and because, in the ready-made cant of politics they denounced "federal control." Anyone who knew the Island could distinguish personal animosities, the special interest of "operators" and some of the landed gentry; and there was the silent complicity of which Professor Stein wrote in the *American Scholar*: the "question of threshold . . . precisely the key to the Zeitgeist that encourages and condones what otherwise would be consciously disavowed."

More general causes of opposition might be found in the nature of society itself following the abandonment of liberal education in the schools except for lip service now and then, and the ascendancy of the sales pitch of television. ". . . The objective of most schools, including graduate schools, is social conditioning rather than development of the individual," writes René Dubos in *A God Within*. This is it precisely; and social conditioning comes out as conformity. Whereas "the satisfaction of every want creates a higher want" has presumably been true always in the life of man, this principle has heretofore operated in the slowest of slow motion as compared to the turnover and escalation of today.

No account of the Island controversy could satisfy anyone involved, but what history can record objectively is that in the two years following the introduction of the Trust bill, and the somewhat longer period following the Metcalf & Eddy report, the uniqueness of the Island's rural splendor was lost for good and all. The most that could be said from now on would be "There are still places worth saving." What was gone was the entirety.

The Island had gained a trailer park, grouped condominiums almost on the water's edge, summer homes barely perched above beaches, and such a host of "developments" that they outran ordinary observation. Wherever one went, new dirt roads led off to right and left, in almost every instance to gridiron or strip or spider-web subdivisions and developments, each lot representing not only a future house but prospective automobiles, congestion, and pollution.

The plains that Charlie Brown and Beriah Hillman had debated about years ago were captive to the speculative drive. A summer-resident landowner feared that "federal control" would reproduce the conditions of Fire Island on the Vineyard; but local control, which was the least control imaginable, had suddenly turned Lobsterville, site of the earliest up-Island fishing settlement, into a caricature of Fire Island.

Apart from the heat of controversy, the Trust bill offered no affront to local independence. It established three categories of land use—Forever Wild, Scenic Preservation, and Town Planned—with an administering commission heavily weighted toward local control but with participation by the Interior Department and ultimate effectiveness in land use and planning through the principle of compensation in proportion to the degree in which any landowner's right had been reduced.

It was said later by Senator Kennedy's aide in the matter of the Trust bill that there was "no obvious and compelling reason why the state could not legislatively provide for virtually everything" embraced in the bill. But the state hadn't and wouldn't; and it couldn't politically or any other way scrabble around for enough money—a proposed twenty millions—to support the compensatory land provisions critical in such legislation.

When Governor Sargent and his young Commissioner of Community Services finally got around to framing a state bill, it was, in the Governor's phrase, "a planning measure and regulatory bill, not primarily a preservation bill"—and it had come into existence because the "elected officials" of the Vineyard wanted a countermeasure against the Trust bill. Politics and expediency required that the Governor and his Commissioner deal with the "elected officials" as a true arm of democracy rather than a special-interest pressure group conjoined with the activists of enterprise, growth, and profit.

The new planners hired by the Planning and Development Commission produced in the fall of 1973 "An Economic Base Study," which differed most significantly from the Metcalf & Eddy report in its conventional language and documentation as to what shouldn't have happened but in the past few years certainly had happened. "Any economic expansion in Dukes County must be undertaken with considerable care so as not to damage the natural resources on which the lifestyle and economy is [*sic*] dependent." A man-in-the-street gave his own report: "This is getting to be like some place on the mainland—like New Bedford. That place is bombed out."

"Certainly the seasonal tourist economy, both vacationers and second home owners, is dependent upon the Island's rural nature," the Base Study said. But while this conclusion was being reached, the degree and character of development had been set in train which would change "rural nature" into suburban imitation.

The new planners embalmed their study in sixty-two pages of prose, statistics, graphs, exhibits, appendixes—but Edward J. Logue, talking to the Martha's Vineyard Garden Club, boiled everything down to a simple declarative sentence: "What threatens this Island is greed."

Somehow the experts had never got around to the truth poetically expressed by Emily Dickinson that under the scalpel "stirs the culprit—Life!"

I didn't dream of Betty for more than a year after she died, though I thought I might dream of her when the house was emptiest and the sense of parting so strange and keen. Shouldn't there have been some softening of the finality that death brings, some illusion anyway, some backward look, even within oneself, to tide over the confrontation with the irrevocable?

At last, after a year and a half, a dream came when I had no reason to expect it. Betty and I were both present in the dream, though not in a meeting, but, rather, in some chance moment, some slight fraction of opportunity, oblique, tangential.

I said to her, "Even if you are dead, can't we see each other once in a while?"

"No," she said. "They wouldn't like it."

So I didn't see her even then though we were so nearly together, but her answer was characteristic, because in life she so clearly recognized what was allowable and what was not. She judged of that for herself, no matter what rules, laws, and regulations said. Yet in an odd way our roles in the dream were reversed, for she had told me again and again, "Oh, you're so law-abiding!" The difference was in one's standard, or whether obedience to law and custom made sense.

The dream was an end after the end. I knew I would never see her again, and even in the dream I had not really seen her, though I had heard her voice.

In one of her last hospital stays in Boston she read paperback copies of Lawrence Durrell's *Alexandria Quartet,* and I have the *Balthazar* she held in her hand when Dr. John F. Sullivan came into the room to see her. She had been examined by an oculist, and Dr. Sullivan said he wanted her to stay longer instead of going home with me that morning.

She asked what the oculist had found. Dr. Sullivan, making no fuss or excuse about it, drew a small sketch in the margin of page 19 of *Balthazar*—an artery showing the direction of blood flow until it reached a short stretch that Dr. Sullivan inked in solidly, then the artery again with an arrow showing flow in the opposite direction toward the block. Betty listened and made no fuss about it, either, and I went out, got the car from a nearby parking lot, and went back to the hotel to register for another day and night.

Now and then I take *Balthazar* from the shelf and read a few pages. On page 15 there is a stain, not blood, I think, but some medicine. Also on page 19 Dr. Sullivan had written the figures "8" and "1.2 plus." I don't know what those meant.

Then there was a sunny day in Edgartown when the roses were blooming in our front yard in the beds as we used to have them, and Betty and I were sitting in the warm air. Dr. Sullivan and his family had sailed to Vineyard Haven on vacation in their boat. They drove to Edgartown especially, found our house, and he said, while we both leaned over the roses, "Mrs. Hough's circulation is precarious." I appreciate his kindness still, though I already knew.

The dreams I remember have not been many—only four, I think, that I remember always. Others come up in fragments now and then, I suppose, disappearing quickly without substance. The first was the one with the flying monster that seemed a red lobster with the red feelers that gave it the name whippoorwill for me. This was in the downstairs guest room at Fish Hook, where often I heard the night call of the whippoorwill.

The second was one I recognize now as my first sex dream. I was asleep in my bed at Campbell Street. I have no idea of the year, but I must have been approaching puberty, and in the dream I drifted gently down a river in velvet darkness broken by distant lights somewhere peacefully away. It was my state of perfect bliss that I remember always, continuing moment by moment, beyond longing or misgiving or past or future. When I awoke it was with a feeling of serenity and wonder.

Another dream, the most recent of the four, showed me a train, a few cars drawn by an old-fashioned engine, passing through an untroubled countryside of beautiful hills with copses, slopes, and comfortable distances. The sun was shining, but without glare. In my dream I felt that the countryside was familiar, though when I woke I knew it wasn't, and somehow it concerned a journey back in time.

Hiram Haydn interpreted this dream as signifying—death—though I don't think he was aware at the time that I was the one who had dreamed it. He may have been right, but I think that sex, which had come to me by boat on a gentle river in a velvet night so many years ago, took its departure by train in a late and remembering time of my life.

Of course it isn't accepted that one should speak of any diminution of sexual power, particularly in the male, so long as life lasts. On the contrary, both men and women are encouraged to continue sex acts indefinitely, and if a senior citizen of 100 and 101 can beget a child, he wins world recognition. I regard all this with an open mind, though I doubt if these November and December antics of the elderly can ever be illustrated to any advantage—for comedy or romance or even sheer eroticism—in the pages of *Playboy* or on the screen.

There is nothing in age that can be changed or mitigated by pretending to be young. I am not speaking here of desire, which is eternal; but desire apart from fulfillment, the wooing of life for its own sake, is the true romance of age. Age at last is free. Time shortens and needs to be taken slowly so that the best may be realized from it; lest its precious reality be wasted. I had always disbelieved that parting, for the young, could be sweet sorrow; but for the old, loving or even longing may be sweetness enough when they keep life company on the downward slope.

I had learned that two logbooks or journals of my grandfather's voyages were in the Nicholson Collection in the Providence Public Library, and since the age of transportation, which makes it easy to journey to far places, makes it impossible to travel comfortably next door, I despaired of ever reaching Providence to look at them. So I wrote a letter, and Miss

Virginia Adams, curator of special collections, generously helped me out.

My grandfather had kept a journal on the *James Andrews* from June 14, 1851, to November 2, 1853: so many incidents remarked, most of them mishaps. "Lost two lines, four irons, one lance when whale sounded and fouled line." "Two men down with scurvy, mate sick, and one man with fits." "I shall be very glad when this bark is safe alongside of N. Bedford wharf." "Spanker boom broke, it was half rotted off."

Then at Pico in the Azores he wrote:

> I found no letters from home and what the reason is I don't know, my officers and boat steerers got quite a number. But none for me. I never had but one that wrote much to me and when she stops I have to go without. I hope she is alive and well, feel quite uneasy about it.
>
> Sept. 30 I feel about discouraged. I don't know as I have one friend in the world. It don't appear as I had. I don't see as it is any use for me to try any longer, might as well give it up. I have not anything encourage me at all. Hope deferred has made me sick. Henry W. Beetle.

As I was typing this long-ago expression of my grandfather's despair, the telephone rang at my elbow. A voice said, "Mr. Hough, this is Bruce Colman in San Francisco." Exasperating thing about communication—too much, too little, once in a while just right. San Francisco is a lot farther away from Martha's Vineyard than Pico, in the Azores, where the *James Andrews* dropped anchor in 1853.

We waited days to hear from Aunt Addie and Aunt Ettie after the San Francisco earthquake. It was when I was at Columbia that everybody seemed to be singing "Hello, Frisco!" and there was a gathering at Earl Hall to listen to that remarkable achievement, a transcontinental conversation.

Who had the best of it all, I wonder—my mother, whose life began after one of my grandfather's homecomings from sea and extended until the time of the Great Depression? My father, whose abundant energy found purpose and satisfaction through the final decades of individualism, before the Age of Mass Man? Surely not I, witness of a society and a world in decline.

At the end of my grandfather's journal he wrote:

List of books that I want if I can afford to buy them:
Washington's writings, 11 volumes
Hart's female prose writers of America
The Leaflets of Memory 1852 by Royall H. Coates
Human Prudence
Commentaries on the Bible
Modern Philosophy by Tuppes
Histories Ancient and Modern
The Crock of Gold
Sunny Side & Shady Side by Mrs. Margaret Maitland

So he did still look ahead. I can't suppose that he ever acquired any of these books or that he would have thought he had time to read them. But looking ahead at the books one might read is one of the good prospects that remain.

I join my experience to the conclusion shared by so many humane and qualified observers, for instance Barbara Ward and René Dubos in *Only One Earth,* who wrote: "If all man can offer to the decades ahead is the same combination of scientific drive, economic cupidity, and national arrogance, then we cannot rate very highly the chance of reaching the year 2,000 with our planet functioning safely and our humanity preserved." In *A God Within* Dr. Dubos said he thought man would act in time. I'll bet man won't.

Considering everything, I should be sorry to have these memoirs end with the slightest note of optimism. Selfishly, I am sorrier about Martha's Vineyard than about the world.

I should have liked to see Halley's Comet again. Ambrose Maguire and I talked about the prospect in the lane opposite our Campbell Street house in 1910, and I wonder if he is still living. One draws in one's hopes as one grows older, no matter how the world behaves.

INDEX